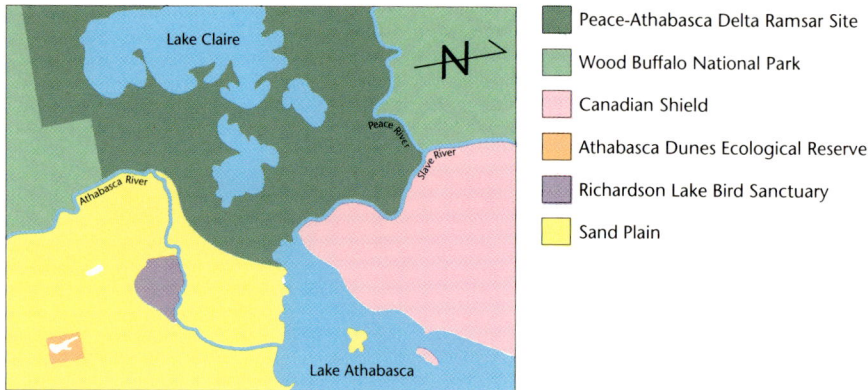

Legend:
- Peace-Athabasca Delta Ramsar Site
- Wood Buffalo National Park
- Canadian Shield
- Athabasca Dunes Ecological Reserve
- Richardson Lake Bird Sanctuary
- Sand Plain

The above diagram is an orientation to the satellite photograph inside the covers. This photograph of the north-east corner of Alberta shows an area of extreme landscape diversity as well as sites protected by four different park-related designations.

The top-half of the photograph lies within Wood Buffalo National Park. Surrounding Lake Claire is the Peace-Athabasca Delta Ramsar Site. Just below is the Richardson Lake Bird Sanctuary. This area is one of the world's largest freshwater deltas. To the left of Lake Claire, the land slopes upward toward the Birch Mountains and is blanketed by coniferous stands of the boreal forest.

The two white crescent shapes in the lower-left corner are active sand dunes, the larger protected as the Athabasca Dunes Ecological Reserve. Numerous kettle lakes are clearly visible below the Reserve, and above, is an extensive sand plain of glacial outwash. The entire area in the vicinity of the Reserve has been subjected to a recent forest fire. The redder tones are wetter sites such as the valley of the Richardson River between the areas of active sand that did not burn.

Between Lake Athabasca and the Slave River are the granite outcrops of the Canadian Shield. The long narrow configuration of many of the small lakes is the result of glacial erosion along faults in the bedrock. *(Alberta Transportation and Utilities/ Radarsat International)*

Alberta's Parks – Our Legacy

Published by Alberta Recreation, Parks and Wildlife Foundation

Edmonton, Canada. Copyright 1992.

Edited by Donna M. von Hauff, Edmonton, Canada

Front/Back Cover photographs by Rosemary H.L. Calvert, Calgary, Canada

Design by Wei Yew Studio 3 Graphics, Edmonton, Canada

Printed and bound by D.W. Friesen, Altona, Canada

Distributed in Canada by Lone Pine Publishing, Edmonton, Canada

96 95 94 93 92   5 4 3 2 1

Canadian Cataloguing in Publication Data
Alberta's Parks — Our Legacy

Includes index.
ISBN 0-7732-0649-3

1. Provincial parks and reserves — Alberta.
I. von Hauff, Donna, 1952-   II. Recreation, Parks & Wildlife Foundation

FC3663.A53 1992   971.23   C92-090354-1
SB484.C3A53 1992

Alberta's Parks – Our Legacy

Fred Vermeulen

Edited by Donna von Hauff

Published by Alberta Recreation, Parks & Wildlife Foundation

TABLE OF CONTENTS

Lupine *(Kåre Hellum)*

CARING FOR THE LAND

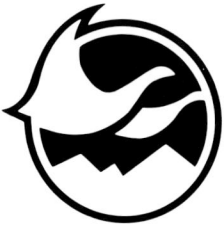

In 1992, Alberta's provincial parks celebrate their 60th anniversary, and we are proud to join this celebration with the publication of *Alberta's Parks — Our Legacy*. The book traces the development of parks within Alberta, and the contributions of past and present generations. These parklands are our wealth — a legacy to be enjoyed now with a promise for the future.

Research, education, recreation, tourism and personal well-being depend on the parkland that surrounds us. The Recreation, Parks and Wildlife Foundation is committed to expand and enrich Alberta's parkland through partnerships and community cooperation. To do this, the Directors of the Board of the Foundation volunteer their efforts to bring representation from all over this beautiful Province of Alberta.

The many contributors to the book, touched by the beauty of the land, take us on a tour of Alberta with stories and images. They sketch a gentle story of caring for the land. Reading and enjoying the book with our children will prepare them to take their part in this continuing saga of stewardship.

PARKS...A TRADITION

The CIBC is pleased to support the publication of the Alberta Recreation, Parks and Wildlife Foundation's book, "Alberta's Parks — Our Legacy". Our sponsorship is made in recognition of the 60th anniversary of Alberta Provincial Parks, and the role the park system has played in the lives of so many Albertans, Canadians and visitors from abroad.

In 1992 CIBC celebrates its 125th year of providing financial services to the people of Canada. CIBC, one of the country's oldest and largest financial institutions, has played an important part in the economic development of Alberta and Canada. We continue to occupy a leadership position today. Our involvement in this book is one way of saying thank you.

The book contains spectacular pictures of Alberta's parks, as well as historical, geographical, contemporary and anecdotal information. It also features wildlife, ecological areas and the five national parks within this province's borders.

CIBC believes that respect for the environment is important to everyone. We are committed to making sure that we do our part in preserving renewable and non-renewable resources. We are continuously striving to conserve our use of nature's resources and to reduce waste caused by our day-to-day operations. We do this not only out of respect for our environment, but also because it makes sense and is good business.

We are pleased that this book will be distributed by the Foundation to Alberta schools. The revenue raised by the sale of the remaining books will revert back to the Foundation for its good work.

Parks and wildlife are a Canadian and Albertan tradition. To recognize this 60th anniversary milestone, we are pleased to sponsor this special limited edition book on Alberta's world renowned parks. We trust this book will help people enjoy our parks even more.

Sincerely,

R. Donald Fullerton
Chairman

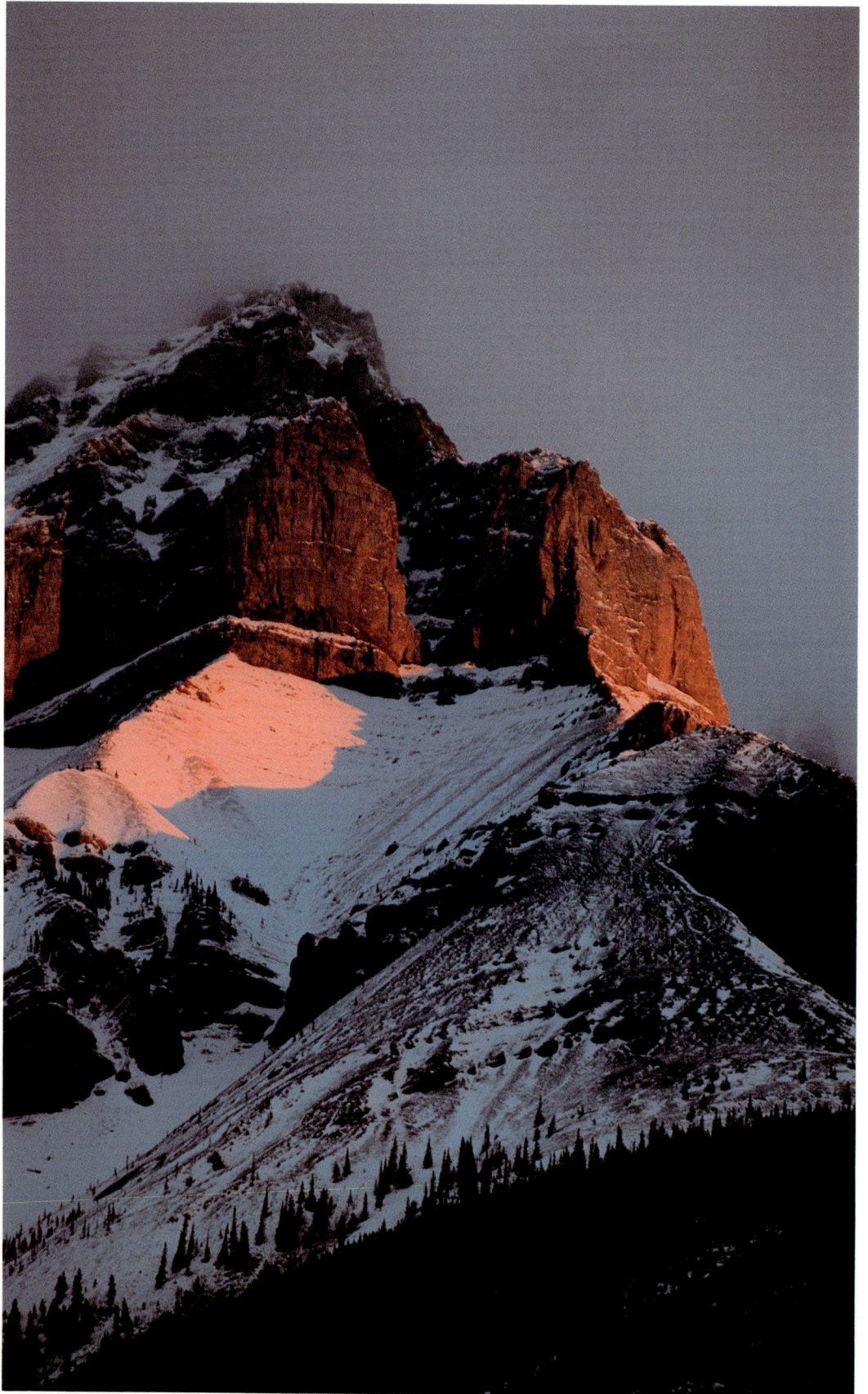

Sunrise over Alberta's Rocky
Mountains *(Rosemary H.L. Calvert,
FRPS)*

A CHANCE TO REFLECT

Anniversaries can be joyful occasions, overflowing with good food, good will, tall tales, fun and laughter. Nobody would knowingly refuse such fine birthday fare on the occasion of the 60th anniversary of Alberta's provincial parks — but gaiety is not enough. There is a serious responsibility about a birthday celebration. It should be a time for review that will mirror the varied events of 60 or 100 years as the situation demands, not overlooking the reverses, the mistakes, the triumphs, the warnings and the lessons which should be a prominent part of all exposures to history.

The same anniversary occasions should invite friends and servants to re-declare their support and loyalty to the cause for which the organization exists, in this instance, to parks, forests, soil, water, animal life and other resource treasures. Such rededication will surely bring a fresh determination to speak more boldly about parks, conservation, environment and the high calling of caretakership on God's good globe.

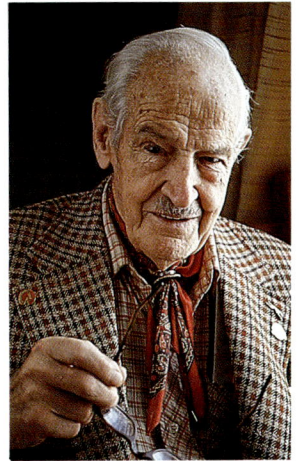

Dr. Grant MacEwan, 1991
(Rosemary H.L. Calvert, FRPS)

The tide of popularity is presently quite pronounced in favor of guardianship of the earth. Even members of the politician crowd appear eager to climb on the bandwagon. They should be encouraged to stay, but the best line of defence in protecting the environment will be those who long ago found spiritual and practical reasons for unspectacular and unfailing devotion to the principle of helping Nature rather than destroying it.

We appear to have got ourselves into the position where there is no sure and easy cure for our environmental ills. Canadians are going to insist upon having 12 million or more cars even if they are polluters. Ocean-going tankers are going to have accidents and spill a million barrels of oil and destroy countless wildlife now and again. And the temptation to raid nature's storehouses and sell the contents for money that may not be needed, is not going to go away. Many of our citizens are likely to be difficult to convert to conservation and the sanctity of the environment. The best candidates for the needed philosophy of guardianship of the earth may be today's kids. They are talking about it and they deserve to be encouraged in the way that spokesmen for parks and conservation can do it.

Now there is the promise of a new and useful book, *Alberta's Parks — Our Legacy*, with contents to make the task of carrying the message to where it is needed, easier and more effective. "The book", says Donna von Hauff, editor and publisher, "will be both educational and 'a good read'."

There is assurance that the book's contents have been selected from park histories, workers past and present, naturalists, writers and philosophers, all of whom have seemed proud to have been drawn into it. Much of the time and effort was given voluntarily, making it "a labor of love".

May this writer be among the first to offer congratulations to all who had a part in the creation and production of this book.

Grant MacEwan

GROWING A BOOK

Nowhere in North America can you find such a diversity of landforms as in Alberta. From the lofty mountains of Kananaskis Country to the dark, shady forests of Lakeland; from the native grasslands of Kennedy Coulee Ecological Reserve to the rugged foothills of Beauvais Lake; from the ghostly hoodoos and badlands of Writing-on-Stone and Dinosaur Provincial Park to the storm-swept beaches of Lesser Slave Lake — Alberta's natural heritage is preserved in parklands.

Alberta's Parks — Our Legacy celebrates 60 years of provincial parks, and the myriad of plants and animals that live in them. It also pays tribute to the many dedicated citizens and parks personnel who helped shape the political will to protect these and other natural heritage landscapes including the national parks and wilderness areas.

Through the years, prominent figures have staunchly backed the development of parks in Alberta. Premier Brownlee pioneered the Provincial Parks Act. William Aiken, the first Secretary of the Provincial Parks Board, spent his spare moments corresponding with park movements all over the world. And Dr. Vi Wood, the first Deputy Minister of Alberta Provincial Parks, argued for and guided, between 1951 and 1974, its rapid expansion.

No less important are Alberta Provincial Parks Service rangers, clerks, maintenance workers, planners and administrators who have been part of the development and stewardship of our parks. They should be proud of the legacy that is entrusted to their care.

In one short year, an idea for a book to celebrate the 60th anniversary of Alberta's parks grew to include hundreds of essays and countless photographs. All of the authors and photographers have contributed freely of their time and talents. The success of this edition has, in fact, set the stage for more to follow.

Alberta's Parks — Our Legacy contains the premier showing of work by world-class photographers Rosemary Calvert, Fred Vermeulen, Tom Webb and botanical artist, Kåre Hellum. These individuals have captured the beauty of the land, visually. Award-winning naturalists and writers, Joy and Cam Finlay, join with others to educate and challenge us to protect and preserve these landscapes, in perpetuity, as parks.

Recognizing the interconnectedness between the environment and our economy, often symbolized by parks, the Alberta Recreation, Parks and Wildlife Foundation and the CIBC have made the publishing of this book possible. More of these links between the business community and organizations committed to protecting parks are vital to our ongoing stewardship of Alberta.

As in all projects, some individuals have made an outstanding contribution to guarantee its success. During the past 12 months, it has been my privilege to work with Archie Landals, a talented researcher and writer, Hiske Gerding, who acted as the link to the volunteer contributors, and Glenn Martin, who, as the senior editorial consultant, cheerfully imparted advice and experience. In addition, the essays, often handwritten, and when stacked exceeding a metre in height, were painstakingly inputted by Val Poirier and Cora Trompetter. To all the essayists and photographers, whose names appear next to their contributions, and whose words and visions add so much to this book, I am very grateful.

Wei Yew, Hiske Gerding, Donna von Hauff, Maxine McDowall and Archie Landals *(AV and Exhibit Services)*

I would like to personally thank Julian Nowicki, Deputy Minister of Alberta Tourism, Parks and Recreation and Dave Chabillon, Assistant Deputy Minister of Parks for their unconditional support. Likewise, Jim Acton, Tom Drinkwater, Vi Wood, Lynne Steele, Chuck Moser, Ted Hart and Ray Rasmussen provided valuable insight into the development of Alberta's system of parks. I would also like to thank Bob Mills of Westbrook Elementary School for his assistance in shaping the contents of the book so that it can be used to teach youngsters about Alberta's natural regions.

Special thanks go to Dr. Natalia Krawetz of the Environment Council of Alberta for seconding Archie Landals to this project, and to Harvey Alton, Deputy Minister of Alberta Transportation, for allowing Ed Hammond and Irene Shiu to prepare the mapping and satellite photography. Trevor Weins and Glen Semenchuk were extremely helpful during this process — they got all of our computers talking the same language.

The search for the book's designer and printer was most capably conducted by Alberta Public Affairs staff Karen Stewart, Maxine McDowall, Dan Wouk and Ray Ledda under the leadership of Annie Re. Studio 3 Graphics, internationally recognized for their outstanding book designs, and D.W. Friesen, printers of fine quality books, were selected.

Alberta's system of parks is an evolving legacy. From ecological reserves and wilderness areas that focus on protecting Alberta's natural heritage, to provincial parks and recreation areas which afford opportunities for outdoor recreation and heritage appreciation, Alberta's parks are world-class. Join with Albertans to celebrate, enjoy, learn about, understand and appreciate the legacy of parks that has been entrusted to our care!

Donna von Hauff, *Editor*
Alberta's Parks — Our Legacy

B O R E A L F O R E S T

Alberta's largest natural region, the boreal forest, consists of broad plains and discontinuous hill systems. The climate of the region is variable and plays a major role in vegetation patterns. The more moderate southern areas support mixed-wood forests of spruce and poplar. Stands of jack pine grow on sand dunes and coarse-textured well-drained soil. In the northwest corner of Alberta the climate is significantly cooler and extensive areas of permafrost occur. Some areas, too cold to support forests, are covered by moss and shrubs. The prevalence of wetlands is a major characteristic of the region with widespread muskeg on flat, poorly drained sites. Because of the diversity of habitats, the boreal supports a variety of wildlife including moose, caribou, wolves and bears.

Boreal forest in autumn *(Rosemary H.L. Calvert, FRPS)*

Calling Lake Provincial Park

Calling Lake Provincial Park is situated on the southern shore of Calling Lake, north of the town of Athabasca. The park is classified as a natural environment park which provides recreational opportunities such as swimming, picnicking and boating. Interest in forming a park at this site began as early as 1948, but it was not until 1958 that the government placed a reservation on lands along the south shoreline to preserve the area as a future provincial park site. In 1964 the Athabasca Chamber of Commerce requested that a provincial park be created. The 738-hectare park was formally established in 1971.

Can You Eat These?

I was the ranger in charge of Calling Lake Provincial Park in 1986. The park is in a mixed boreal forest dominated by spruce trees, prime mushroom habitat. As a result, people travel for many miles for the great mushroom hunt.

One day in the late summer, I noticed a middle-aged couple picking mushrooms. The gentleman, in his late forties or early fifties, was about five-foot-seven with strong hands and a body used to hard work. The lady with him appeared to be about 10 years his junior. She kept searching for mushrooms while the man and I talked.

Balsam poplar *(Kåre Hellum)*

Boreal Forest

The conversation eventually got around to mushrooms and I jokingly said that I hoped they knew the difference between edible and non-edible varieties. The gentleman replied that he was fairly certain of the mushrooms he should, or should not, pick and added, "It doesn't really matter because I get my wife to try them first. By the way, this is Velma, my second wife." — *David Vetra*

Mushroom Magic

Walking in fields or woods, you can hear birds sing and squirrels protest; you can see grass, trees and small plants, and you might also see mushrooms! These fungi play a very important role in nature's housekeeping. But if mushrooms are here today and gone tomorrow, why are they so important?

A mushroom is the fruiting body of a fungus; you could compare it to an apple and an apple tree — when the apple is picked, the tree lives on. Thread-like tissue in leaves, wood or in the ground is the living-on part of a fungus. When the time is right, little knobs form on this tissue and develop into mushrooms.

We cannot do without fungi. First, many fungi are recyclers of fallen leaves and branches, dead trees, grass, manure, etc. Without fungi and insects, dead material would pile up everywhere. Second, almost all plants — from the largest tree to the smallest herb — have a fungal partner. The thread-like tissue (mycelium) forms a glove around the rootlets of plants and the partners exchange food. Fungi contribute minerals to trees which they cannot get themselves, they also extend the root system. In return, trees provide essential compounds that fungi cannot produce themselves. Because of this exchange, marvellous forests can grow on very poor soil.

It's important to be respectful of fungi. Even the tiniest mushroom has as much mycelium as a big one. The next time you're in the woods, follow a path and look for mushrooms! — *Helene M.E. Schalkwijk-Barendsen*

An Evolving Legacy

The story of parks in Alberta is an evolving one, closely tied to our relationship to the land. Just as our society and lifestyles have been shaped by the natural resources of the province, Alberta's landscapes and resource base have been altered by our activities through the years. Agriculture, forestry, mining and urban development have changed the landscape, forever. The natural environment, with its ecological processes, and our economic activities are intrinsically linked. Our continued prosperity — even our survival — is dependent upon striking a balance between the economy and the environment.

Fly amanita. One of the poisonous mushrooms of the boreal forest
(*Archie Landals*)

In Europe, parks emerged as enclosed pieces of ground stocked with game and held by Royal decree. Later these tracts of land, with their manicured gardens and lawns surrounded by woodland and pasture, were used as game preserves and for recreation. Today the term "park" can mean an area of land — urban or rural — identified for outdoor recreation or protected for its ecological values.

People are involved in all aspects of parks — their establishment, management and use. Direct and indirect benefits of parks accrue to present and future generations. But parks are more. They are refuges for the many species of plants and animals that depend on the habitat of these protected landscapes.

Prickly rose (*Kåre Hellum*)

Boreal Forest

Indian paintbrush (Kåre Hellum)

Alberta's boreal forest provincial parks provide many shady campsites. (Archie Landals)

Carson-Pegasus Provincial Park

Located on the southern flank of the Swan Hills, nestled amongst rolling hills and mature stands of timber, is Carson-Pegasus Provincial Park. The Swan Hills are a pre-glacial upland plateau dissected by glacial action. The underlying bedrock is capped by a tertiary conglomerate that is resistant to erosion. In most places, the landscape is covered with a rocky glacial till which blankets the underlying bedrock. The lakes are kettles formed by ice-blocks that were buried in the till and later melted. At present Carson-Pegasus encompasses 1,210 hectares, 25 per cent of which is covered by the waters of McLeod and Little McLeod Lakes.

These lakes have had several name changes. Early maps of the area show a single, large lake named McLeod. In 1931 the new Federal Sectional Map showed only one large lake named Carson Lake. Mobil Oil, which was operating on the north shore of the smaller lake, renamed it Pegasus after its company logo.

When Carson-Pegasus Provincial Park was established in 1982, it was named after the then-named Carson and Pegasus Lakes. In 1985 the names were changed back to McLeod and Little McLeod in response to a request by the local historical society.

The three lakes in the park — McLeod, Little McLeod and Laura — are home to a wide variety of flora and fauna. Numerous loons and grebes inhabit the lake. It is not uncommon to see an osprey, soaring above one moment, and the next, diving into McLeod Lake and resurfacing with the catch of the day. Naturally occurring population of northern pike, whitefish and yellow perch are sought year-round in Little McLeod; anglers prize the rainbow trout stocked in McLeod. — *Carrie A. Lanz*

Cold Lake Provincial Park

The Chipewyan called it *thooway-show-tway* or Big Fish Lake. The Cree called it *takikawew-sahigan* or Cold Lake. Whatever name is used, there are many stories about big fish in Cold Lake. A Chipewyan native, it is said, passed by a lake where big fish were churning up the water. When a young Cree

Conquering the Land

When the early explorers and fur traders came to what is now Alberta, they harvested fur, hunted, fished and used whatever they needed to survive. Their relationship to the land was much the same as that of the native people they encountered. These early explorers, like the natives before them, regarded the endless wilderness and its resources with awe. They made little attempt to tame or change the land. Some sketched and painted the landscape, many were inspired to comment in their journals. In 1789, Alexander Mackenzie recorded: "The valley ... is about three miles in breadth and is confined by

French Creek. Cross Lake Provincial Park displays the diversity of the boreal forest. *(Dave Dodge)*

two lofty ridges of equal height, displaying a most delightful intermixture of wood and lawn, and stretching on till the blue mist obscures the prospect. Some parts of the inclining heights are covered with stately forests, relieved by promontories of the finest verdure, where the elk and buffalo find pasture. It was in the month of September when I enjoyed a scene, of which I do not presume to give an adequate description; and as it was the rutting season of the elk, the whistling of that animal was heard in all the variety which the echoes could afford it." The scene described was the Clearwater River Valley, east of present-day Fort McMurray.

As agriculture spread westward, the relationship between these pioneers and the land changed. Like the fur traders and explorers, early settlers and promoters viewed the land as a limitless, vast, unoccupied territory. These frontiersmen, however, saw the land as something to be tamed and developed. Generally, the natural resources were considered free — to be used to create economic growth, profits and employment.

Boreal Forest

Limestone outcrops on the Clearwater River are the core of Whitemud Falls Ecological Reserve. *(Archie Landals)*

The Birth of Parks in Alberta

It was, in fact, these sentiments that led to the establishment of Banff as Canada's first national park. The government of the day recognized the economic value of these mineral hot springs and set them aside to protect and develop them into a first class resort, one which would rival the health spas of Europe. The hot springs, it was reasoned, had the potential to attract a wealthy clientele who would use the recently completed Canadian Pacific Railway. In the words of Sir John A. Macdonald, these tourists would "recoup the treasury".

The Rocky Mountain Park Act of 1887 officially created Banff as Canada's first national park and the first park to be designated in what would later become the province of Alberta. *The said tract of land is hereby reserved and set aside as a public park and pleasure ground for the benefit, advantage and enjoyment of the people of Canada. — Sir John A. Macdonald*

Although the initial impetus was to protect the mineral hot springs because of their tourism value, the park was soon enlarged to protect vast tracts of wilderness. Visitors and adventurers such as Mary Shaffer came to explore and to conquer unclimbed mountain peaks.

Red-breasted merganser (*Blaine Landals*)

Undeveloped beaches are common in the boreal forest. (*Archie Landals*)

native, who lived and hunted in the area, crossed the lake, a huge fish rose from the depths and swallowed him, snapping the canoe in half. The next day pieces of the canoe were found floating in the lake. The Chipewyans believe the *kinachuk* (Big Fish) died when its sides were punctured from swallowing a bull elk with horns.

Long before the fur-trade brought European settlers to Cold Lake, the Beaver and/or Slavey hunted and fished in the area. As the importance of the fur-trade grew, the Chipewyan and Cree moved into the region. The Catholic Church arrived in the area in the mid-1800s and first settlers between 1905 and 1911. Portions of the park were cleared by settlers for farming, and even now, large grassy fields, homesteaders' cabins and farm machinery including the remnants of a sawmill can be found within its boundaries.

During the 1920s, Cold Lake established itself as a fishing paradise. Lake trout were even exported to the eastern United States. By the late-40s, however, few trout remained and even a once-flourishing mink farm, located on the lake, was forced to close because of the low fish population.

The unspoiled natural areas of Cold Lake Provincial Park, formally established in 1976, abound with wildlife. Over 220 species of vascular plants, 190 bird species, 40 different mammals and at least seven amphibians and reptiles have been recorded within the 398-hectare park. —*Steven Cooney & Kevin Bamber*

Naturalists came to study plants, wildlife, geology and glaciology. Arthur Oliver Wheeler, a monumental figure in the parks movement, first came to the Rockies to work as a Dominion Land Surveyor. Almost single-handedly, he provided the inspiration for the founding of the Alpine Club of Canada in 1906. He later went on to serve on the executive of the fledging Canadian National Parks Association now known as the Canadian Parks and Wilderness Society.

Artists, poets and writers were inspired by the grandeur of the mountains and wilderness. At the invitation of guide and outfitter Jim Simpson, the now famous wildlife artist, Carl Rungius first visited Banff in 1910. He was so impressed with the Rockies that he returned annually for many years to sketch and paint the wildlife and scenery.

Wild sarsaparilla (*Kåre Hellum*)

19

Boreal Forest

Cross Lake Provincial Park

Officially named Steele Lake, the old-timers and locals have always called it Cross Lake, probably because of its shape. Prior to the 40s, the area around Steele Lake was used for trapping and some farming. Fish, mainly northern pike, were abundant. At that time, a few residents lived around the lake on acreage leases. Carl Browning, Les Callahan, and later Max Jacobi and family were trappers and mink farmers in the present park development area. George Richardson lived across the lake on what is still referred to as George's Point.

In the 1950s, residents of Flatbush and Fawcett formed the Cross Lake Booster's Club to promote the development of a picnic area by the lake. Cross Lake Provincial Park was officially established in 1955.

Situated 55 kilometres north of Westlock, this 2,076-hectare park is representative of Alberta's northern boreal forest with examples of marshy areas, black spruce bogs, pure pine stands, mixed-wood areas and mature poplar stands. Steele Lake continues to be a good fishing spot for northern pike and perch. Blue herons, bald eagles and osprey nest around the lake, and deer and moose are often seen. — *Sidney Allen, Wilton Allers, Victor Bratt, Mike Bosma, Darryl & Kathie Buss*

Garner Lake Provincial Park

Homesteaders, migrating north and east of Smoky Lake during the early 1900s, were the first to settle in the vicinity of Garner Lake. There were no roads with the exception of an old winter trail which ran through the northwest corner of what is now Garner Lake Provincial Park. The lake was named after George E. Garner who began to homestead one mile east of the lake in 1904.

The lake, surrounded by a mixed-wood forest, steep hummocky moraines with rough and irregular knob and kettle topography, was soon recognized by local residents as having great potential for both public and private recreational use. In 1927 the Alberta government reserved some 55 hectares of land which is now part of the park. In 1930 Garner Lake was included on a list of possible park sites by the newly formed Provincial Parks Board. In 1953 the area was officially established as a provincial park. The 74-hectare park, covered with a mixed-woods of aspen and balsam poplar, provides habitat for birds common to central Alberta, moose, the occasional black bear, deer and smaller mammals. — *Glenn Harvey*

Alberta's parks provide time for quiet reflection *(AV and Exhibit Services)*

Boreal Forest

Gregoire Lake Provincial Park

Gregoire Lake Provincial Park was established to provide outdoor recreational opportunities for the rapidly growing population of Fort McMurray. The 696-hectare park was officially opened in 1973.

In 1939 the provincial government reserved lands at the east end of Gregoire Lake (originally called Willow Lake) for later development as a recreational area. This reservation was renewed in 1944 for a 10-year period but was cancelled in 1951 when the lands were required for local school purposes. Regional concern about the lack of natural recreational areas surfaced in 1968, and the creation of either a municipal or provincial park was considered. A Provincial Parks Planning Branch survey revealed that 80 per cent of the households contacted were already using Gregoire

The History of the Provincial Park Movement

While the establishment of Banff National Park by the federal government signalled the birth of parks in Alberta, the province had to wait another 45 years before it had full legal status for its resources. Just after the boundaries of Banff were consolidated and Waterton Lakes, Jasper, Elk Island and Wood Buffalo established, the Alberta Natural Resources Act of 1930 was passed giving the province jurisdiction over its resources. Anticipating the official transfer, the Alberta government passed the Provincial Parks and Protected Areas Act on March 21, 1930.

The passage of this legislation was very much a result of the commitment of John E. Brownlee, then premier of Alberta. In 1928, Brownlee led a trade delegation to Europe and the British Isles. Upon his return, he said: "We stand in Alberta today with the greatest heritage of natural beauty in the world, a potential source of wealth which, in the years to come, will yield a greater wealth than we are today obtaining from the flood of grain that is pouring in to our granaries. Beautify our towns. Beautify our highways. Inspire our people with a sense of beauty in their surroundings that they may leave a more splendid heritage to coming generations."

Lake for recreation. On the basis of this information, the government approved creation of the provincial park.

A five-kilometre cross-country ski trail is maintained during the winter, and holes in the ice indicate where fishermen have tried their luck. Pike and walleye are common species but lake whitefish and perch can also be found. Moose and bear have been seen in the area. Woodchucks, squirrels and birds abound in the park. — *Dennis Spackman*

The Sun Shines and the Water Runs at Hilliard's Bay Provincial Park

At one time, the centre of the Peace River district was Grouard, a place that saw many people come and go. Natives, trappers, traders, miners, prospectors, settlers, writers and poets brought their culture to the area and left a part of their life story. Seven kilometres to the east of this historic settlement, on the shore of Lesser Slave Lake, is Hilliard's Bay Provincial Park. Both the quiet bay the park is situated on and the park are named after the family that first homesteaded there.

The Woodland Cree displaced the Beaver Indians, who once inhabited the area. The Cree developed a symbiotic relationship with the European traders, exchanging beaver pelts for supplies and guns. However, once the Beaver Indians acquired guns, and smallpox had taken its toll on the Cree, their hostilities ended at Peace Point (Uchaga) which is how the Peace River got its name.

Alexander Mackenzie learned about Lesser Slave Lake from the Beaver Indians, but it was David Thompson who, in 1799, established the first fur-trading post for the North West Company at the lake's east end. In 1802 the Company built another post, Blondin's House, and in 1815 the Hudson Bay Company built their first post, Fort Waterloo, also at the east end of the lake. One year later, a fierce competition ensued when Fort Waterloo burned down and was rebuilt beside Blondin's House. The two companies eventually merged in 1821 and Blondin's House, renamed Lesser Slave House, continued to trade until 1926.

By 1912 there was so much traffic in the Peace River district that five railways were planned. The community of Lesser Slave House, renamed Grouard in honour of the resident priest, Bishop

Cattail *(Kåre Hellum)*

Meadows of fireweed add color to the boreal landscape. *(Maureen Landals)*

23

Boreal Forest

Grouard, sprouted in anticipation of the coming railway. However, the tracks of the Edmonton-Dunvegan railway, built in 1914, were laid straight to High Prairie and completely bypassed Grouard. The centre's plans to become the metropolis of the great Peace River Country were soon forgotten.

While planning Hilliard's Bay Provincial Park in 1978, the thought occurred that visitors should have the opportunity to experience the Grouard Trail along the north shore of Lesser Slave Lake. The route, a natural and cultural-heritage link between Lesser Slave Lake Provincial Park on the east shore and Hilliard's Bay on the northwest shore of this mighty lake, traces the same steps taken by Alberta's early explorers. — *Carter Cox & Roger Reilander*

Yes — There's Hope for Kimiwan Lake!

Diary entry — June 1988: I walked out through the mudflats by McLennan to inventory shorebirds. I'm about 300 metres past the 1986 shoreline. There's a moonscape — unvegetated mudflats circling the lake for several square kilometres — marked only with soft craters. I've crawled the last 60 metres on my knees: the mud is up to my hips. The usual 50 American avocet are visible, ducks and other shorebirds are out in the thousands. The lake is less than 15 centimetres deep.

Kimiwan Lake was an oval lake originally about six-and-a-half kilometres wide and nine-and-a-half kilometres long. The town of McLennan is located on its south shore. Rated in the Canada Land Inventory as one of Alberta's top waterfowl breeding and staging areas, many of McLennan's older folk learned to swim and even to dive in this lake. What happened?

Kimiwan Lake has a relatively small, shallow drainage basin and a gradually sloping shoreline which makes it very susceptible to water level fluctuations. Moreover, the forest cover surrounding the lake and its uplands has sharply decreased since 1945 due to agricultural and forestry practices. This, coupled with several years of low rainfall, began a significant decrease in water levels. In the five years or so before 1984, Kimiwan water levels dropped from over three metres to half a metre. The existing canal between Winagami and Kimiwan Lakes was not effective for adding spring run-off water because of its shallow grade and the vegetation in it. Once Kimiwan became this shallow, it began to evaporate.

Mushrooms surrounded by wild strawberries *(Archie Landals)*

Active beach dunes in Lesser Slave Lake Provincial Park. *(AV and Exhibit Services)*

Northern pike are popular sport fish in Alberta parks. *(Maureen Landals)*

Many homesteads in the boreal forest have been abandoned due to poor soils. *(Blaine Landals)*

A few of the McLennan residents took notice and in 1983, the "Save Our Lake Committee" was formed to lobby politicians and government agencies for help. In 1985 Kimiwan Lake and the surrounding area was proposed as a Natural Area and I was sent to inventory the birdlife in 1986, 87 and 88. The commitment to raise the water level of the lake grew. In 1987 the Winagami-Girouxville Canal was upgraded and the amount of precipitation in the fall of 1988 allowed the water level in the lake to rise.

Water is now coming into Kimiwan Lake from the improved canal. McLennan has almost finished a major bird walk and park on the south shore of the lake and it now calls itself the "Bird Capital of Canada". Yes . . . there is hope for Kimiwan Lake! — *Chel Macdonald*

Aspen Beach Provincial Park was established on November 21, 1932, signalling the beginning of Alberta's provincial park system. While Aspen Beach is regarded as Alberta's first provincial park, Gooseberry, Park and Sylvan Lakes, Saskatoon Island, Lundbreck Falls, Ghost River and Hommy were, in fact, established at the same time. Additionally, Dillberry, Elkwater and Vermilion, although not officially established, operated as provincial parks.

The events surrounding the passage of the Provincial Parks and Protected Areas Act and the establishment of the first parks was recorded by William Thomas Aiken on September 30, 1935.

The Provincial Parks and Protected Areas Act of Alberta was in large measure the result of observations made and impressions received by former Premier the Honourable J.E. Brownlee while on a visit to the British Isles on government business during the year 1928. The Premier, while investigating the possibilities of farm immigration to Alberta, was greatly impressed by the attachment of the British farmer to the beauty and surroundings of his home land, and he returned to Alberta with a firm resolve to see what could be accomplished towards beautifying the landscape of his own province, thus making rural life more attractive.

Lakeland Provincial Park

Lakeland Provincial Park, situated east of Lac La Biche, encompasses steep ravines, ridges, open slopes, hummocks, bogs, marshland and relatively flat river floodplains. Alberta's newest provincial park is characterized by a boreal forest of spruce, poplar and pine, and old-growth forest stands. Numerous lakes within the 14,700-hectare park were formed by glacial activity. Long sandy beaches line portions of many lakes in the region, the best to be found at Touchwood and Pinehurst Lakes. "The designation of Lakeland allows for the careful development and management of recreational opportunities within this northern area," stated Dr. Stephen C. West, the parks minister responsible for establishing the area.

His impressions were conveyed to the people at various meetings, which he addressed throughout the province, and through the medium of the press. His viewpoint met with general approval and the first step was taken by the Government when they appointed a Supervisor of Town Planning and passed the Town Planning Act at the session of 1929. This Act, as its name implies, was for the purpose of assisting urban authorities in the better planning of subdivisions and buildings for the beautification of town properties. But in order to complete this plan it was necessary to consider ways and means for the creation and development of a system of rural improvement such as the

Alder *(Kåre Hellum)*

Boreal Forest

The western portion of the park encompasses a complex of lakes which represent a unique and valuable wilderness resource. The lakes — Jackson, Kinnaird, Dabbs, Blackett, McGuffin and Helena — were created by melting glacial ice intermixed with till, gravel and other debris. These lakes, known as ablation till lakes, are characterized by irregular shorelines and lake bottom contours with till shores, few beaches and shallow-to-steep-treed shorelines.

The park area is home to a rich variety of wildlife including moose, deer, timber wolves, red fox, lynx, martens, otters, fishers, arctic shrew, silver-haired bats and porcupines. Woodland caribou have been observed. Many of the lakes offer important nesting and feeding habitats for waterfowl such as ducks, pelicans, cormorants, wading and shore birds. The larger lakes are staging areas for numerous migrating species.

Diving waterfowl such as common goldeneyes, lesser scaups, white-winged scoters and loons feed and nest on Pinehurst, Seibert and Touchwood Lakes. Ospreys nest around these bodies of water, and eagles and pelicans feed in the area. Other significant species that have been sighted in the area include turkey vultures, pileated woodpeckers, northern pygmy owls and great grey owls. An active great blue heron colony can be found on Pinehurst Lake and there is a large common tern colony on Ironwood Lake.

Several species of reptiles and amphibians including the tiger salamander, Dakota toad and chorus frog are found in the park. Angling is one of the most popular recreational activities in the Lakeland area. Seibert is a designated trophy lake. Walleye, northern pike and yellow perch are among the most common fish caught.

Potential exists in the Lakeland area for uncovering archaeological findings of provincial, if not, national significance. Artifacts have been found at one site in the Touchwood Lake area. Further study may shed light on the movements of early hunters and gatherers in this region of Alberta.

Bracted honey suckle *(Kåre Hellum)*

Moose are frequently seen by visitors to Lakeland Provincial Park. *(Archie Landals)*

Life Is a Beach

Like an ocean of freshwater, Lesser Slave Lake stretches to the horizon, a vast shimmering expanse of water that is so unexpected in northern Alberta. Lesser Slave Lake Provincial Park lies along the lake's east shoreline. It preserves and protects 7,557 hectares of boreal forest.

The Lesser Slave Lake area has attracted people since the last ice age and perhaps beyond. Its waters and surrounding forests provided food, shelter and clothing for nomadic native tribes. In fact, the name "slave" comes from a Cree word. The Cree came from eastern Canada armed with the whiteman's fire sticks (guns) and upon encountering the natives of Lesser Slave Lake, drove them away. They were called the "slave" or "slavey" by the Cree as an expression of ridicule.

Europeans came to the area in search of furs. In 1799 members of the North West Company, a vigorous and entrepreneurial fur-trading company based in Montreal, established the first fort in the area.

Even 125 years after the first fort was established on Lesser Slave Lake, the demands of northern travel were not taken lightly. His Excellency The Duke of Devonshire, Governor-General of Canada, was warned of the inconvenience of travel in the north. He was, however, determined to visit the present day site of Lesser Slave Lake Provincial Park.

He wrote in his diary: "Sunday, September 12, 1920. Arrived at Sawridge at 8 and started out at once by motor for the lake (Lesser Slave) two miles off. After some delay a big motorboat was got underway [sic] and we went for a very nice trip. Saw a lot of ducks."

The first recorded interest in the lake's recreational potential came from the Canadian Pacific Railway (C.P.R.) in 1922. They had their eyes on an exceptional stretch of white sand beach at the east end of the lake. This was at a time when outstanding natural features, like the hotsprings at Banff National Park, were protected under legislation and became the destinations of the wealthy and privileged. The railway was anxious to develop the lake as a future summer resort for the citizens

Cotton grass grows in wet boreal meadows. *(Archie Landals)*

development of provincial parks.

With a view to carrying out this policy the Premier, on May 28, 1929, appointed a special committee for the purpose of investigating the possibilities of park development in the province. The committee was composed of Mr. J. D. Robertson, Deputy Minister of Public Works, Chairman; Mr. H.L. Seymour, Director of Town Planning; and Mr. R.A. Smith, Solicitor to the Executive Council.

The committee was directed to: (1) arrange for the transfer of certain lands to be donated by the Calgary Power Company for park purposes at Ghost River, to investigate the possibility of acquiring title to any additional land which might be desired for development at the location, and to submit estimates and plans for development of the Ghost River Park; (2) make a survey of the province and report to the Executive Council on sites suitable for the development of fairly substantial parks; and (3) report on sites adjacent to provincial highways suitable for camp sites.

The committee prepared and submitted its report to the Premier on November 7, 1929, recommending the purchase of property and development of park sites at Aspen Beach on Gull Lake, Ghost River and Gooseberry Lake, and submitted a list of desirable sites, recommending

Red-eyed verios inhabit Alberta's forested parks. *(Tom Webb)*

that the purchase or reservation of property at the same be given future consideration.

As a result of this report, property was purchased at Gooseberry Lake, Gull Lake and Sylvan Lake, and work commenced on the erection of a pier at Aspen Beach, Gull Lake. At the 1930 session of the provincial legislature the Provincial Parks and Protected Areas Act was passed. This Act made provision for the appointment of a Board of Management to be known as the Provincial Parks Board, and for the appointment of a Board of Management for any particular park where such might be deemed necessary or advisable. In the spring of 1930, the Executive Council appointed a Provincial Board of Management in accordance with the provisions of the Provincial Parks and Protected Areas Act. The personnel of the new board was the same as that of the Committee appointed on May 28, 1929, with the exception that Mr. R.A. Smith, Solicitor to the Executive Council, was replaced by Mr. A. Paton, Landscape Gardener in charge of the Government's grounds at Oliver Mental Institute.

The fall of 1929 saw the commencement of the economic depression, and the Government, faced with decreasing revenues and increasing financial burdens for unemployment relief, was reluctant to vote public funds for park purposes.

of Edmonton. A beautiful sand beach was just the ticket that was needed to increase revenues and develop traffic on the Edmonton, Dunvegan and British Columbia Railway. This railway had reached Sawridge, now the town of Slave Lake, in 1914, and by 1922 it was in serious financial trouble.

The scheme never came to fruition and the area's recreational potential was ignored until 1960 when E.P. Shaver, Provincial Parks Commissioner, informed the minister of lands and forests that the Grouard Constituency Social Credit Association had passed a resolution recommending the east end of Lesser Slave Lake be developed as a provincial park. Lesser Slave Lake Provincial Park was established in 1966.

The park has the distinction of protecting the white sand beach that so interested the C.P.R. Every summer, Devonshire Beach, named in honour of The Duke, plays host to the Alberta open sand castle building championships. — *Frank Fraser, Chris Bruntlett & John Doll*

Long Lake Provincial Park

Long Lake has always been a popular fishing spot. As early as 1919 there was a small resort on its southeastern shore, and as many as seven saw mills had operated on the western shore. Lumbering activities, however, ceased by 1940. In 1956 the County of Thorhild requested that a provincial park be established at Long Lake. The County offered a cash grant for beach development and a further amount for road improvement. Local residents volunteered labour. The provincial government, in light of the community's interest, established Long Lake Provincial Park in 1957. The park encompasses 769 hectares of aspen-covered landscape interspersed with some balsam poplar and spruce forest, prime habitat for over 90 species of birds and 18 species of mammals. The lake's large northern pike attract fishermen year-round. — *Rick Johnson & Nancy Keith*

Moonshine Lake Provincial Park

Moonshine Lake was a small, mint-scented slough for many years, a detour on the old Moonshine Trail so named because of the vocation of some of the settlers along its course. One story has it that

Viewing platforms allow visitors to experience fragile resources in Alberta's provincial parks. *(Archie Landals)*

Jack Campbell and Harry Hanrahan — well-laden with product — were climbing up the steep incline on the north edge of the pothole when some of their brew spilled and ran back down into the pond. Thereafter, the slough was known as Moonshine Lake.

This pond, however, did not resemble a lake. The grasses always grew lush around it and when children rolled in them, the aforementioned spices permeated both the air and children. Because the trees standing sentinel around that spot were some of the most scenic in the area, it became a favorite picnic spot for the locals.

The area's residents were persuaded by Jack Bird, George Esselink and Lawson Scott to form an association to promote the development of the site into a park. Donations were solicited and two-

---

The activities of the board were, therefore, confined largely to consideration of various projects and reservation of certain lands for future development. The sites in various parts of the province have been proclaimed as provincial parks, and at four of these, namely Aspen Beach, Park Lake, Gooseberry Lake and Dillberry Lake, a certain amount of development work has been carried out as indicated in the descriptions which follow.

In the early part of 1933, Mr. Seymour resigned as Town Planning Commissioner, the result of a Government policy of retrenchment, and later in the year the board suffered a severe loss by the death, after a long illness, of Mr. J.D. Robertson,

Chairman. For a period of approximately one year following Mr. Robertson's death the work of the Board was looked after by the Department of Public Works, and during this period, property for park purposes was purchased at Rochon Sands on the south shore of Buffalo Lake.

On June 2, 1934, the Provincial Executive appointed a new Provincial Parks Board composed of Mr. C.A. Davidson, Highway Commissioner, as Chairman, Mr. A. Paton, and Mr. W.T. Aiken as Secretary. The new board is giving attention to the establishing of new parks at Taber, Fish Lake, Buffalo Lake, Elkwater Lake and Saskatoon Mountain. These projects have been held in

dollar tickets were sold. The locals complained that they couldn't enter a store without being asked to buy a ticket. The lordly sum of $384 was soon raised. Money was also earned from Sunday skating parties on the small pond (the music was supplied by Bird's P.A. system) and lunches were sold. With this money and volunteer help, the top-soil was pushed into two islands at the east end of the proposed lake and the outline of the shore established. Land was even cleared for a ball park.

Jack Bird encountered little difficulty in persuading the local Member of the Legislative Assembly, A.O. Fimrite, to designate the area as a provincial park. Moonshine Lake Provincial Park, established April 9, 1959, was intended to serve an area south of the Peace River, east to the Little Smoky River and west to the B.C. border. As it turned out, large numbers of people from Dawson Creek, Grande Prairie and B.C. became regular users of the park. The Moonshine Lake Athletic Association, organized in 1960, built and operated a concession booth to raise funds for local activities. Manning the booth was considered a popular sport by the ladies of the district.

Moonshine Lake has seen a lot of changes over the years. The 847-hectare park, mostly a boreal mixed-wood forest, provides opportunities for fishing, swimming, picnicking, horseshoes, hiking, baseball and volleyball. In winter, visitors can cross-country ski on groomed trails, ice fish or skate on the regulation size rink. Moonshine Lake — a park for people by people — is a tribute to the pioneers who made a dream come true. — *Wilma Bird & Rob Spelliscy*

Harebells occur throughout Alberta. *(Archie Landals)*

Moose Lake Provincial Park

Approximately 10,000 years ago, the Keewatin Ice Sheet receded north of Moose Lake releasing huge quantities of water to the south. The water carried with it a heavy load of coarse glacial sands which were deposited in the area of the park. The very thin soil layer above the sand deposits created the unique, fragile ecosystem which characterizes the park. The earliest known white settlement in Alberta, a trading post established by the Hudson's Bay Company, was built on the north shore of Moose Lake in 1789. Archaeologists, however, have been unable to find the exact location.

The 735-hectare park, established in 1967, offers visitors year-round outdoor recreational opportunities. Files at the park and folklore from neighboring pioneers chronicle early trappers' cabins and trails. — *Martin Paetz*

Notikewin - Alberta's Frontier Park

The vast green expanse of spruce and poplar forests of northern Alberta stretched east, virgin wilderness in the truest sense of the word. Looking west, the agricultural frontier — a checkerboard of fields, brilliant gold squares of canola interspersed with patches of pale blue flax — intruded into the forest. Below lay the deeply incised valley of the Peace River, up ahead a ribbon of silver merged with its muddy waters — the Notikewin River.

It was August, 1974 and we were flying the lakes and rivers of northern Alberta to complete the final phases of the Canada Land Inventory for Recreation. We were also responding to a request by the Hawk Hills Agricultural Society and the Manning Fish and Game Association to establish a park at the confluence of the Notikewin and Peace. That day, we performed the preliminary reconnaissance survey.

The name, Notikewin, was derived from the Cree word for battle. The river was the setting for a series of battles between the resident Beaver Indians and the invading Cree during the 1700s. In 1793 Alexander Mackenzie passed by on his epic voyage to the Pacific. From 1866 to 1897 the Hudson's Bay Company operated Battle River House on the south bank of the Notikewin. Steam-

abeyance by difficulty in the acquisition of the desired areas, but it is anticipated that a satisfactory settlement will be reached shortly.

William Thomas Aiken, the first secretary to the Provincial Parks Board, was a person of considerable vision regarding a future park legacy for Alberta. During his leisure hours, he corresponded with a number of fledgling park agencies and formulated a strategy for the establishment of a three-tiered provincial parks system. Aiken's submission included Class A parks for the preservation of large areas of natural beauty where citizens of the province would have the opportunity of becoming

Fireweed *(Kåre Hellum)*

Boreal Forest

powered, paddle-wheelers plied the river for another 50 years carrying missionaries such as Bishop Grouard, trappers, early settlers, and supplies for the Hudson's Bay Company and the North West Mounted Police.

It was easy to see why the locals wanted to protect this area as a provincial park. The valleys of the Peace and Notikewin cut 150 metres and more into the surrounding uplands. In fall, the hillsides are a mosaic of golden aspen, red shrubbery and green conifers. The rivers provide a sanctuary for the Canada geese that feed in nearby grain fields.

The area is diverse — spruce covered islands, forests of aspen and balsam poplar, sand dunes with scraggly jackpine, open muskeg and wetlands. Relict stands of self-regenerating old-growth forests are dominated by white spruce 30 metres tall and 200 years old. Pileated woodpeckers, boreal chickadees, golden-crowned kinglets, western tanagers, orange-crowned warblers, barred owls, black-throated green warblers, bay-breasted warblers and other species depend on these forests. Ostrich ferns two metres tall grow in the moist glades. Horsetails surround clear, cold springs. Fossil shells and petrified wood erode from the sandstone cliffs.

On November 20, 1979 an area of 9,697 hectares was established as Notikewin Provincial Park. This natural environment is protected forever because local residents realized the majesty of the frontier would not last. — *Archie Landals*

Chipmunks are not shy of park visitors. *(Archie Landals)*

O'Brien Provincial Park

O'Brien Provincial Park is located just south of the town of Grande Prairie. As early as 1917 the town council proposed formation of a park on the Wapiti River. The call for park status was renewed in 1939, and while the needed land was reserved, no provincial park was created. Nonetheless, the Grande Prairie Board of Trade undertook the development of these recreational facilities.

In the late-40s, the efforts of local residents to create an official park at the site were dealt a serious blow. The provincial government decided to abandon all thought of the project since there were numerous adjacent provincial parks. In 1954 the issue was re-examined and seen somewhat differently, and O'Brien Provincial Park was formally designated. Today the 65-hectare park remains a favorite picnic spot for locals.

Pembina River Provincial Park

The Pembina River Provincial Park area has long been associated with local recreational use. In 1948 a local landowner attempted to purchase crown land that abutted his, with a view to starting a tourist camp. This move so alarmed local officials that they immediately petitioned the government to create a provincial park at the site. In 1949 the province reserved the land and in 1953, it formally established Pembina River Provincial Park.

The 167-hectare park, set in the valley among aspen and spruce, provides ample opportunities for swimming, fishing, picnicking and camping. In the southeast quadrant of the park, visitors can find a stand of white spruce trees, many with a diameter of 40 centimetres.

Sir Winston Churchill Provincial Park

The history of this island park is almost as old as its trees. Located in Lac La Biche, the island attracted the attention of voyagers and fur-traders as early as the 1700s. David Thompson is credited with establishing the first fort, in 1798, where the present community of Lac La Biche is located today.

The island gained protected status after the 1919 fire. This blaze spread over a 245-hectare

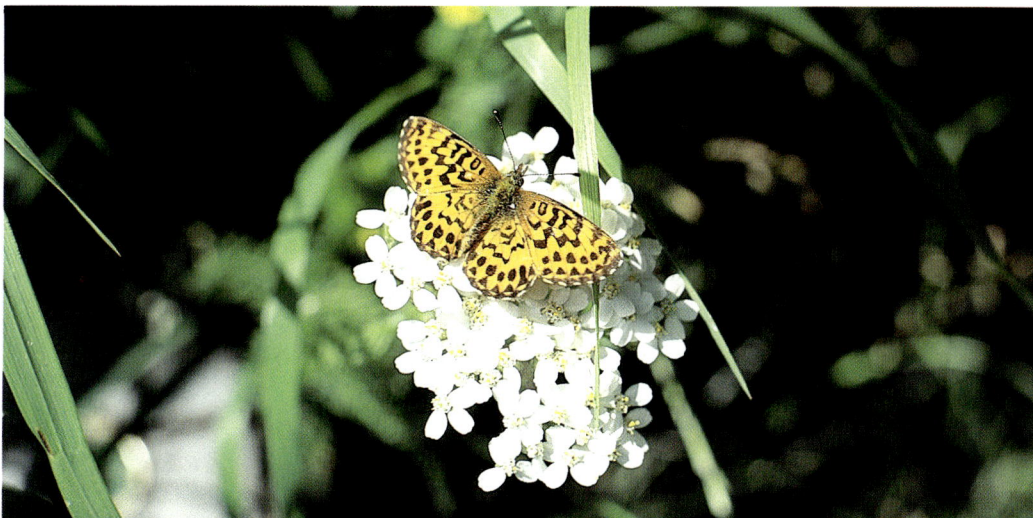

Butterflies and flowers in Alberta's provincial parks are a treat for nature photographers. *(Archie Landals)*

area from the south and west, wiping out the town except for the church, inn and priest's residence. The entire population took refuge in the lake.

From the charred ruins of the shoreline, people stared at the island's tall green trees and lush wetlands, now home to hundreds of birds and animals. The survival of the wildlife prompted the residents to prod the Dominion Government into establishing Big Island (as it was known then) as a bird sanctuary.

Although it was known locally as an important bird sanctuary, interest grew and a delegation from the Lac La Biche Board of Trade and Lions Club requested that the island be examined for its suitability as a provincial park. On September 29, 1952 Big Island Provincial Park was established, and in 1965 it was renamed Sir Winston Churchill Provincial Park for a public figure who advocated parks for the people.

The old-growth forests are an integral part of the island's habitat. It is an important area for pileated woodpeckers, boreal chickadees, fox sparrows and the 230 other species of birds that nest there. Sir Winston Churchill Park attracts bird-watchers from all over North America. The island's sandy beaches and warm, shallow water make it a haven for swimmers. — *Phil Cohen, Donna-Lee Ost & Karen Stroebel*

refreshed and invigorated by contact with the healing powers of nature; Class B parks were to provide recreational facilities especially associated with bathing beaches; and Class C parks were intended to increase the enjoyment of the motorist by providing opportunities for full enjoyment of particularly beautiful glimpses of the landscape, and the establishing of picnic grounds where he may enjoy a few hours and an out-of-door lunch with his family and friends. It was envisioned that these parks would be located along the primary highways of Alberta at 30 to 60 kilometre intervals.

With Alberta's economy suffering from the effects of the Great Depression, the provincial park system got off to a rocky start. Support for Ghost River, Lundbreck Falls and Sylvan Lake faltered and they were later deleted from the system. Hommy, although retained "on the books", was ignored for many years. Little money was available for the few parks that did survive. Capital expenditures for all areas that operated as provincial parks for the six-year period 1929 to 1935 amounted to under $40,000. Of this total, a significant portion was for the purchase of property.

Thunder Lake Provincial Park

Thunder Lake Provincial Park resulted from a request from Barrhead area residents. Although no previous recreational use seems to have been made of the lake, several proposals for swimming facilities and cottage development emerged in the early to mid-50s. In 1956 the government reserved the land but remained unwilling to develop it because of the low local population, the proximity of other parks and the poor access roads. The Kinsmen Club of Barrhead responded by upgrading the existing road, and the Barrhead Chamber of Commerce immediately went to work to raise funds for the future park. They also prepared a beach. Thunder Lake Provincial Park was established in 1958. The 208-hectare park presents opportunities for camping, swimming, fishing, picnicking, motor boating and golfing.

The Way We Were — Pitcher's Cottage

When I was a little boy, I played with my neighbor Peter Pitcher, and because little boys like to take their friends with them, I spent many summers at his family's cottage at Lake Wabamun. His father built it during the 1920s before the present-day Lake Wabamun Provincial Park was established on Moonlight Bay. As soon as school was out, the whole family, Mrs. Pitcher, Lucy, Peter, Mary, Peggy, Bobby the fox terrier and I, would be loaded into the Overland 90 with supplies for a summer at the lake.

In the 20s, the drive to the lake in itself was an adventure. The first cottagers on Lake Wabamun went out by train. The road west to Wabamun had the typical one-chain (66 foot) right of way with 33 feet of dirt piled up in the middle by horses pulling fresnos or scoops. Gravel roads were a luxury still a few years off. Surveyors followed the old pack-trails and wound around the sloughs and larger hills, and when they couldn't avoid a muskeg, they corduroyed it.

We were the only cottage on the bay and we drank the water from a common dipper that hung over the pail. The girls did the washing and the boys took out the slop pail, which was called the "Widow's Cruise" after some forgotten reference known only to the Pitcher family. The outdoor

Willow *(Kåre Hellum)*

Autumn reflections at Long Lake Provincial Park. *(Maureen Landals)*

privy was located strategically behind the woodpile, and over the years, I watched, through its door, a spruce tree grow until it towered over the back of the cottage. Ice was cut from the bay in the winter and put up in sawdust in an ice house.

In the evening, after the dishes were washed and the "Widow's Cruise" taken out, the fire would be started in the fireplace and the coal oil lamps lit. Mr. Pitcher would read to us from *Pilgrim's Progress*. Later as we learned to read, we all took a turn. We slept on the porch and were lulled to sleep by the birds — the laughing grebes and every now and then, the lone cry of the loon.

When the Alberta government realized that Prohibition wasn't going to work, they allowed hotels to set up beer parlors. A chap called Walker built a small hotel in Wabamun. He put up signs along the highway, "Don't pass us up." But in those days there weren't many tourists to pass him up, and his beer parlor, which wasn't very large, was more like an English pub for the locals to have their pint. Summer visitors were tolerated. When we got to legal age, or just about, we would hike across the trestle for 10-cent glasses of Mr. Walker's cold draft beer.

Great grey owls inhabit undisturbed forests. *(Tom Webb)*

Norman Pitcher died shortly after World War II. Peter, after the army, became a mining engineer who travelled the world. Lucy married a Church of England minister and moved to the south of Ireland, and Mary, who had been in the WRENS, stayed east as a dietician. That left only Mrs. Pitcher and Peggy, and when Mrs. Pitcher offered to sell me the cottage, I jumped at the chance. After the stress of the Battle of the Atlantic, the little cottage and the tranquillity of Moonlight Bay eased me back into civilian life. After supper on the screen porch with the onshore evening breeze stirring the branches of the trees planted 30 years before, the soft light of the setting sun and the calls of the birds on the water, I would think back to my early days as a little barefoot boy with Peter and his sisters. — *Rodney Pike*

Wabamun Lake Provincial Park

Wabamun Lake has been popular as a resort since settlement began in the district around 1909. The summer communities of Kapasiwin, Fallis and Seba Beach were developed by private enterprise. When the Member of the Legislative Assembly for Stoney Plain requested that the government create a provincial park on the north shore of the lake in 1931, he was refused on the grounds that private development had made the investment of public funds unnecessary.

In the early-50s, the government began to consider creation of a park on the lake because of increasing public pressure on the privately developed beaches. Of the three prospective park sites considered, Moonlight Bay had the most recreational potential and could be acquired from the municipal district at no cost. Once additional lands were purchased from private sources, the government established Wabamun Lake Provincial Park in 1955. The 229-hectare park, situated 65 kilometres west of Edmonton, is one of the most heavily used recreational parks in Alberta.

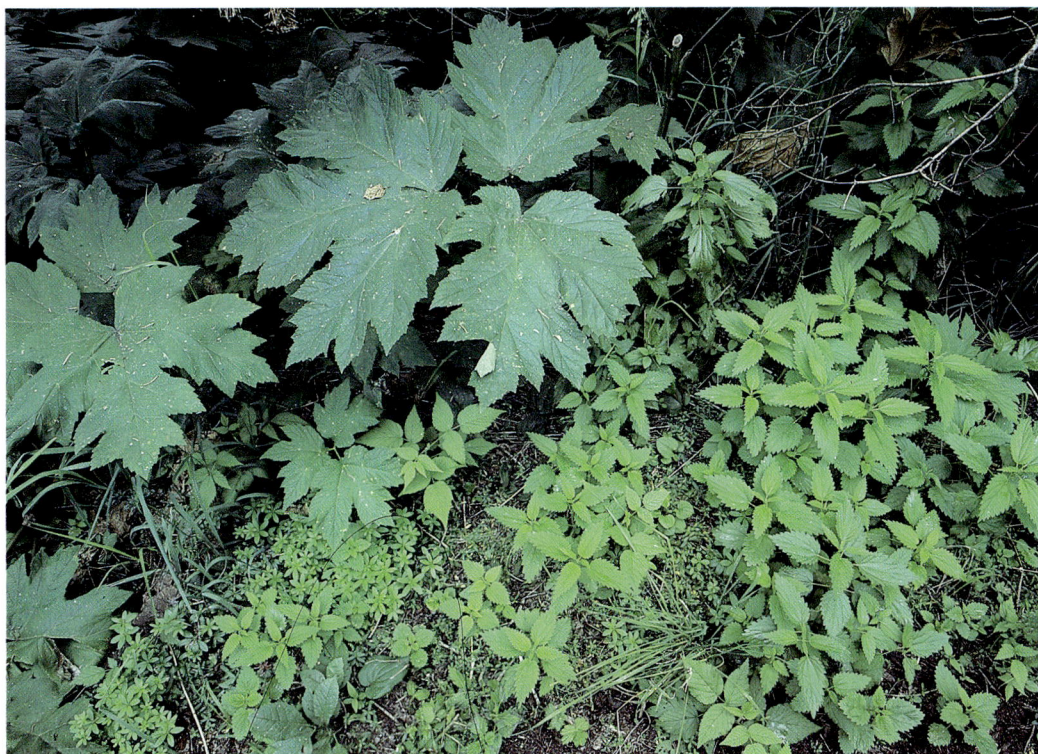

Lush understorey of moist boreal forest. Sir Winston Churchill Provincial Park. *(Dave Dodge)*

Boreal Forest

Williamson Provincial Park

Williamson Provincial Park is centred on Sturgeon Lake, an excellent recreational resource and commercial fisheries body of water just west of Valleyview. It attained park status in 1960.

The impetus behind development of this land as a recreational site came from the Grande Prairie Member of the Legislative Assembly, Ira McLaughlin. He wished to see a highway campground established on a three-hectare site between Highway 34 and Sturgeon Lake. It later became known that the parcel in question was not for sale. The Parks Board investigated the property, declared it suitable for park development and acquired it in 1960. The 17-hectare park is known throughout the province for its whitefish.

Winagami Lake Provincial Park

The haunting calls of loons echo across the water, bald eagles soar overhead and blue herons wade near the beach. These are the sights and sounds of Winagami Lake Provincial Park. Located in northwestern Alberta, the park is home to over 200 species of birds during the summer months. Bordered on the west by Winagami Lake and on the east by South Heart River, the park is situated in the midst of productive farmland. Bald eagles are year-round residents while others — yellow warblers, Baltimore orioles and kingbirds — are seasonal. Nature's curious mating rituals amongst birds can be observed in the park in spring. The everyday character of the male ruddy duck is transformed as his bill becomes a bright iridescent blue to better attract a mate. The rhythmic beating of the male ruffed grouse drumming his wings to entice the female can be heard resounding through the trees. The arrival of autumn is signalled by the cacophonous chatter of migrating geese, ducks, swans and cranes.

Community Spirit

Park development was due, in large part, to community pride and volunteer efforts. The first parks were small. They served the Sunday afternoon needs of nearby communities. Local advisory committees were set up to guide the operations of these parks. Residents donated time and material to construct ball diamonds, horseshoe pits, beaches, toilets, tables and other facilities. Perhaps nowhere was this community spirit better demonstrated than at Park Lake Provincial Park, where volunteers, in 1932, planted 15 acres with approximately 4,500 trees and shrubs.

Lesser Slave Lake stretches to the horizon like an inland sea. *(AV and Exhibit Services)*

Boreal Forest

Local folklore has it that Winagami is a word of Cree origin meaning "Stinking Water," not an auspicious beginning for a provincial park. In 1952 a dam was built on the South Heart River to allow water to be diverted to Winagami Lake to freshen it. Soon after, a group of residents from the neighboring areas travelled to the lake bearing axes, shovels and picks with a common purpose in mind. Their combined efforts resulted in a hand-cut trail to Winagami Lake and a cleared section of lakeshore for a beach. At one point, 125 people became marooned at the site for several days when a large amount of rainfall prevented them leaving. Helicopters were used to fly in provisions to the stranded and air-evacuate those who became ill.

The Winagami Lake Beach Association continued to make improvements to the beach and lake. Soon the area was so popular and the workload so great that the Association asked the Provincial Parks Board to designate it as a provincial park. Winagami Lake Provincial Park was formally established in 1956.

The 1,211-hectare park, which also has a 72-lot cottage subdivision within its boundaries, presents a wide range of opportunities for the young, young at heart and physically challenged. The park's bird-viewing trails and two viewing platforms with spotting scopes encourage visitors to see nature at its best. — *Shannon Reed-Caron & Rob Hugill*

Young's Point Provincial Park

Young's Point Provincial Park was established in 1971 near the town of Valleyview close to the Sturgeon Lake oil fields. About a decade before, the Provincial Parks Board had investigated the condition of the lands that now form the park and had suggested that they possessed considerable recreational potential. Further impetus for park reservation came in 1967 from the local member of the legislative assembly. When it became known that the owner of the lands in question, Frederick C. Young, was willing to sell the land for below market value as long as the name of the park contained a reference to his surname, the government quickly made the purchase.

Gull eggs *(Archie Landals)*

44

This 1,090-hectare park is considered one of the best water-based resources in the Peace River country. There are over 150 species of birds including great grey owls and barred owls found within the park.

A Visit to the Park on July 1, 2010

Roots reached for our feet, branches clasped at our shoulders, the massive trunk of a white spruce swelled from the ancient terrace, pierced the green canopy and reached for the sky. Cutting through the bush and out onto the gravel bank beside the creek, we pitched our tents on the sand where the vegetation would not be harmed, sprawled and considered the trees. The grove of spruce far outstripped their poplar neighbors. These spruce, found only in a few parks, range from two to three hundred years old. They greeted the first Europeans, and sheltered the Indians and forest animals long before that.

Glaciologists assure us that the glaciers retreated from this area about 10,000 years ago. Pedologists state that soils developed slowly in these cool steppe climates. Climatologists claim that the rainfall in this area was once 700 millimetres per year. Botanists impart that the spruce-poplar complex is mutually interdependent and that the history of the site can be read from the rings of the trees. Ecologists insist that the whole is greater than the sum of the parts and that the forest is a giant web. Environmentalists say that a forest community is a living, breathing whole.

Somehow, someone or something created the wonders of this park. Whoever created it fashioned a cathedral with vaulted ceilings where the cries of birds are hushed by the banners of moss, the trickle of the stream is music and the fruit of the bushes is an offering to those who visit. Here, in this park, the species live together in a harmony that has endured for thousands of years, each drawing from the strength of the other to form a community in the truest sense of the word.

We will endure — but these spruce may not. They may be sacrificed for our progress and when they are gone, so too will be the other denizens of the park and with them, our hearts and souls.
— *Chip Ross*

Provincial parks remained small and local in focus until after the end of the Second World War, no doubt a result of the social and economic climate of the time. Alberta's population was relatively small and predominantly rural and people continued to have close ties to the land. Hunting, fishing, berry-picking and similar outdoor pursuits were a part of everyday life.

Besides, Alberta had the national parks. Albertans of the day were indeed fortunate to have the spectacular scenery of the Rocky Mountains available as national parks. Early tourists were blessed with the mountain national

Aster (*Kåre Hellum*)

CANADIAN SHIELD

The Canadian Shield extends only into the northeast corner of Alberta in the vicinity of Lake Athabasca. The area north of the lake is characterized by granite outcrops, while south of the lake, extensive sand plains and dune systems occur. Jackpine and lichen woodlands cover much of the sand plain while black spruce bogs dominate the depressions between the rock outcrops which support only scattered pine trees. Reflecting the cool climate and poor diversity of vegetation, wildlife is scarce. Clear lakes and rugged scenery make this an attractive region for wilderness recreation.

Granite outcrops of the Canadian Shield. *(Archie Landals)*

Yellow Heather. Athabasca Dunes Ecological Reserve. *(Maureen Landals)*

F O O T H I L L S

The Foothills Natural Region consists of the belt of folded and faulted sedimentary rock that lies along the eastern edge of the Rocky Mountains. Topography varies from rolling in the east to rugged along the mountains in the west. Vegetation reflects a transition between the Rocky Mountains and the boreal forest. Lodgepole pine forests cover much of the area, graduating into stands of white spruce and aspen toward the boreal forest. Although lakes and marshes are relatively uncommon, the foothills contain some of Alberta's finest trout streams.

Wildflowers blanket Whaleback Ridge in the southern Alberta Foothills. *(Cleve Wershler/Provincial Parks Service)*

Parks and People — A Natural Relationship

The tendency nowadays to wander in wilderness is delightful to see. Thousands of tired, nerve-shaken, over-civilized people are beginning to find out that going to the mountains is going home; that wildness is a necessity; and that mountain parks and reservations are useful not only as fountains of timber and irrigating rivers, but as fountains of life. Awakening from the stupefying effects of the vice of over-industry and the deadly apathy of luxury, they are trying as best they can to mix and enrich their own little ongoings with those of Nature, and to get rid of rust and disease.
— *John Muir (1901)*

Beauvais Lake Provincial Park

Beauvais Lake, located in the southwestern part of the province, was named after Remi Beauvais, a local rancher who had moved to the area after the passage of favorable lease laws in 1881. These ranchers, having small holdings, were more akin to the mixed farming homesteaders who entered the area between 1898 and 1909. The ranchers ran their cattle on the hillsides and used the lake for watering stock. Soon many local settlers were using the lake for recreational purposes as well. The potential conflict between these users prompted the government to consider the establishment of Beauvais Lake as a provincial park. A local advisory committee oversaw activity at the lake. By 1948 there were about a dozen cottages whose owners were largely responsible for local road improvements.

Gallardia *(Kåre Hellum)*

49

Small herds of elk, eight different amphibian and reptile species and more than 110 bird species are found within the 706-hectare park. Habitats such as spruce and pine forests, aspen woods, grasslands and wetlands are found within the park. Rainbow trout have been planted since 1947. One of the six historical sites within the park is said to be the grave of one of General Custer's scouts.

Big Hill Springs Provincial Park

Spring water, wood, shelter and a cliff thought to have been used as a buffalo jump drew prehistoric people to the site of Big Hill Springs Provincial Park. In 1881 a grazing lease was issued on the land and in 1891, Alberta's first commercial creamery was established in the coulee of Big Hill Springs by D.M. Radcliff.

Although the area had been used as a recreational area for picnics and similar outdoor activities since the turn of the century, this was not the reason the provincial government became interested in its development. Rather, the stream that ran through the area had a considerable reputation for trout production, and in 1941, the government seized upon the idea of making this the site of a new fish hatchery operation. The hatchery, however, was a failure. Big Hill Springs Provincial Park was established on the site in 1957. Today the 26-hectare park, located west of Calgary, provides visitors with the opportunity to view typical prairie birds, mink, coyote, Richardson's ground squirrels and pocket gophers.

Chain Lakes Provincial Park

Chain Lakes Provincial Park was developed because of the creation of a reservoir resulting from the damming of Willow Creek. During the 1940s, the Prairie Farm Rehabilitation Act authorities and the Lethbridge Northern Irrigation District council sought a means of ensuring a sufficient supply of water in the district south of Calgary. Although these and other interested groups agreed on the nature of the problem, they could not decide on a suitable location for the reservoir. Finally, a 1957 engineering report indicated that it would be feasible to back Willow Creek into the Chain Lakes to ensure a supply of water to the communities of Claresholm and Granum as well as to irrigation projects west of Granum. But this decision aroused local ire as ranchers complained about the adverse effect such a project would have on their springs and grazing areas. Right-of-way discussions occupied the next several years as development proceeded cautiously. The reservoir was finally completed in 1965.

Ranchland is part of the attractive cultural landscape of the Southern Alberta Foothills. *(Rosemary H.L. Calvert, FRPS)*

That spring, the local member of the legislative assembly stated that development of the reservoir was arousing interest in the creation of proper recreational facilities. Other people queried the government on the site's possibilities as a fishing resort if it were to be stocked with appropriate species. These enquiries worried local ranchers and the concept of a provincial park at the reservoir was raised. In 1969 Chain Lakes Provincial Park was formally established.

The park comprises 409 hectares, and according to Joy and Cam Finlay, Alberta's premier bird-watchers, "The developing marsh below the dam attracts a diversity of wetland plants and birds." The park is held in high value by anglers and other recreational visitors from the Calgary region. — *N. Campbell*

Foothills

A Commemoration

I walked this ground long before you came
And mapped the way before it had a name;
I dug pits and mounds by the forty chain score
And forced the township grid across the prairie floor.
The Meridians, the Base Lines, the Correction Lines I drew
And carved them in the land as westward I flew,
Chiselling the section posts and marking them clear
For the coming homesteaders who always were near.

I mapped out your soil, the type and how deep
And showed you the coverage, the trees and how steep,
And where there were rivers and also the sloughs,
The trails and ridges — all topographical news.
The creeks and the mountains bear the names of my men
And in towns and hamlets, street corners can
Tell you the history of long time ago
When we marked out the land so that it might grow.

Gordon L. Haggerty

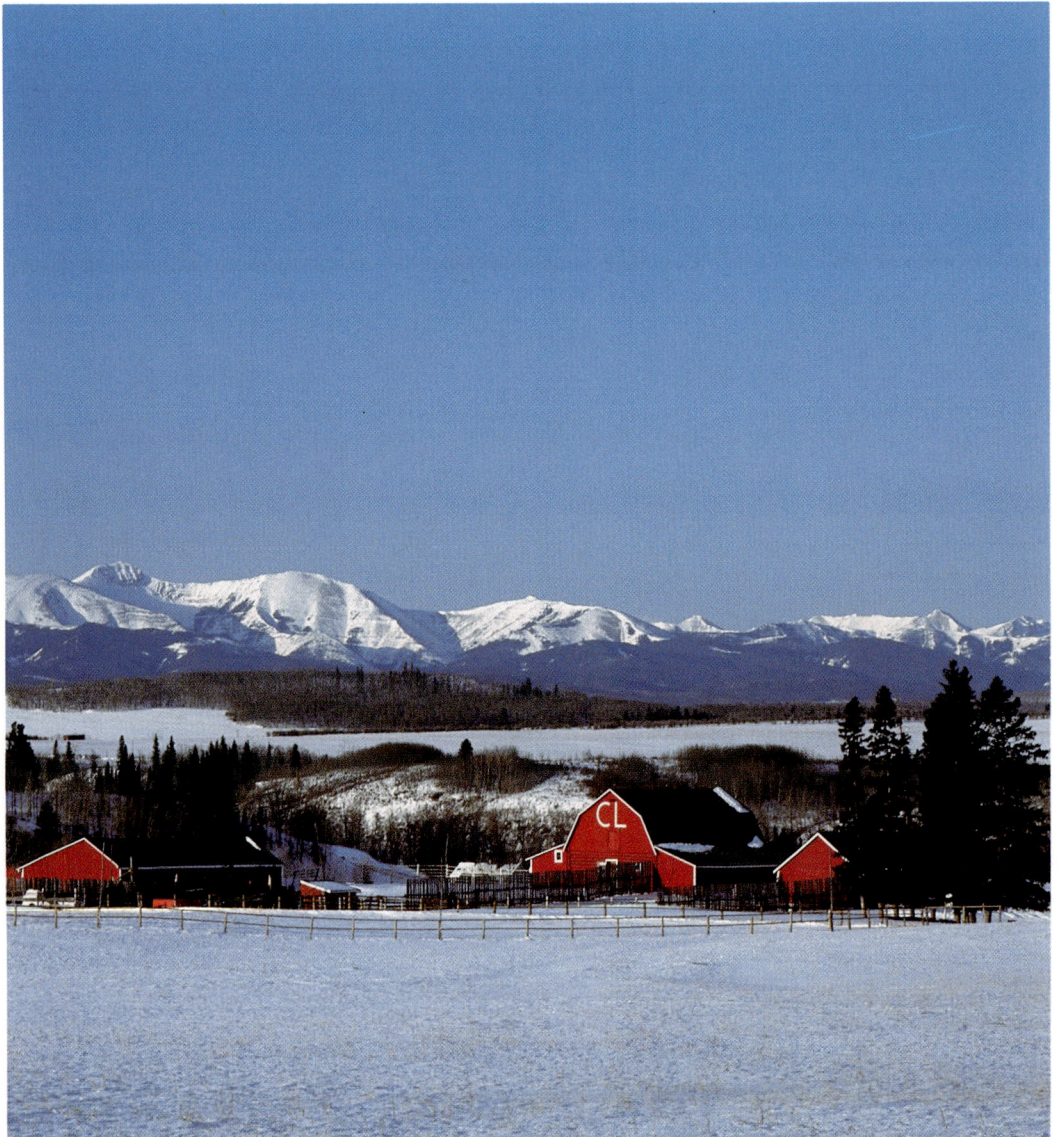

Crimson Lake Provincial Park

In 1912 Jack Mooney was working with a survey crew in the area and discovered the lake at sunset. The striking colors of the setting sun reflecting on the waters caused him to name it Crimson Lake. The lake has played an important recreational role in the lives of Rocky Mountain House residents since the 1920s. A cottage subdivision was established in 1932. Given the growing interest in the area, the Rocky Mountain House Board of Trade asked the provincial government to create a provincial park. Crimson Lake Provincial Park was officially opened in 1951 and at that time encompassed 688 hectares. The park has grown over the years to its present size of 3,209 hectares providing increased protection to the wildlife and the unique land base found in the area.

The surrounding land is a transitional forest area that developed on sand dunes left by the glaciers. Here three types of natural regions come together — boreal forest, aspen parkland and foothills forest. In addition to lodgepole pine, black spruce, white spruce and tamarack, several species of orchids as well as lilies, fireweed, Labrador tea and Indian paintbrush grow in the park. Mammals include: black bear, moose, elk, deer, wolf, cougar, hare, red squirrel, chipmunk and beaver. Song sparrows, sandhill cranes, blue herons, loons, robins, ruffed grouse and osprey are a few of the species of birds found in the park.

The recently opened Amerada Trail offers an excellent opportunity for people who wish to explore a larger portion of the park. The 10-kilometre trail starts at the day-use area and encircles the entire lake. Amerada Minerals Corporation, which hold leases on oil wells within the park, sponsored the building of the trail, the first development of its kind in Alberta's park system.

Southern foothills ranchland.
(Rosemary H.L. Calvert, FRPS)

William A. Switzer Provincial Park

The Hinton Chamber of Commerce called for establishment of a provincial park near Jarvis Lake in 1958. Recent improvements to Highway 16 and the interest of local sportsmen were factors that were taken into account by the Provincial Parks Board, and in 1958, Entrance Provincial Park was formally created. The park was renamed in the early-70s as a tribute to William A. Switzer, the local member of the legislature.

After a master plan was completed for the park in 1970, the government began to phase out lease-holders. This was an exceedingly complex question which took some time. Included in the park

---

parks but their descendants were faced with the task of establishing destination parks in other parts of the province. This task became more difficult with each passing year as land was dedicated to other uses.

Statistics specific to Alberta are not available prior to 1901. It is estimated, however, that 25,000 people lived in what is now Alberta in 1885, the year that Banff National Park was established. Probably over 90 per cent of these Albertans were rural folk. A vivid image of southwestern Alberta at that time is painted by rancher Frederick Ings. In his 1936 autobiography, the pioneer rancher recounts the spring

cattle round-up of 1884: "On the trail, as far down as the cattle might have drifted, we passed through an absolutely unsettled land; no towns, no farms, no fences, just one big grass-covered range, such grass as we never see now. The buffalo had been gone for years, and what cattle there were wandered at will from Sheep Creek (just south of Calgary) almost to the border. We followed the old Macleod Trail used by freighters and bull trains. We passed Trollinger's Stopping Place on Mosquito Creek, The Leavings, another such place where Granum now stands, and then nothing to Macleod where a few settlers clustered about

Fire is part of the natural evolution of the Foothills landscape. *(Fred Vermeulen)*

were a Royal Canadian Air Force survival training school, a forestry service reservation with picnic facilities, a North West Pulp and Power timber reservation, a Kiwanis youth camp and a Junior Wardens' camp reservation.

Within the 2,685-hectare park there are five lakes — Cache, Blue, Graveyard, Jarvis and Gregg — Jarvis and Gregg being the largest, and the Blue Lake Leadership Training Centre. Over 150 species of birds including at least 13 raptors have been noted in the park such as nesting ospreys and pygmy, barred and great grey owls. Over 30 mammals including coyote, beaver, red fox, pine marten, river otter, elk, moose, mule and white-tailed deer are also known to live in or around the park area.

the post. Here the south wagons joined us and on again we went through vast emptiness to east of where Lethbridge is now built. We went as far as we found cattle and worked back. It might take about a week to get there and two months to return with the cattle we had gathered."

After World War II, Alberta underwent a period of rapid change. Oil was discovered at Leduc and Turner Valley – the economy boomed. Industrial development began to predominate in the previous agricultural economy. Alberta's population increased. Soon more people lived in the cities and towns than on farms. The standard of living for most Albertans improved. People had more leisure time and money to spend on recreation and tourism. The family automobile became the norm — no longer a luxury. A network of modern highways soon linked all parts of the province. The average Albertan's appetite for travel, out-door recreation and tourism became insatiable. There was little sense of the need to protect diverse landscapes. The general public perceived Alberta as still largely an unoccupied wilderness.

Yellow monkey flower *(Kåre Hellum)*

G R A S S L A N D

Alberta's grassland natural region is a flat to gently rolling plain that stretches across the southern part of the province. Major rivers such as the Red Deer, Bow, Oldman, South Saskatchewan and Milk flow across the region from west to east. In places, the valleys are carved deeply into the bedrock, and extensive badlands have developed. As its name implies, the vegetation is mostly grasslands, with some exceptions. Cypress Hills, because of its elevation above the surrounding plains, receives enough precipitation to support stands of aspen, pine and spruce in the wetter north-facing valleys. Riparian forests of plains cottonwood and willow stretch like ribbons along the rivers. Sagebrush flats occur along the valley bottoms further back from the rivers. Stabilized and active sand dunes scattered throughout the region support a variety of rare plants and occasionally, desert animals such as the kangaroo rat. Pronghorn antelope and mule deer are the major ungulates. Wooded river valleys and coulees are highly productive and provide nesting sites, food and shelter for three-quarters of the bird species that inhabit the area.

The Great South Circle Tour

There's more to the soul of Alberta than mountains. For example, the Great South Circle Tour is 1,000 kilometres of ferries, badlands, dinosaurs, antelope, owls, deer, cacti, bison jumps, mountains and ptarmigan, endless images that will stay with you forever.

Leave Calgary and drive northeast to Drumheller. The smaller roads cut through wheat fields and farms. Take Highway 840 through Standard and Rosebud and discover the famous Rosebud dinner theatre. Continue on a gravel road east of 840 to cross the Rosebud River. The next stop is Drumheller. Visit the Royal Tyrrell Museum of Palaeontology nestled in the badlands of Midland Provincial Park. Follow the Dinosaur Trail north to the Bleriot Ferry and cross the Red Deer River on an old wooden car ferry. Camp under the stately cottonwoods along the river.

Head north to Dry Island Buffalo Jump Provincial Park. Sit on the high valley walls above the park at sunset and watch the deer move below along the Red Deer River. The evening rays highlight the incredible erosion of the badlands.

Picture perfect skies over Dinosaur Provincial Park. (Rosemary H.L. Calvert, FRPS)

Wild bergamot (Kåre Hellum)

Cross the river north of the park at MacKenzie Crossing and head back to Highway 56. Visit Rumsey Ecological Reserve, over 33 square kilometres of rolling aspen parkland set aside to protect a landscape that has been largely cultivated because of its productive soils. Head south toward Drumheller, then southeast to Little Fish Lake Provincial Park where you can camp for the night. Spend the evening wandering through the fescue grasslands of the nearby Hand Hills Ecological Reserve. Imagine what this prairie landscape was like without fences, teeming with buffalo.

In the morning, head southeast through Alberta's prairie ranching country to Dinosaur Provincial Park. If you leave early, you'll see antelope and mule deer. Little snippets of badlands will begin to appear and then suddenly, Alberta's past will confront you. Drive down into the valley and lounge in a stream shaded by poplars. The temperatures can soar to over 40 degrees Celsius. Scoop up the coarse sand and look for bits of fossils. Step in squishy bentonite mud as you walk up the creek. Rainstorms transform the park. Large waterfalls form over dramatic shelves in minutes. Gray water

The impact upon parks was profound. Urbanites overran the provincial parks such as Aspen Beach and Park Lake. The local advisory committees and their entourage of volunteers could no longer cope; full-time staff were required.

Starting in 1951, Alberta Provincial Parks underwent a period of profound change. A comprehensive new Parks Act was passed and the administration of parks was transferred from Public Works to Lands and Forests. This legislation established a new, three-member Provincial Parks Board. Dr. Vi Wood, an agricultural economist, became board chairman, a position he would hold until 1966 when he was appointed Deputy Minister of Lands and Forests. The 50s and 60s were the formative years for Alberta's formal system of provincial parks. During this period, the reversal of the urban-rural split prompted the mass reservation of land for recreational purposes. "We reserved land just to have it," said Wood, "even if we didn't have the money."

In the 1952/53 fiscal year, there was a substantial increase in park expenditures. A total of $125,000 was appropriated for park purposes. The annual report of the Provincial Parks Board summarizes the focus of these expenditures. "During the fiscal year, a considerable portion of

Sandstone cliffs capture the evening sunlight in Writing-on-Stone Provincial Park. *(Cleve Wershler/Provincial Parks Service)*

spews from sinkholes and the bentonite hills become mounds of axle grease. Take an evening boat trip to watch deer and beaver, or a day boat trip down to the Old Mexico Ranch where cacti grow on mud roofs and large bull snakes wind through the grass and corrals.

The landscape gets flatter and drier as you drive to Cypress Hills. Except for the irrigated cropland around Brooks, ranching is the dominant industry. Oil wells dot the landscape. Cypress Hills is a cool refuge in summer — it's much higher than the surrounding land. Travel a back road to Manyberries and then on to Writing-on-Stone. Look for Pakowki Lake. On some maps the entire shoreline is dotted indicating there isn't much water. If you go there, perhaps there will be some water for the tundra swans, although their heads and breasts will be stained red from the iron oxide of the slough. The view — raw, open and untouched — stretches for hundreds of miles. Hidden in front of the Sweetgrass Hills is the Milk River.

---

the provincial parks vote was utilized for capital expenditures. The major improvements consisted of five picnic shelters, two each at Cypress Hills Provincial Park and Garner Lake Provincial Park, and four miles of new roadways at Cypress Hills, Garner Lake, Crimson Lakes and Beauvais Lake. In addition, gravelling and road maintenance were carried out on many miles of roadways within provincial parks, and buildings and other structures were maintained either by caretakers or voluntary labor from residents of the area. Several steel stoves of improved construction were purchased and distributed to various parks, and playground equipment, which proved to be

a major attraction to the children, was supplied to twelve parks."

The new Act also provided for full-time staff. Charlie Harvey was the first to be hired, and as Superintendent of Provincial Parks, his first undertaking was to find out where the parks were, what was there and who had looked after them, then to prepare budgets for their upkeep and operation. Two further parks staff members, a warden and an assistant warden (renamed "rangers" in 1974), were appointed to Cypress Hills Provincial Park, which at that time, was the largest provincial park in Alberta. The early years in parks, though, were a labor of love, albeit a

Grassland

Interpretive walks compliment a visit to the Tyrrell Museum, Midland Provincial Park. *(Fred Hammer)*

Migrating snow geese, Little Fish Lake Provincial Park *(Provincial Parks Service)*

Snowdrifts and roadside grass *(Rosemary H.L. Calvert, FRPS)*

very frustrating one said Mr. Harvey. "It was a constant uphill battle to even attempt to do those things for which the Parks Act stated that parks were established — namely, preservation of nature and environment."

Responding to the demand of the motoring public, Alberta developed a system of campsites and rest stops at intervals along all the major highways. Clean, convenient picnic sites and overnight campgrounds were provided for auto tourists. Quickly, these way-side-stops became the pride of the province and the envy of the country. According to Tom Drinkwater, who followed Wood as deputy minister, "The

paving of the Alberta's highways and secondary roads forced us to get serious about our parks."

A total of 46 provincial parks were established in the 20 year period 1951 to 1971. Although there were a few notable exceptions such as Dinosaur and Writing-on-Stone that were set aside to protect their resources, most of these parks were selected on a recreational basis. Development focused on family recreation including picnicking, camping, beaches, playgrounds, boating and fishing. A rule-of-thumb was to locate parks within 80 kilometres of the population centres. All site improvements were to blend visitor developments with the

Writing-on-Stone Provincial Park doesn't fully reveal itself until you're on top of it. The hoodoos are strange and magical looking. Take time to observe the bird life. Perhaps a pair of golden eagles will soar over the Mounted Police Outpost. The Sweetgrass Hills reflect orange sunlight as the moon rises behind them in the evening. Deer can be seen moving in single file along the river. On the valley wall coyotes yip and howl in unison. There are places along the Milk River that are time-less — unchanged for 10,000 years or more.

Travel west on Highway 504 toward wild prairie vistas and infamous spots like Whiskey Gap. Just before sunset, the land seems to spring forth deer and antelope. Drive down the road to Police Outpost Provincial Park just as the sun goes down and see a vision of what heaven might look like — no foothills — just prairies meeting mountains. If it's early, continue to Waterton Lakes National Park and camp in Beauvais Lake Provincial Park.

The next morning, head out for the Crowsnest Pass area. You'll find a lot of mining history and varied native prehistory. The terrible Hillcrest Mine disaster is movingly portrayed in a slide show at the Frank Slide Interpretive Centre, a wind-blasted gnarled-tree montane zone and the gateway to the final day of your trip. Take Highway 940 to the Highwood Pass in Kananaskis Country. Travel through forests over creeks, rivers and past Livingston Falls. Climb into the beautiful alpine environment of the Highwood Pass where the tree-line is close at hand. A relatively short self-guiding trail takes you through the features of this fragile yet rugged country to Ptarmigan Cirque where, within seconds, you're transported to a true high alpine environment of rocks and scree. Look for picas, marmots and ptarmigan. The trip becomes somewhat of an anti-climax once you leave Kananaskis and head toward Calgary. You could, however, take your time and travel Highway 68 through Sibbald Flats and perhaps take the forestry trunk road that cuts off from the highway to Bragg Creek.

The week-long circle is complete and you're back in Calgary. But now that you've tasted southern Alberta . . . turn your eyes north. — *Mark Hamill*

Tiger swallow-tail. *(Archie Landals)*

Grassland

Cypress Hills Interprovincial Park

Looking down from space, one would get quite a different impression of the Cypress Hills. The details would not be discernable, only the broad patterns and features. The roadways, campgrounds and fencelines would be gone as would the man-drawn line that divides Alberta and Saskatchewan. The Hills would appear — as they have for more than 40 million years — one geographical feature.

Between 1911 and 1930, the management of the Hills was unified; they were managed as a Federal Forest Reserve. When the responsibility for natural resources was transferred from the federal government to the provinces in 1930, management practices began to diverge. Alberta's Hills continued to be managed as a forest reserve until 1951 when it became a provincial park. Saskatchewan, however, designated their Hills as a provincial park in 1931.

The Cypress Hills were considered, in the 1960s, a candidate site for a national park. But another two decades passed before their management was once again unified. The Cypress Hills Interprovincial Park Agreement, signed on August 25, 1989 by Stephen West, Alberta's minister of parks and Colin Maxwell, Saskatchewan's minister of park, was an achievement in itself. Although similar agreements have been signed between nations, this was the first formal interprovincial park agreement to be signed in Canada. The agreement recognized four broad program areas — resource management, tourism, marketing, and interpretive and information activities — where coordination could be improved between the provinces, and with Fort Walsh National Historic Park which is also located in the Hills. Alberta's Cypress Hills Provincial Park celebrated its fortieth anniversary in 1991. Dora MacKeage, a long term resident of Elkwater, the townsite within the park explained: "The park has become a place where people meet to enjoy the outdoors in a variety of beautiful settings."

The extensive parklands present opportunities for educational and recreational activities and nature appreciation. Some enjoy the bustle of the beach and activities in Elkwater, others prefer the more secluded wilderness of Graburn Gap. Cypress Hills Interprovincial Park has achieved its place in provincial park history as one entity, one geographical feature, one unique and valuable ecosystem, and now — one park. — *Keith Bocking, Kelty Otto, Mike Klassen & Heidi Breier*

Prairie crocus in Gooseberry Lake Provincial Park. *(Archie Landals)*

natural environment.

Social conditions in Alberta continued to change and demand for parks escalated. The Parks Act was amended in 1964. The scope of parks was enlarged to include historic sites, natural and wilderness areas. Additional provisions were made for the purchase and expropriation of land, and for the authority to provide grants to local governments for park development. Another early architect of Alberta's park system, Jim Acton, summarized the rationale of establishing parks: "Just as parks served a purpose for people to gather and enjoy recreation, politicians recognized the significance of having a place for people to gather."

The urbanization of Alberta occurred in two distinct ways, each with very different ramifications for the growing system. During this first period of growth, many Albertans who had grown up on the farm moved to nearby towns and cities to find employment or retire. When these families felt the need to flee the city, chances were they still owned a nearby piece of the countryside. Barring this, being the first generation off the farm, they still had relatives or friends with a vacant "back forty" suitable for a family picnic or ball game. However, as the population of Alberta grew and urbanization

Cypress Hills includes vegetation typical of Foothills natural region. *(Rosemary H.L. Calvert, FRPS)*

To experience the moods of Dinosaur Provincial Park, the visitor should be there at all times of the day. *(John Walper/Alberta Parks Service)*

continued, this scenario changed. People flocked to Alberta from other parts of Canada seeking employment with the booming oil industry. Immigrants continued to arrive from all corners of the globe. With no immediate ties to the land, these new Albertans were far more dependent on the emerging park system to satisfy their outdoor recreational needs and their desire to experience, enjoy and understand their new home.

During this same time period, general access to the countryside was being further restricted. Wide belts of country residential subdivisions and hobby farms were springing up around the major cities. The owners of these rural estates were individuals who wanted to escape the hustle and bustle of the cities; they were not predisposed to the general public using their property for recreation. "I remember a lady from Cooking Lake crying as she explained how the rural landowners were being overrun by urban pleasure seekers," recalled Dr. Wood.

Throughout the 50s and 60s, while the parks system was making a valiant attempt to keep up with the demand for outdoor recreation, another phenomenon was occurring. The general public was becoming more aware of the environment and increasingly concerned for its wellbeing. Landmark works such as Rachael

From Past to the Present on a Bus

"Badlands are areas of high erosion rates, moonscapes of v-shaped valleys, knife-edged ridges, hoodoos, rills and soft sedimentary rock. With each intense rain storm, all the loose sediment washes down the barren, steep-sided slopes and fills normally dry stream beds with muddy water. These streams then flow into the Red Deer River. Three million tonnes of mud, sand and silt is carried from Alberta into Saskatchewan each year! Close to one-half centimetre of the badlands is eroding away each year. In 20,000 years or so, depending on the climate, they'll have completely eroded away, we'll be out of a park and I'll be out of a job!"

Some groans and laughter, it's the start of another Badlands Bus Tour of Dinosaur Provincial Park. It's a journey into the heart of the Natural Preserve — a place accessible only with a guide — where pristine beauty, fossil treasures and rare habitat is appreciated and enjoyed by all who visit.

The bus tours began after the park's first ranger, Roy Fowler and Charlie Sternberg, a world-renowned palaeontologist, excavated a Corythosaurus (duck-billed) dinosaur. It was left exactly the way it was found, in a slab of sandstone, but with the fossilized bones exposed. The next park ranger, Jerry Tranter, began taking folks to the site. Jerry and a pick-up truckload of park visitors would drive out past the Petrified Tipi, and if they were really keen, take a short walk to the Valley of the Moon. So began the evolution of the Badlands Bus Tour into a fragile, natural landscape in southern Alberta. Visitors gasp at the beauty of large mushroom shaped hoodoos filling a valley surrounded by greenish popcorn textured hills.

"Those hills are made up of bentonite clay, a weathered and altered volcanic ash. It absorbs water when it rains, swelling up to fill the cracks, making the greasiest, slipperiest mess ever seen. Bentonite has many commercial uses. It's used as drillers' mud, for clearing wine and filtering dye out of purple gas, as a glaze for pottery, for making toothpaste and as an emulsifier for peanut butter and ice cream. The distinct layers of volcanic ash found in the park are used to date the sedimentary rock containing the dinosaur remains. A radiometric age of close to 75 million years has been calculated.

Carson's *Silent Spring* exposed the risk of indiscriminate use of pesticides. Television brought nature-films into many homes. People began to realize that they were living in a rapidly shrinking world. Moreover, there was an awakening to the dependence of human survival on the environment. "Concern was building about our resource base," recalled Wood. "It was realized that we no longer had to conquer the natural resources — we had to care for them."

Albertans were not immune to these external influences. At home they were getting a first-hand look at a rapidly changing province. Increased mobility, more leisure time, a passion

Prairie cone-flower *(Kåre Hellum)*
Prickly pear cactus flower *(Fred Hammer)*

Grassland

"Dinosaur Provincial Park, a UNESCO World Heritage Site, is unique for its palaeontological resources, the threatened cottonwood river valley habitat and the animal species it protects. Birds like the golden eagle and ferruginous hawk nest here. The other species of birds found here, however, winter elsewhere in the world where they may not be protected. Remember, the loss of natural habitats anywhere — affects our own backyard. When you go home, think globally, but act locally. I hope you all enjoyed the tour. Come back and visit us again." — *Heidi Eijgel*

A Ranger's Ramblings — Dinosaur Provincial Park

I remember the excitement and anticipation we felt — Sharon, my wife, Clinton, our three-year-old son and me, a "rookie" park warden — as we headed east out of Lethbridge to our new home in Dinosaur Provincial Park. It was April 3, 1966. Over the next 18 months, we met people from around the world. Moreover, we had the privilege to help raise public awareness for this precious resource — Alberta's badlands.

1966: On my first visit, I was taken by the park's raw beauty. My predecessor, Roy Fowler, the first warden and a self-taught palaeontologist, had accumulated great quantities of natural and historical artifacts. I was amazed how very few people knew about this place. Albertans must hear about it, this was my first challenge.

The first three months passed quickly. I spent long days exploring, meeting neighbors and getting "tuned in" by my park foreman, Adam Yuschuk, an old miner. Prior to my arrival, he had used dynamite to loosen a large portion of a ridge containing the skeleton of a duck-billed dinosaur. After the slab was slid down to a flat location, palaeontologists carved away the rock and soil to expose the skeleton. On May 3, 1966 Canadian photographer Roloff Beny toured the badlands with me. I had never realized photographs could be taken at so many angles and elevations and still turn out.

As the early spring days became warmer, the badlands put on their green coat, and back came the migratory birds, mosquitoes and people. Word filtered down that "Feds" were interested in a trade with Alberta. They would trade all or part of Wood Buffalo National Park for all of Dinosaur Provincial

A relic of Alberta's past *(Maureen Landals)*

Fire Truck, Fish Creek Provincial Park *(Susan Parenteau)*

Park Service Ranger *(AV and Exhibit Services)*

Alberta's grasslands are famous for their big skies. *(Rosemary H.L. Calvert, FRPS)*

for travel and a new network of highways encouraged people to discover parts of the province they never knew existed. The perception of Alberta as untouched wilderness faded. People were alarmed at the proliferation of oil-exploration roads and seismic-lines in the eastern slopes of the rocky mountains. It was seen as an incursion into the wilderness — a wilderness that few Albertans had experienced, but one that all held dear. They valued its scenery, wildlife and most of all its pristine watershed. People still romanticized about month-long trail-rides without encountering the signs of modern civilization.

As well as the loss of wilderness in the mountains and foothills, Albertans began to worry about the loss of wetlands and the disappearance of wildlife as the prairie grasslands and aspen parkland were converted to cropland. About three-quarters of the grasslands was now cultivated, few large areas of aspen parkland remained. The public began to heed the alarms of early environmental "evangelists." Support for the protection of Alberta's landscapes swelled.

People asked for larger parks, the setting aside of wilderness, preservation of wildlife habitat and a more protection-oriented focus in the management of existing parks. Debate

Grassland

The Milk River badlands have been regarded as a magical place for centuries. *(Lawrence Halmrast)*

Park. A contingent of federal park staff inventoried the facilities. The next day, the visitors were guided into the reaches of the badlands to take photographs. I never heard another word about a trade.

Collecting camping fees was new to me. About seven o'clock each evening, my foreman or I would drive around the campground, collect the fees, pass out information and offer to take the campers on a tour of the badlands in the back of the park's half-ton truck. Since there were no other women and children living in the park, Sharon and Clinton usually tagged along. With three in the cab (normally reserved for the elderly and ladies) and up to 10 in the back of the truck, we toured the wilds. I stopped to provide commentary when we passed vistas or wildlife, but often learned more from the visitors than they learned from me. Moreover, I soon noticed that I had an interpreter along

raged over the need to set aside natural areas. Responding to these concerns, four wilderness areas were set aside: Willmore Wilderness Park (1959), Siffleur Wilderness (1965), White Goat Wilderness (1965) and Ghost River Wilderness (1967). A number of parcels of Crown land, primarily in the settled part of the province, were set aside as natural areas.

Public knowledge, understanding and appreciation of the environment continued to grow, and by the early-70s, Albertans began to articulate a clearer vision for their parks. The Provincial Parks Service was forced to put more emphasis on reconciling preservation and recreation. While the provincial government was articulating a new policy for its provincial parks, provision was also being made for improved protection, management and presentation of Alberta's historic resources.

Between 1956 and 1974, the Provincial Parks Service established and maintained 25 historic sites. These remnants of Alberta's past included places of archeological significance such as Head-Smashed-In Buffalo Jump; fur-trade posts such as Fort George-Buckingham House; early private endeavors such as Shaw's Woollen Mill; sites that commemorate events such as the Frog Lake Massacre; and places that pay tribute

in the form of my young son. Having picked up the main points of the tour, he offered a running commentary. It was his inquisitiveness and unending questions that resulted in the names several features retain today. We dubbed one rock, shaped like a tent, the "petrified Indian teepee."

On one of the tours, a visitor asked a great number of questions about the area. Arnold Brunner, who wrote for the Toronto Star Weekly, had stumbled on the park by accident. Brunner assured me that he was going to write about the park. The following January, I received a telegram: "Obtain a copy of March 25 Star Weekly. Story as promised." In an article called "Canada's Best Kept Secret," Brunner wrote: "Suddenly, with dizzy abruptness, there is a valley, a monstrous canyon in full color with fearful depth. An awful force has gouged it out of the platter-like Alberta prairie. The

Guided interpretive tours in Writing-on-Stone Provincial Park help ensure the protection of the petroglyphs. *(Provincial Parks Service)*

to historical individuals such as the Rev. George McDougall. Most were small, in private owner-ship and deteriorating, or at risk of being lost to industrial development. The purchase of many of the sites occurred only after extensive negotia-tions. In 1973, these historic sites were brought under the control of the Historical Resources Act and are now an integral part of a comprehensive system of designated historical resources throughout Alberta. Present and future genera-tions are indebted to past Provincial Parks board members and employees, and dedicated citizens who had the foresight to protect these valuable components of Alberta's legacy.

A major position paper, tabled in 1973 by Allan A. Warrack, the minister responsible for Alberta's parks, stated: "The Government's assessment is that the present system in Alberta is inadequate. More park space is needed. Many existing parks are badly in need of upgrading. There are serious resource development conflicts in certain parks. The most serious defect is location; Albertans in metropolitan centres are seriously disadvantaged in their opportunities to enjoy our provincial parks. The problem is especially acute for disadvantaged Albertans and for senior citizens."

The paper set out a seven-point policy to

Grassland

Cypress Hills is an oasis of forests in the dry grassland region. *(James Martin/ Provincial Parks Service)*

Bull snake *(Archie Landals)*

rains have tortured and gnawed its slopes, leaving them twisted and etched and spired. These are the badlands, the Valley of the Moon. Here the dinosaurs roamed."

July 12, 1966: I was working around the house when the dog barked and I noted a man, boy and dog approaching. The man wore an old straw hat, short-sleeved shirt and shorts. Sporting a bushy beard and a crop of slightly greying hair, he was quite a sight. After exchanging pleasantries, I learned that they were canoeing the Red Deer River from Red Deer to Saskatoon. It was the gentleman's life-long dream to canoe the river all the way. I offered to drive them out into the badlands for a better view of what they had seen from the river. When he left, W. Hugh Arscott said he was going to write a book about his trip. In 1969 he published *Down a Wet Highway* and included a chapter on Dinosaur Provincial Park.

The summer of 1966 wasn't over yet. I was working in the shop one day when a beat-up Volkswagen drove into the yard and a lady jumped out. Talking very excitedly with a French accent,

address public concerns and desires. Financial commitment for provincial parks more than tripled over the next three years resulting in a dramatic expansion of the system. Parks were selected, planned and developed to emphasize opportunity for outdoor open-space recreation and to preserve and, where possible, improve the ecological character of the area in perpetuity. The philosophy of "parks are for people" — a guarantee of accessibility — was adopted. Reconciliation of resource development and park use became important. The development of recreational opportunities by private enterprise was encouraged and a drive for larger parks was initiated. Moreover, integrated planning amongst agencies responsible for national and municipal parks, forest reserves, tourism-promotion, management of public, historical and cultural-heritage programs, wilderness areas and other potential recreational sites was endorsed.

Several significant initiatives grew out of this policy. In 1974, the Urban Parks Program was announced. Bold, farsighted and innovative, this initiative, backed by the province, enabled cities to acquire land, a difficult task to achieve in high density developments. Reflecting on the program's success, Premier Don Getty stated:

Hand Hills Ecological Reserve protects a remnant of Alberta's prairie landscape. *(Provincial Parks Service)*

Richardson's ground squirrel *(Rosemary H.L. Calvert, FRPS)*

she asked if there was a place to pitch a tent where there were no snakes. She explained that she had her tent pitched in the park's campground until she saw a huge snake climbing a tree. I had to see this. Sure enough, wound around a big old plains poplar was the biggest bullsnake I'd ever seen. Being a macho park warden, I told the visitor that the snake was harmless and that I would relocate it. No such luck. That snake was as thick as my forearm and it wouldn't budge. Since that day, Estelle Lamontagne has written stories and photographed many of Alberta's special places.

As summer came to a close, I concentrated my efforts on improving the facilities and exploring more of the park's 8,900 hectares. Winter set in and suddenly it was Christmas. The

"Building legacies for Albertans is the essence behind Alberta Urban Parks. Communities throughout our great province have created extensive urban-park systems for friends and families to enjoy for years to come."

The area known as Kananaskis Country is the most significant outcome of the commitment made by the Alberta government to integrate provincial parks with other programs. The "Country" concept affords the widest possible spectrum of park and outdoor recreational opportunities. Resort hotels, golf courses, ski hills and off-highway vehicle areas were developed. At the same time, sites were set aside for total

Grassland

temperature dropped and a layer of snow made everything look clean and crisp. I stepped out the front door about midnight and watched a dozen mule deer feeding on the lawn. In the distance, coyotes set up a chorus that echoed across the valley.

1967: In March, we hosted a CBC camera crew that was filming the badlands for a future show. We also watched the spring thaw bring Sand Hill Creek up to the edge of the maintenance yard and the pumphouse. Spring came with a rush. We planted flower beds around the administrative site, trees around the buildings, and landscaped and seeded the new lawn in the south shelter day-use area. The spring rains started in late April, just as we started construction of a new display building at the south parking lot. Hauling concrete building blocks — not to mention the sand, gravel and cement — up the bentonite hillside became a major challenge. The rains continued into summer and the prairies and river valley blossomed into colors not seen for years. It was a great year for wild flowers including the prickly pear and pin cushion cactus. The berry crop was plentiful, especially pin-cushion cactus berries for jam.

We nearly lost the irrigation pump several times in June. Rains raised the upper reaches of the river as much as two metres a night. With all the rain, the prairie wool (grass) grew quickly. It was time to move the range cattle to their summer pasture. Riding with my neighbor and cattleman, Albert Irwin, we drove his herd of several hundred head through the badlands to the park's southern prairie. I knew these times would end soon. Pressure was already building to protect the park's resources.

I used horses for patrolling the park. It was much faster than on foot or by driving 15 to 30 kilometres around the deep canyons to check out strange vehicles. Usually they belonged to fossil hunters. Yet another summer — with visitors like Bruno Engler — passed.

We left our first park home on December 13, 1967 to accept another posting. I returned once more to the "Valley of the Moon" in an official capacity. On June 19, 1980, I watched, as a member of the Parks Mounted Patrol, the official dedication of Dinosaur Provincial Park as a World Heritage Site. My hopes for this park — to be recognized for its rare and valuable resources — have been achieved beyond my wildest dreams. — *Gerry Tranter*

Bison once roamed Alberta by the millions. *(Archie Landals)*

protection, wildlife habitat enhancement projects undertaken and large areas restored to their wilderness character. Kananaskis Country, covering more than 4,000 square kilometres, is integrated into a single management and administrative unit and can be considered an entire park system. Seldom, if ever, has such a major park develop-ment been undertaken in such a short period of time. In less than one decade, an area equivalent to a major national park was planned, designed and constructed.

The Municipal Recreation Areas program, initiated in 1981, was designed to make parks more readily accessible to local communities.

Frosty prairie sunset *(Rosemary H.L. Calvert, FRPS)*

Grassland

Kinbrook Island Provincial Park

Originally established in 1912 as an irrigation project, the creation of Lake Newell resulted in one other very important landmark — Kinbrook Island. What was once dry prairie, local organizations and the Provincial Parks Service have turned into a long strip of cool, shady summer oasis.

In 1914 a flood exposed a beach on the east side of the lake and created a spot for the locals to spend a relaxing afternoon or weekend. By 1954 the area became Kinbrook Island Provincial Park, taking its name from the Kinsmen in Brooks who helped to establish the campground.

With the help of causeways and dikes, a marsh was created between the island and the mainland providing a year-round habitat for many species of birds as well as shelter for white-tail deer. The marsh attracts numerous species of birds including Canada geese, ducks and cormorants. In the middle of the lake, pelicans scoop up supper in their huge bills. The night air is punctuated by the chorus of coyotes and hoots of great horned owls. — *Angela Fryberger & Morris Gorko*

Little Bow Provincial Park

Southeast of Calgary, hidden within the agricultural heartland of the province, is the cool, green oasis of Little Bow Provincial Park. Now a favorite spot for boating enthusiasts and family campers, we really must thank the Lions Club of Champion for its inception and early development.

Homesteaders settled in and around the future park in the early 1900s. The area, however, experienced a series of climatic disasters that prompted many of the settlers to declare bankruptcy. Not until the Canada Land and Irrigation Co. of London, England began large-scale irrigation in the area in 1909 did wheat farming become important. The Prairie Farm Rehabilitation Act (P.F.R.A.) assumed the responsibility for irrigation projects to supply water to 80,000 hectares of land in 1915 when their predecessor experienced financial problems.

Eventually, water from the Bow River was diverted into McGregor Lake and then into the Little Bow Reservoir. This, however, was a tenuous process; 20 kilometres of canals connected the two lakes. Thus, in 1951, the P.F.R.A. began construction of the Travers Dam on Little Bow River as a means of replacing the canals and providing additional water for irrigation. At the same time, the Champion Lions Club was investigating possible locations for a park to fill the community's recreational needs. After checking several locations on McGregor Lake and the future Travers Reservoir, they chose the current site of Little Bow Provincial Park. The Provincial Parks Board was approached for assistance and the park was formally established on January 20, 1954. The Lions Club continued to put more improvements into the park, including the planting of 2,000 trees.

Little Bow Provincial Park offers a diversity of recreational activities and facilities. The Travers Reservoir is an excellent location for water-skiing, windsurfing, fishing and sailing. Mammals such as the Richardson's ground squirrel, antelope and the occasional badger, and a variety of birds common to the prairies in summer are found within the park. — *Barrie Rennick*

Midland Provincial Park was once a prosperous coal mine. *(Provincial Archives of Alberta)*

Grassland

Little Fish Lake Provincial Park

The Little Fish Lake area was investigated by officials of Public Works in the late-1920s for its suitability for a provincial park. The Parks Board, not satisfied with the initial information, requested further information. In 1932 a district engineer recommended the reservation of all land surrounding the lake since it was already being used by locals for recreational purposes. Although interest in the park waned during the Great Depression and Second World War, locals began to make extensive use of the lake by the 1950s. The government formally established Little Fish Lake Provincial Park in 1957.

The 61-hectare park, situated in the Hand Hills of southeastern Alberta, is an important waterfowl staging area for snow geese, Ross' geese, white pelicans, common loons, whistling swans and common mergansers. Mammals include: pronghorn antelope, mule deer, white-tailed jackrabbits, Richardson ground squirrels, badgers, coyotes and long-tailed weasels.

Midland Provincial Park

The stark but beautiful badlands adjacent to Drumheller are the setting for a park with a unique story. Here, along the banks of the muddy Red Deer River, people can experience the colorful history of Alberta's coal mining era in a landscape that has also yielded the fossilized bones of nearly 20 species of dinosaurs. This unusual mix of recent industrial and ancient natural history heritage is protected within Midland Provincial Park.

The origins of the Midland story date back to 1912 with the opening of the Midland Collieries Ltd., just west of Drumheller. One of the principal investors was Col. Seneca Lent McMullen, who came west from Nova Scotia. Drumheller was in the midst of a coal boom and the mine prospered. A second mine site was opened in 1926. By the time the Great Depression arrived in the early-30s, Colonel McMullen was the sole owner and the company operated as the Midland Coal Mining Co. Ltd.

Syd McMullen started working at his father's company in 1934 and eventually became the vice-president and general manager in 1946. The company prospered, riding the demand for coal during World War II and reaching maximum production in 1947. Despite vigorous and creative

Toad flax *(Kåre Hellum)*

Capital work grants of up to $100,000 were made available to municipalities for local park development. The minister responsible for parks at that time, Peter Trynchy, summarized the essence of the program: "The grants are intended to help municipalities provide additional recreational facilities and opportunities for rural Albertans. The grants are used to develop day-use facilities including parking, drinking-water supplies, playgrounds, picnic and beach areas, and boat launch sites."

Ten provincial parks have been established since 1973. All ten are nature-oriented to some degree and many have fulfilled the province's commitment to larger parks. Peter Lougheed Provincial Park, established in 1977, is Alberta's largest, incorporating slightly over 50,000 hectares of alpine and sub-alpine landscapes. Notikewin, a frontier park established in 1979, protects almost 10,000 hectares of the scenic and varied landscapes of the Peace River valley. Lakeland Provincial Park, established in 1992, adds almost 15,000 hectares of diverse boreal forest communities, crystal-clear lakes and abundant wildlife to Alberta's park system.

New parks that previously would have focused on a single recreation activity are now nature-oriented as well. Carson-Pegasus

Cliff swallows build their mud nests on the sandstone cliffs along the Milk River. *(Archie Landals)*

advertising, coal markets began to shrink in the 1950s as Albertans shifted to the new energy sources of oil and natural gas. In 1959 Midland closed its operations and merged with another company to form Amalgamated Coal Ltd.

Throughout the 1960s, the property waited for a final decision on its future. Buildings and equipment were sold, torn down for scrap lumber or lost to fires. By 1970 only the mine office remained. Mr. McMullen, who fondly remembered "running up and down the hills, and sitting on cacti" as a boy, wanted to see the land protected for the enjoyment of succeeding generations. "I wanted the site to be left in as natural state as much as possible," he explained. "I wanted to see it kept intact." The park was formally dedicated on September 12, 1979 in a ceremony that included a tribute to the McMullen family.

The gift of the McMullen family to the people of Alberta can be appreciated as you explore its 599 hectares. Amid the cacti and sagebrush-covered slopes stands the mine office. Only foundations and some equipment remain where hundreds of men once toiled to extract coal. The hills have been explored for fossils which reveal clues about life long ago. In particular, the sandstone and mudstone layers have produced high-quality fossilized bones of nearly two dozen species of dinosaurs. The search for these treasures dates back to the time of the

Provincial Park was established because of its popularity as a rainbow-trout fishery. Whitney Lakes Provincial Park was the result of demands by the region for improved camping and swimming facilities. Each of these parks incorporates well over 1,000 hectares of natural landscape, thus affording opportunities for the visitor to experience, understand and appreciate Alberta's natural heritage.

Additionally, older parks have been made larger and more nature-oriented. Dillberry Lake and Miquelon Lake provincial parks were originally established to cater almost solely to camping and swimming — both have been en-

larged. Miquelon is now over 800 hectares and Dillberry is over 950 hectares. These two parks provide the best opportunities within the system to experience the aspen parkland, a natural region which has been altered by agriculture.

Recent additions to Beauvais Lake and Writing-on-Stone have also increased their significance as protected natural landscapes. Beauvais now encompasses 760 hectares of rugged foothills terrain, providing opportunities for hiking or nature-appreciation. Writing-on-Stone has been expanded to over 1,700 hectares, three times its original size. This significant increase includes additional sandstone canyons,

great Canadian dinosaur rush from 1910 to 1917. McMullen recalled, ". . . my father telling me that during the excavation of an airshaft in 1912, the skeleton of a duck-billed dinosaur was uncovered. Charles Sternberg from the Geological Survey of Canada persuaded my dad to delay the construction until it was safely removed."

The park not only protects ancient forms of life but it also provides valuable habitat for wildlife and plants. During the summer months, a host of wildflowers bloom on sun-baked arid slopes or under the cool shade of riverside cottonwood trees. Bird-watchers can observe the activities of over 65 species including hawks, warblers, and waterfowl. Keen eyes are rewarded with glimpses of mule deer, ground squirrels and cottontail rabbits.

Six years after its dedication, the park marked another milestone in its history. On September 25, 1985 the Royal Tyrrell Museum of Palaeontology opened its doors to the people of the world. Located in the west end of the park, this facility attracts over 400,000 visitors each year. The story of Midland is indeed unique. Through the efforts of private citizens, a piece of Alberta's natural and cultural heritage is protected for future generations. — *R. Fred Hammer*

Alberta's Milk River Canyon

Before the arrival of European settlers, grasslands teeming with bison and other wildlife stretched unbroken from western Canada to Texas. Most of North America's native grasslands, however, have now been destroyed by cultivation. The Milk River Canyon in southeastern Alberta is one of the few large tracts of grasslands found anywhere, a tribute to the management of local ranchers. Its size, unique geology and diverse ecosystems make it a national treasure. There is an astounding variety of landscapes from rolling grasslands to extensive badlands, rugged coulees and the spectacular Milk River Canyon. These habitats support a diversity of plants and animals including many rare species.

North America's grasslands evolved with grazing by large herbivores, like bison. While not exactly the same, properly managed cattle grazing simulates the uneven grazing conditions that once existed under the bison. Many grassland species prefer a moderate level of grazing. Several species

Gulls and pelicans at Kinbrook Island Provincial Park. *(Archie Landals)*

Grassland

of native wildlife and plants thrive in the tall, dense grass cover of ungrazed sites. Others seek out the short, sparse grass cover of heavily grazed areas. As recently as 1975, some large ranches in southern Alberta each leased hundreds of square kilometres of public grazing land, areas large enough to allow for all levels of grazing. There was a 155-square kilometre unfenced area on the Lost River Ranch with commanding vistas of the rugged plains, badlands and Sweetgrass Hills.

New legislation in the early-70s, however, restricted the amount of land which one lessee could hold. Larger ranches were broken up. The lease reductions forced more intensive management. Fences and dugouts now impair the views. The romantic notion of the West's wide-open ranges is a myth in today's highly managed cattle industry.

On March 21, 1984 people from all over Alberta and from many walks of life met in Lethbridge to show their support for the proposed Milk River Canyon Ecological Reserve, one of the first proposed by the Province. Ecological reserves are highly protected natural landscapes set aside to preserve functioning ecosystems and genetic diversity for future scientific research. Most briefs presented to the Ecological Reserves Advisory Board supported the proposal. Others, mostly ranchers, farmers and hunters — people who had lived near the Milk River for generations and in some cases had leased and maintained the area — felt threatened and betrayed.

To resolve this conflict, the Milk River Canyon Task Force, comprising local citizens and provincial conservationists, was established. They were asked to develop a plan to "protect the ecological character of the Milk River Canyon." The task force showed great concern for the area. Almost everyone opposed roads, pipelines or cultivation which would disturb the native grassland

"sod." Although hunting, vehicle access and legal aspects of designation and management were contentious issues, the task force was determined to make the process work — the burden of failure would have been too much to bear.

Conservationists pushed for a better deal for the ranchers including long-term tenure to ensure sound management and ecological stability on their leases and in the proposed ecological reserve. They also suggested that the government contract the ranchers to manage the area.

The task force recommended the establishment of a 73-square-kilometre natural area. No grazing would be allowed in the sensitive wetlands, the Kennedy Creek valley or the adjacent uplands. Elsewhere, levels would be lower than normally recommended for public grazing lands. Recreational facilities, roads, oil and gas drilling, pipelines, power lines, cultivation and disturbance of archaeological sites would be prohibited. The task force also recommended that local citizens and conservationists be responsible for overseeing the long-term management of the site and encouraged scientific research.

In 1987 an area of 1,068 hectares was established as the Kennedy Coulee Ecological Reserve. The surrounding 5,344 hectares was designated as the Milk River Natural Area. A management committee including provincial conservationists, government personnel and local residents was struck to prepare an operational management plan for the area.

The success at Milk River has demonstrated that ranchers, hunters, academics, organized conservation groups and local authorities can achieve conservation goals through cooperation. Protecting Alberta's natural legacy is everyone's responsibility. — *Cliff Wallis*

Grassland

Park Lake Provincial Park

The reservoir known as Park Lake was constructed by the Lethbridge Northern Irrigation District as an integral part of their irrigation system. In July, 1930 the reservoir was officially opened by Premier Brownlee and christened Park Lake. At that time, the premier promised to give serious consideration to the request to designate the lake a provincial park.

During the 1930s, the park began to take shape. Most of the early development was made possible through the volunteer efforts of local farmers and school children.

From the Lethbridge Herald - May 14, 1932

While there may be a temporary shortage of finances for appropriations for provincial government parks, there at least is no lack of good will in the promotion of work at Park Lake Park. Trees by the thousands were planted on Saturday by volunteers, boys and men of the community, ably assisted and directed by Dr. W.H. Fairfield, M.L. Freng and P.M. Sauder of the Advisory Committee for the park.

Approximately 4,500 trees and shrubs, gathered from various places nearby were set out, and all the prepared area amounting to about 15 acres was fully covered. A striking feature of the work in connection with Park Lake Park is the enthusiasm of the committee who not only perpetually boost but are unafraid to take off their coats and demonstrate their faith by actual work with shovels.

The people surrounding the park and throughout the district have volunteered in large numbers each year for the work of caring for and planting trees, levelling ground, irrigating and other necessary work, but it is especially encouraging to see the school children taking such a great interest. The following boys are commended for their excellent work last Saturday; John Brenton, Alex Davidson, Leslie Smith, Truman Sherret, Donald Brown, Fred Sauder, Orval McDermott and Robert McDermott.

Following this outstanding community effort, then-Premier John E. Brownlee wrote the following letter to the members of the Park Lake Advisory Committee.

Volunteers planted 4,500 trees and shrubs in Park Lake Provincial Park in 1932. *(Provincial Archives of Alberta)*

associated rock art as well as prairie grassland environments. At Dry Island Buffalo Jump, a large block of private property purchased by the Provincial Parks Service, and Crown land along the Red Deer River are being incorporated into the park. Eventually, a 16-kilometre corridor of badlands along the Red Deer River will be available for visitors to explore and enjoy.

In 1980, the Wilderness Areas Act was amended to enable the establishment of ecological reserves which, in part, addressed the public's concern that more must be done to protect the province's biological resources. The total diversity of Alberta's resources, it was

Frosted heads of brome grass
(Rosemary H.L. Calvert, FRPS)

reasoned, could not always be incorporated within traditional provincial parks. Some important sites, such as the Plateau Mountain ice caves, are extremely fragile. By 1987, Alberta had designated its first ecological reserves. Presently, there are 13 such reserves encompassing a total of 270 square kilometres.

"The establishment of ecological reserves will ensure that the beauty and ecology will be preserved for the enjoyment and education of present and future generation." — *Norm A. Weiss, Minister of Recreation and Parks (1987)*

". . . The objective is to create representative areas of each of the province's natural regions for preservation and appreciation, as well as research and education. Ecological reserves permit natural processes to occur with a minimum of human interference." — *Don Sparrow, Minister of Forestry, Lands and Wildlife (1987)*

Over the last decade, Alberta's system of parks has focused on both ends of the spectrum — recreation and protection. Bringing parks to people has been a major achievement. The urban parks and the municipal recreation area programs have resulted in readily accessible outdoor-recreation facilities. At the opposite end of the spectrum, the ecological reserves

Grassland

"On behalf of my Government and on behalf of the people of Alberta, I desire to express to you my sincere appreciation of the voluntary assistance which you have given towards the development of the provincial park at Park Lake. The spirit of cooperation which is being shown by the residents of your community, gives assurance of the ultimate success of their venture and I feel sure that in the not too distant future you will feel proud of the part which you played in the creation of a beauty spot for the enjoyment of the citizens of this province."

The following letter, dated June 21, 1932, was received by Brownlee from J.I.McDermott, secretary of the Park Lake Advisory Committee.

"I am enclosing two snapshots, one showing school boys who went to Park Lake, in response to an appeal for volunteers, actively engaged in hoeing the thousands of young trees planted in the park; the other a close-up of these boys. One gazing at these young people industriously laboring in an effort to beautify this park could not help but be inspired by the sight. Amidst the no doubt discouraging difficulties which face you in your high office and which face us at this time, it is good to see that our young folks have that wonderful spirit of cooperation, good will and desire for community improvement, without which our community and our Province could not progress. This provincial park, which you dedicated in 1930 (the lake), is being steadily improved and will in the course of a very few years be one of the most beautiful spots in southern Alberta, and I enthusiastically and actively support your splendid idea of beautifying our Province in this way."

Park Lake Provincial Park, officially established on November 21, 1932, is located approximately 15 kilometres northwest of Lethbridge. The lake contains northern pike and perch, and is a popular recreational spot for wind-surfing, sailing, kayaking and canoeing. — *Grant Moffatt*

Police Outpost Provincial Park

In 1891 the Boundary Creek detachment of the Northwest Mounted Police (N.W.M.P.) was established at Outpost Lake to deter whisky smuggling into Canada. The population of the area totalled 48, mostly Americans. Four constables built a house, kitchen, stable, oat-shed and a corral. The following year, Inspector Steele of Fort MacLeod (under whose jurisdiction the Boundary Creek detachment was) wrote to the commissioner of the N.W.M.P. in Regina, urging that the land in the Boundary Creek be subdivided into sections and quarter-sections so that settlers could lay claim to title. In 1893, after the survey was complete, Steel obtained a reservation on the lands which are now part of Police Outpost Provincial Park.

The N.W.M.P. were generally hard put to find men willing to enter their ranks, and the number of men posted at Outpost Lake decreased until, in 1899, "it was found necessary, in consequence of the paucity of men and the buildings of Boundary Creek requiring a greater outlay of money than they were worth, to withdraw the detachment from that point, and to place a mounted constable at a neighboring settler's . . . ."

---

program is now firmly established — special places set aside to protect their natural value. These areas, dedicated to scientific research, will ensure that the benefits from Alberta's natural heritage are there for the future.

Grassland

The post remained vacant until 1902 when a party of 12 Indians, some with smallpox, were directed into Alberta by the Indian agent at Browning, Montana. Unable to get them back into the United States, the Mounties established a quarantine at the site of the Indians' encampment. Thereafter, a constable was stationed at Boundary Creek until 1909 when once again, a manpower shortage forced the post to close. In 1915 a patrol from MacLeod was stationed at the old Boundary Creek post to "patrol the international boundary and to prevent enemy aliens from crossing into the United States of America." The post was last used in 1916.

Between 1910 and 1932, numerous grazing leases were let. In 1939 the provincial government, which by then controlled its own natural resources, granted agricultural leases on the land now included in the park. The southeast quarter was disposed of on a 10-year cultivation lease to the Hansen family who renewed the lease every 10 years until 1970. At the same time, yearly grazing leases were granted on the north half to George and Ernst Salt. They maintained the lease until 1951 when it was granted to J. Allan Wilcox. In 1959 the land was disposed of under a grazing permit to the Boundary Creek Grazing Association and the Parks Board reserved it for future use. In 1970 an area of 223 hectares was officially designated as Police Outpost Provincial Park. — *Wanda Nadasde & Beth Cornish*

Taber Provincial Park

The valley of the Oldman River has always been a picnic ground for Taber. In 1934 the Board of Trade requested that the government designate the land adjacent to the McLean Bridge as a provincial park. While the government did not formally accede to this request until 1954, an agreement in principle existed as early as 1936. An active citizens' advisory committee administered park developments including swimming facilities, picnic shelters and landscaping. Severe flooding damaged the park facilities in 1942 and 1953, and in 1964 flooding carried away the outdoor privies and the old pump-house.

A dense stand of large cottonwoods can be found within the 51-hectare park. These trees, remnants of the those that grew on the flats prior to the arrival of white men, range from 17 to 23 metres tall, some with trunks over one metre thick.

Natural grasslands are home to pronghorn antelope. *(Rosemary H.L. Calvert, FRPS)*

Tillebrook Provincial Park

Like a mirage rising out of a desert, Tillebrook Provincial Park is an oasis located between the towns of Tilley and Brooks. For motorists, it is a welcome stop after crossing the scorching prairies. Tillebrook, officially established July 20, 1965, is just one of a series of campgrounds situated along the Trans-Canada Highway.

A person cannot fully appreciate the lush beauty of Tillebrook Provincial Park until they discover what difficulties were overcome to bring water to this prairie landscape. Just over one kilometre is evidence of this — the Brooks Aqueduct. Built in 1914 and made entirely of concrete, it supplied water to the Eastern Irrigation District. Today an adjacent canal provides water to quench the thirst of the prairies. Through the cooperation of the Eastern Irrigation District, the Alberta Parks Service and Alberta Culture, a hiking trail was built linking Tillebrook to this concrete landmark. Walk along this trail and you will witness the prairie ecosystem at its natural best. — *Angela Fryberger & Morris Gorko*

Willow Creek Provincial Park

Willow Creek Provincial Park developed around the nucleus of a dance pavilion that was constructed during World War II. It became a family-oriented resort with playgrounds, swimming and picnic areas. The park was administered by the municipality until its official establishment as a provincial park in 1958. Both the narrow leaf and black cottonwood can be found within this 109-hectare park.

Woolford Provincial Park

Woolford Provincial Park, situated near the site of an early North West Mounted Police post (St. Mary's, 1883), was created in 1948. For of some years, the island, which forms the main body of land in the park, was the subject of a protracted dispute about ownership. The island was claimed by two local ranchers, one of whom was seeking an assured source of water for his cattle in the winter (the island has natural springs) and the other, a shelter belt. When the disagreement appeared close to resolution in 1947, the citizens of Woolford petitioned the government to establish a park on the island. In 1948 the Director of Lands and Forests officially reserved the land for park purposes and

Thickets of thorny buffalo berry in Wyndham-Carseland Provincial Park are important bird habitat. *(Archie Landals)*

Grassland

allowed the two ranchers continued use of their desired island resources. This situation continued until 1961 when the whole island was included in Woolford Provincial Park.

The 35-hectare park is a good spot to view prairie bird species. The river is also used by waterfowl during migration and broods of Canada geese can be found on the river in late summer.

Writing-on-Stone Provincial Park

Set into the valley by the Milk River, Writing-on-Stone Provincial Park offers spectacular sandstone hoodoos carved into a thousand shapes by wind and water. Caves and crevices, cliffs and castles, walkways, tiny pebbles and immense walls, all are scattered in profusion along the river banks, as though tossed carelessly by a giant hand. Long before white men knew about the West, the plains people — awed by the sandstone cliffs, strange hoodoo formations, abundant wildlife, lush vegetation and water — felt the area was inhabited by powerful spirits. They visited to commune with those spirits and, over time, left ritualistic carvings (petroglyphs) and paintings (pictographs) on the rocks as messages to them. Eventually, succeeding generations and nations came to believe these "writings" were made by the spirits and visited to "read" what the spirits had to say.

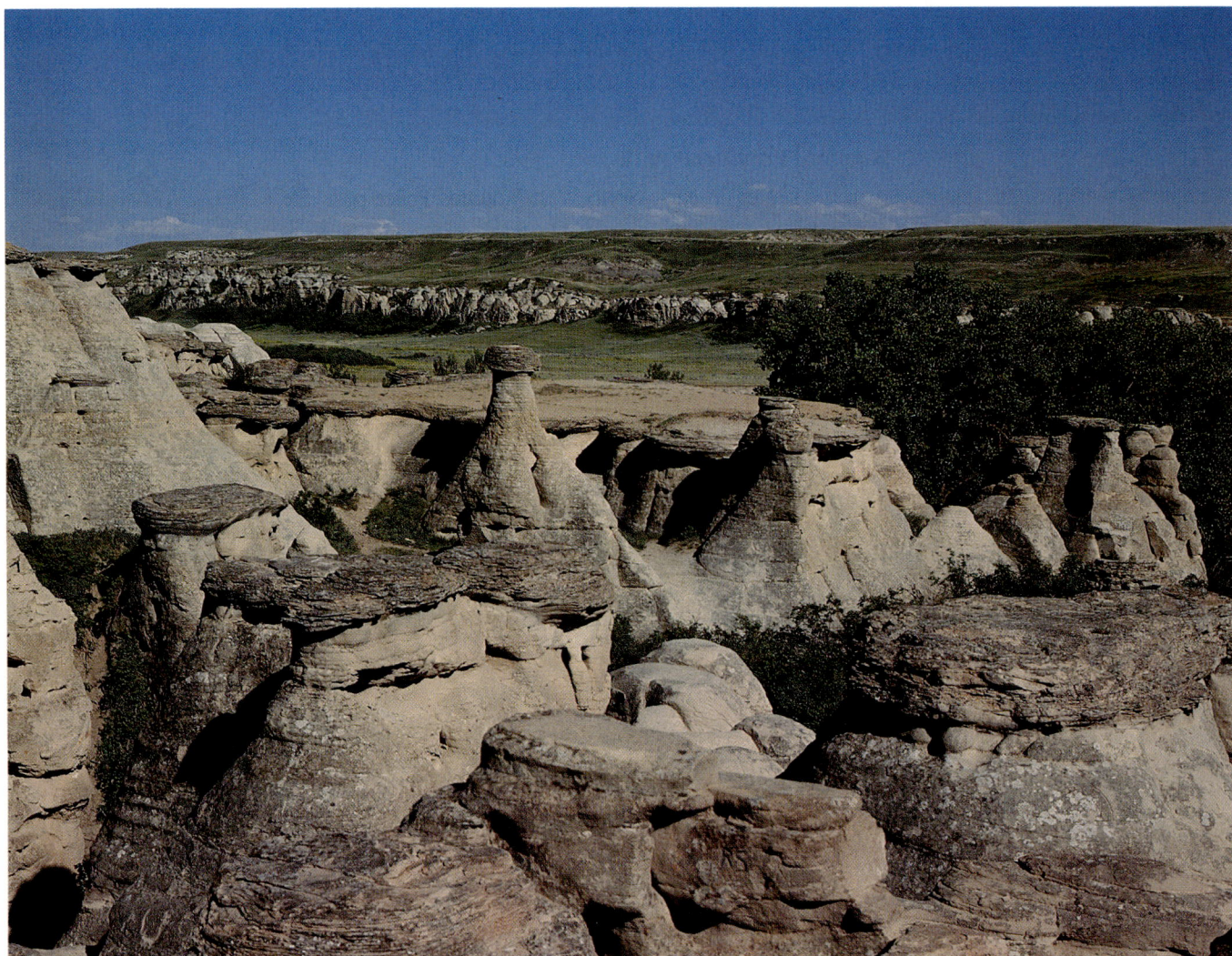

Powerful forces drew the Medicine Men, warriors and buffalo hunters back yearly for hundreds of years to seek spiritual aid in their endeavors. Young boys on their vision quest visited the valley to fast and pray while seeking their guardian spirit. Chiefs and other important tribal members were buried in caves within the tall sandstone cliffs. It is known that the Shoshoni and the Gros Ventre, called by the French, "Big Bellies," were early inhabitants of the area, but they were chased out by the Bloods who obtained horses and guns, and thus, control.

Tales of the power of the spirits at Writing-on-Stone have been handed down for generations in the oral tradition of the plains people. Today the area remains sacred in the hearts of many, a place to be respected, honored and perhaps feared. Not one to be visited casually. Each year native elders still visit the writings, and on several recent occasions, important ceremonies have been conducted at the base of the cliffs. They prepare with prayers before hand, visit the area only for the day, honor the spirits with gifts and leave before nightfall in the tradition of generations past.

Petroglyph. Writing-on-Stone Provincial Park. *(Lawrence Halmrast)*

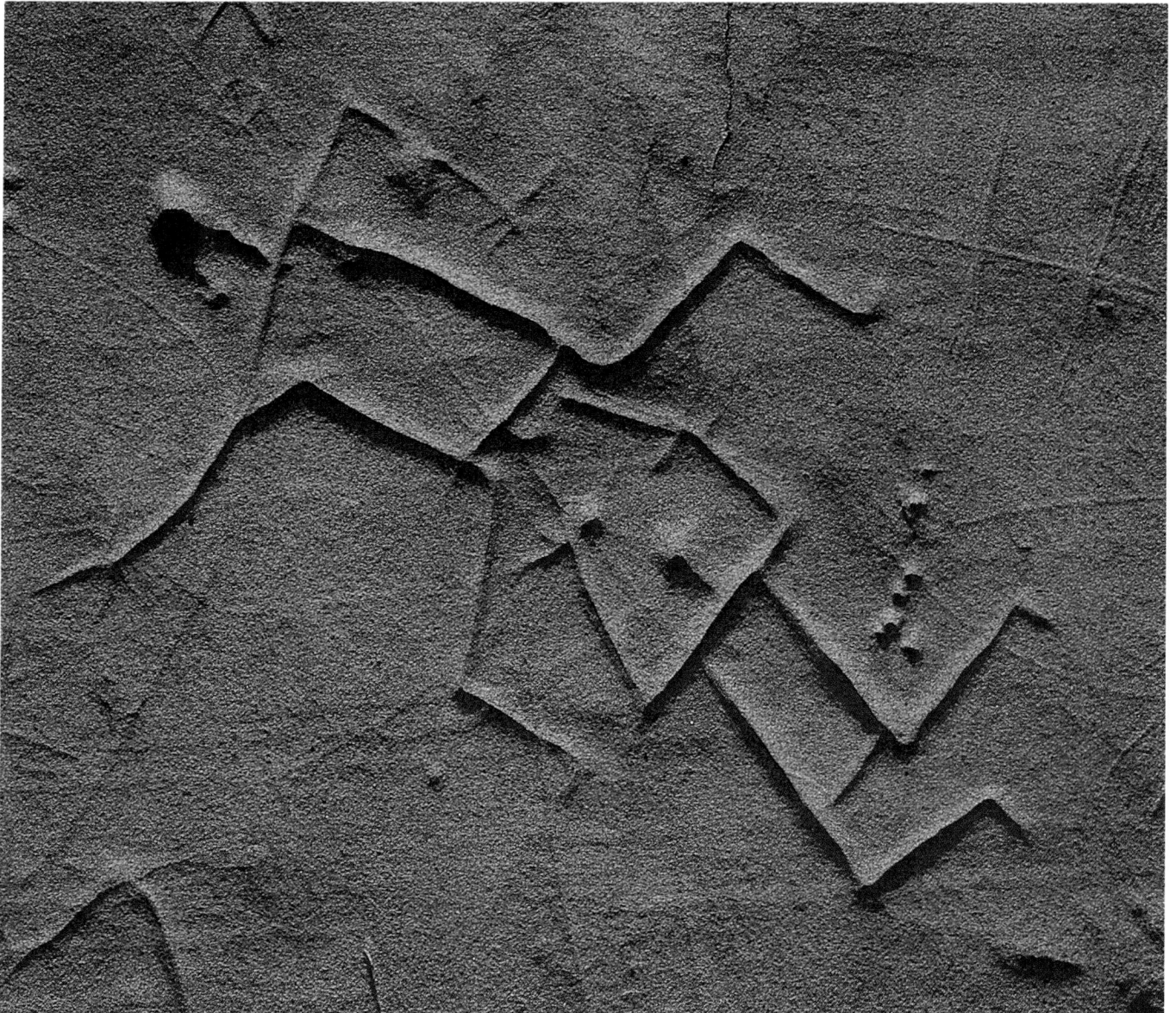

Grassland

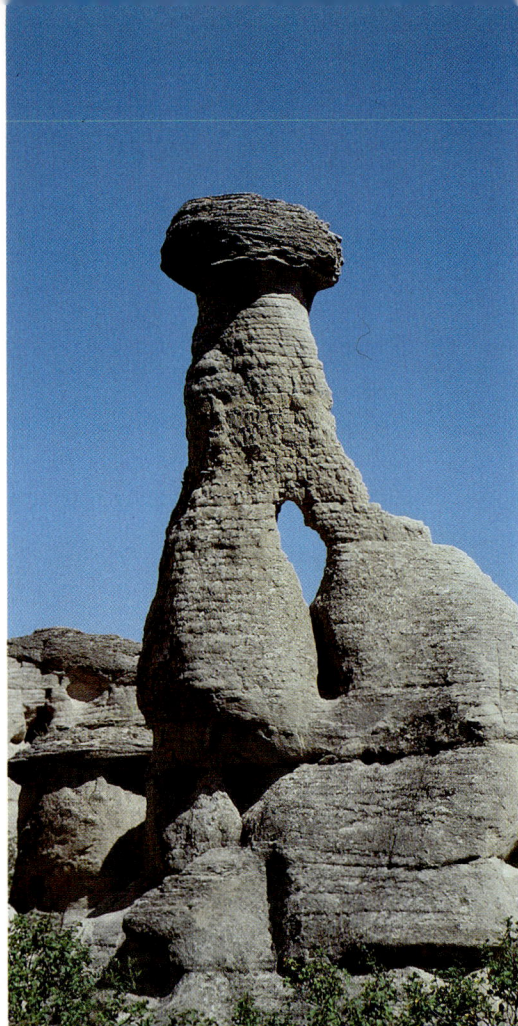

The Sweetgrass Hills in Montana add to the splendid scenery of Writing-on-Stone Provincial Park. *(Maureen Landals)*

Hoodoos come in all shapes and sizes. *(Maureen Landals)*

One traveller, in 1855, mentions seeing "representations of men, horses, guns, bows and shields on smooth walls." A teenage trumpeter with the Northwest Mounted Police (N.W.M.P.), Frederick Bagley, wrote of "ancient pictographs on cave walls" and remarked that "though they must have been very old, the colors were still fresh looking". He further remarked: "Many of us, of course, scratched our names on the rock walls". From 1886 to 1918, the Mounties occupied a border post at the mouth of Police Coulee, directly opposite the area of the most concentrated writings. The many names on "Signature Rock" are evidence of the large number of men who were posted here over the thirty years. Most constables came for only a few months, some stayed longer, a few deserted after a very short stay in this lonely, godforsaken place.

Thomas A. Dickson, a native of Keene, Ontario, arrived at Writing-on-Stone sometime in 1888. Most of his early years of service were spent at this tiny post and he was largely responsible for its construction. On July 25, 1893, Dickson was made the corporal in charge of Writing-on-Stone.

Resolving a Dichotomy

In the early days guides and outfitters including legendary characters — Tom Wilson, Bill Peyto and Jim Simpson provided pack trips, led mountain excursions and catered to natural history expeditions. Undoubtedly, the early tourists had an impact on the natural environment; use levels, however, were low and wilderness abundant. Nevertheless, guides and outfitters realized it was in their best interest to spread the usage out so as to maintain the wilderness mystique.

As use levels increased, conflicts inevitably arose and the dichotomy of recreation and preservation became apparent. Since that time, Alberta's park system, like park systems everywhere, has been faced with reconciling recreation and preservation, with catering to tourism and providing educational opportunities.

Alberta's Provincial Parks Service deals with these objectives under the headings of protection, heritage-appreciation, outdoor-recreation and tourism. These goals, however, are ever changing, molded by public attitudes and values, by the pressure of an increasing population and decreasing natural landscape, and by a sophisticated society that has acquired substantial knowledge and understanding of our

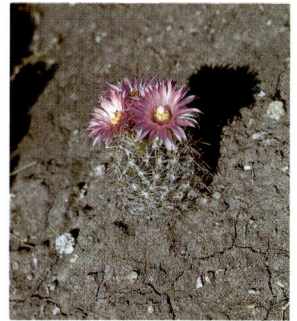

Pincushion cactus *(Archie Landals)*

Grasslands, riverine forests and water result in abundant wildlife at Writing-on-Stone Provincial Park. *(Archie Landals)*

He remained there another three years before an unfortunate case of jealousy regarding a local lady caused the Force to move him elsewhere for political reasons. His unique "stencil-like" carving on Signature Rock is one of the most noticed to this day.

Corporal A.P. White was another Mountie who seemed to have a special fondness for Writing-on-Stone and the Milk River area. Paddy, as he was known, was born in Halifax in 1886. He was posted as a constable at Writing-on-Stone in November 1909 and remained there until 1915, being promoted to corporal in August 1912. During this time he received three commendations from the N.W.M.P. Commissioner for outstanding work on the Stokely murder case, the Harry Simms horse stealing case and for the extraordinary conditions he endured during the winter of 1910 while patrolling to ensure the well-being of the nearby settlers. In 1914, Paddy married a local woman, Pearl Clark, and in 1915, he purchased his discharge from the Police and obtained a homestead southwest of Writing-on-Stone, close to the town of Coutts.

natural environment. Examining how these objectives evolved provides a better understanding of Alberta's system of parks. More importantly, it affords valuable insight into the challenges we face today as we strive to pass on a legacy of parks to future generations.

Protection or resource management in parks has changed dramatically. Early efforts focused on elimination of predators. Bears, wolves and cougars were destroyed so that tourists could more readily enjoy desirable or "charismatic mega-vertebrates" such as elk, deer and bighorn sheep. Fires were suppressed at all cost. During the 1960s, management shifted to

enforcement of regulations and visitor control. On the whole, these were unsuccessful attempts to keep the increasing numbers of visitors from damaging park resources.

Today the philosophy of protection has evolved to one of ecosystem management. Only in those situations where a resource is endangered does the focus shift to individual species or features. There is a growing recognition of the need for a sound scientific basis for resource management. Ecosystems do not respect the boundaries of parks, nor are they apart and separate from visitor use. Ecosystem management strives to integrate the management of

Grassland

Equally captivated were the ranchers and settlers who came to the area around the turn of the century and managed to survive the hard early years. The Penroses, Audets, Turners, O'Haras and their parents and offspring have each had a part to play in the history of the park and of the Masinasin District surrounding it. The children of William and Sara O'Hara, homesteaders on the next bend upriver from the park, spent most of their childhood exploring the Indian writings and discovering burial sites and whisky caches.

The greatest concentration of rock art on the North American Plains is found within the park's boundaries. A rich archaeological array of animals and human figures have been cut into the rock with stone or bone tools. Animals are drawn as naturalistic; boat-shaped with feathery tails; or in delicate, flowing lines with tiny heads. Men are carved in straight lines with pointed shoulders, arms up raised and fingers extended. Another form carries a shield on which a sacred design invokes the aid of spirits in battle. Sadly, much of the rock art — a remarkable record of Alberta's early history — has been badly damaged over the years by graffiti and vandalism.

Few people cared more about the well-being of the rock art than Fred M. "Scotty" Shearer, a long-time park ranger at Writing-on-Stone. Only weeks after he arrived in early 1970, Scotty received a letter from a professor of anthropology which complained about the degree of damage to

the rock art and its lack of protection. Scotty became keenly interested in the rock art. He also saw the value of protecting it in some way. Help finally came for Scotty's cause in 1970s.

Writing-on-Stone became one of the first provincial parks in Alberta with an interpretation program. Informal programming started in 1975 with naturalists rotating between the Cypress Hills and Writing-on-Stone. Interpretation was intended to "ensure that the valuable interpretive resources of Writing-on-Stone are protected from vandalism" by encouraging park visitors "to develop favorable attitudes and values for these resources."

Writing-on-Stone Provincial Park was officially opened on May 20, 1957 and declared an Archaeological Preserve in 1977. Part of it was designated a Provincial Historic Resource in 1981. Today thousands of park visitors marvel at the rock art, discuss its symbolic beauty with interpreters and scowl at the graffiti.

The size of the park was greatly increased during the late-80s from 429 to 1,722 hectares through a land exchange with the Turner-Weir family. This new addition is called the Weir Ranch in honor of the stewardship by the father of Marie Turner (née Weir). Marie, her husband, Ed and son, Doug consented to a conservation easement, one of the first in the province, along an important coulee.

The valley and adjacent coulees offer shelter and favorable conditions for plants and

Fields of grain now grow where once unbroken grassland stretched to the horizon. *(Rosemary H.L. Calvert, FRPS)*

animals, mainly of the grassland species. Rock wrens, prairie falcons, sage thrashers, grouse and hens, raccoons, white-tailed deer, a number of snakes including the prairie rattler, hognose and garter as well as the Bullsnake, short-horned lizards, spadefoot toads, cottontail rabbits and pronghorn antelope abound in the park. Of the over 20 fish species in the Milk River, sauger, ling, northern pike, flathead chub and three kinds of suckers are common. The rare finescales dace and the catfish are among the most fascinating.

Plants found in Writing-on-Stone include the prickly pear, pin-cushion cacti, various sages, rose bushes, low junipers among the rocks, wild berries, a few vines, a mysterious white flower that blooms only at night and is locally called the "Evening Star", an occasional clump of Yucca or Spanish Bayonet and the big cottonwoods that grow all up and down the valley. In a good year, the area bursts with life. In a dry one, the plants and animals hug the earth and wait for a better time. Still, in a quiet moment, a brooding air hangs over the valley, a feeling of those long gone, who left their mementoes in the writings on the rocks. — *Ellen Gasser, Alva C. Bair, Lena Lyall & Michael Klassen*

Wyndham-Carseland Provincial Park

The land now included in Wyndham-Carseland Provincial Park has a divided history. The Wyndham campground, part of today's park, has been used as a recreational area since the 1920s. It was acquired by the local municipal districts, and local people built most of the facilities including a baseball diamond and rodeo grounds. Until the mid-50s, this municipal park remained chiefly a day-use facility. The Carseland portion possesses a history emanating from the construction of the Carseland Weir. This was built in 1910 to divert water from the Bow River into Lake McGregor. The province acquired Johnson's Island, on which the weir is situated, to simplify the construction of the water control structure.

As the popularity of camping increased in the 1960s, more and more Calgarians resorted to Wyndham's limited facilities. This soon resulted in deterioration of local natural resources and in the inability of the municipality to cope. The provincial government was asked for assistance. Wyndham-

natural landscapes, wildlife, ecological processes and human use both within parks and on adjacent lands. However, the ecological integrity of parks cannot be maintained without the cooperation of those who manage surrounding lands. Wildlife species that require large areas must be free to move onto surrounding lands. Conversely, society demands that parks must not be a threat to surrounding land uses. Elk, for example, are hunted in Cypress Hills Provincial Park to prevent the growing herds from competing with cattle on surrounding ranchland.

Decisions, such as a "hands-off" management, allowing ecosystems to evolve on their own, or effecting active management, pose difficult questions that cannot be answered in isolation. Although fires are no longer regarded as something apart from the ecosystem, they cannot always be allowed to burn. The threat to surrounding resources and communities must be considered. In larger parks such as Banff, Jasper, Willmore Wilderness and Kananaskis Country, management strategies include controlled fires that are ignited when conditions are less hazardous. These replace natural fires as part of ecosystem management, rejuvenating wildlife habitat and reducing the risk of

Carseland Provincial Park was established in 1975 from the original municipal park and the beautified grounds of Johnson's Island.

The 178-hectare park is ranked as one of the best fly-fishing spots in the world with rainbow and brown trout often caught in the 50 to 60 centimetre range. Over 120 species of birds are found within the park.

Erosion of the badlands exposes the fossils for which Dinosaur Provincial Park was declared a World Heritage Site. *(Provincial Parks Service)*

P A R K L A N D

The Parkland Natural Region covers about 10 to 15 per cent of Alberta. It is a transitionary area between the drier grasslands of the plains and the coniferous forests of the boreal forest to the north and the foothills to the west. Its topography ranges from essentially flat areas that were glacial lake beds to strongly rolling areas of hummocky moraine. Grassland dominates the drier southern part of the region with aspen groves growing only in sheltered, moist locations. As the climate becomes cooler and wetter further north, the aspen groves begin to merge into forests with only scattered meadows of grass and shrubs. Numerous productive marshlands and pothole wetlands have earned the parkland its status as the "duck factory" of North America.

Aspen turn a brilliant gold during Alberta's sunny autumn. *(AV and Exhibit Services)*

Alberta's First Provincial Park — Aspen Beach

Aspen Beach Provincial Park is located on the southwest shore of Gull Lake. The region around and including the park has a colorful history. It has experienced the topographical changes of the glacial periods, the presence of native peoples, the coming of the white fur-traders, steamboats and railways, the cultural development associated with the settlement of pioneers and, now, extensive recreational use by rural and urban dwellers.

The first reference to the Gull Lake area was an entry in Anthony Henday's journal, dated January 22, 1755. Little is then recorded about this area until after 1799 when Rocky Mountain House was built. A route between Edmonton and Rocky Mountain House, which passed by Gull Lake, was used many times by David Thompson. His records indicate this was also a well-travelled Indian route during the 1800s.

Homesteading in the area began in 1891, yet by 1905 few homesteads remained. William Wiese and his wife, early settlers to the area from Nebraska, arrived in Lacombe and were taken by Mr. J. Ebeling Sr. to a log cabin at the south end of Gull Lake. Wiese, seeing the potential for a lake resort, built a boat-house and rented boats to fishermen and people on holidays. Increased interest by travellers using the new railway between Lacombe and Bentley resulted in its expansion into a resort community known as Wieseville. The community was renamed Aspen Beach in 1914.

Aster *(Kåre Hellum)*

Rumsey Ecological Reserve protects a remnant of the aspen parkland. *(Archie Landals)*

Gull Lake's sandy, accessible beaches and excellent swimming conditions made it a wonderful family resort. On May 28, 1929 the Premier of Alberta appointed a special committee for the purpose of investigating the possibilities of park development in the province. This committee prepared and submitted its report to Premier Brownlee on November 7, 1929, recommending the purchase of property and development of a park site at Aspen Beach on Gull Lake. The Village of Gull Lake donated seven lots and two lots were transferred from E. Sharpe.

The Provincial Parks Service had its formal beginnings on May 15, 1932 with the establishment of Aspen Beach Provincial Park. The park consisted of 6.9 hectares, located just over one kilometre east of the present Ebeling Day-Use Area. Two cottages, which were on the property when it was purchased, were used as bath-houses. A third one was transformed into a public kitchen and a fourth was used as a home for the caretaker.

Over the next 20 years, Aspen Beach Provincial Park struggled to exist. The water level in Gull Lake receded and with it the area's usefulness for a park. In view of this fact, the minister of public works, whose department was responsible for provincial parks, agreed to lease the property to the Village of Gull Lake for one dollar for a period of five years. The deputy minister requested an inspection of all provincial parks in 1947. Inspector McCowan reported Aspen Beach, which was still under lease to the Village, was being fully utilized. In December 1952, Mr. Charlie Harvie, Superintendent of Parks, recommended that an advisory committee be set up to investigate the possibility of reopening Aspen Beach Park to the public. It was formally reopened in 1954.

uncontrollable wild fires.

Parks now require detailed resource management plans that recognize the important ecological components of the park. The elk management plan for Cypress Hills Provincial Park recognizes that the animals migrate onto surrounding ranchlands and across the border into Saskatchewan's Cypress Hills. The ecological boundaries of certain species and ecosystems transcend the political boundaries of parks. Other management plans, like the one being drafted for the Kennedy Coulee Ecological Reserve, are beginning to provide for research and monitoring programs to ensure that

strategies meet the established goals.

Parks as places where users can learn about nature, is a philosophy that has existed in Alberta since the first parks were established. Early scientists were attracted to the mountainous national parks by the lure of the frontier. Geologists came to study the mountains, fossils and glaciers, botanists and zoologists came in search of new species. It was guides, though, who supplied interpretive services for the first naturalists and gutsy adventurers. Much of this early interpretation focused on acquainting visitors with the features of the park. Guides led visitors to view the province's spectacular fea-

Killdeer at Hasse Lake Provincial Park (Tom Webb)

As the popularity of the area grew, so did the park. Between 1955 and 1975 additional land was purchased from Mr. Albert Ebeling, Mrs. Flora Grace Moore, Mr. H.B. Hanson and the Moore estate. The Louis Ebeling family (son of Albert Ebeling) ran a small store and campground on their property for many years. The present Ebeling Day-Use area is named in their honor. A portion of the present Brewer's Campground was named "Moore's Heritage" after the Moore family. The Hanson's property is now the Lakeview campground.

The 216-hectare park continues to be one of Alberta's most popular parks, experiencing upwards of 600,000 visitors annually. Users, attracted by the lake, the beach and ample sunshine, can participate in sailing, power-boating and fishing. — *G.E. Bennett*

tures and gave them rudimentary explanations for these phenomena.

This focus changed little until the tourism boom of the 1960s. Confronted with an inquisitive public, park agencies started to offer formal interpretive programs. Seasonal interpreters, like Eileen Harmon in Banff, were first hired in Alberta's national parks in 1959. By 1963, the first full-time interpretive positions were created in Banff, Jasper and Waterton. Not to be outdone by their federal counterpart, Alberta Parks Service hired their first interpreter in 1968. Bob Townsend was posted to Cypress Hills Provincial Park.

Early programs stressed ecology, the interrelationships of plants, animals and the landscape. By the early-70s, park management issues and strategies began to receive greater attention. The public were eager to know what was happening in their parks and how park resources were being managed. More recently, education and interpretive programs have enhanced visitor knowledge and understanding. The emphasis has remained on ecology and park management. The philosophy, however, has expanded. Parks are used as outdoor classrooms, places where people can develop a greater understanding of the resources of the entire province. Since the

Parkland

Big Knife Provincial Park

Big Knife Provincial Park is located at the junction of Big Knife Creek and the wide scenic valley of the Battle River. Sometime before Anthony Henday explored the area in 1874, a Cree named Big Man and a Blackfoot named Knife fought until both died, hence the name Big Knife Creek. After two trappers were killed by Indians, late in the 1800s, the name of the creek was changed to White Man's Creek. It reverted back to the original name in the 1900s.

Jack Coustain and his two sons were the first to homestead the area in 1902. They erected a log cabin and barn and used thin animal skins for window panes. By 1907, more and more people settled in the area and the Coustains, who preferred the wilderness, moved. Two Swiss brothers, who farmed and entertained the community with their musical talent, moved into the old Coustain building. After a short time the brothers, who were better musicians than farmers, moved to Calgary to pursue musical careers.

Between 1902 and 1907, the area around and west of the park was occupied by Jack Dubois and his gang, convicted cattle and horse rustlers. A variety of people had settled in the area by 1926 including a man named One-Eyed Jack Nelson. In addition to farming the flats and raising cattle, Mr. Nelson had another occupation. He made potato rum and moonshine that was transported as far south as Montana. According to legend, his sales were very brisk. A portion of his cabin can still be found in the park.

"In 1963," recalled Wilton Allers, "I heard the government was going to develop this valley into a provincial park. I applied for a position and was hired along with an assistant, Herb Desjarlais. Our first task was to build a road to the site. Starting out with a tractor, wagon and axe, we camped under the wagon for a night or two until a trailer was provided to live in. Later, heavy equipment and operators were brought in to help with the construction. One day, while clearing brush for a campsite, I fell into a deep hole which turned out to be an old still. Another time, we stumbled upon a small gravesite while building a foot-bridge across the creek. The area was also used as a hideout for cattle rustlers."

The 295-hectare provincial park, established in 1972, is an important recreational resource to the farming district where it is situated. A grove of spruce trees in the park is close to 100 years

Snowshoeing is popular in Blackfoot Recreation Area.
(Archie Landals)

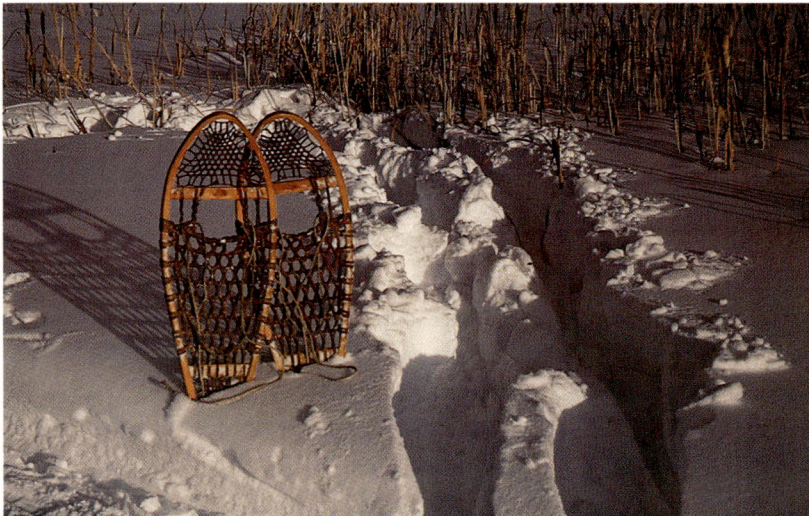

publication of the World Conservation Strategy in 1980 and the Bruntland Commission Report in 1987, parks are being recognized more and more for their unique educational opportunities. Canada's Green Plan of 1990 reinforced the value of protected landscapes by fostering a changed environmental ethic — an ethic of sustainable development.

The evolving philosophy of outdoor-recreation and tourism in parks has been one of turmoil between park visitors and the preservation of nature, a clash brought about by increasing numbers of visitors and heightened by changing social and economic conditions in

old. The rugged river valley supports a variety of wildlife such as bald eagles, elk and moose — all uncommon to the prairies. — *G.E. Bennett, Teresa van Hienen & Wilton Allers*

Cooking Lake-Blackfoot

The Cooking Lake-Blackfoot area has seen intensive resource use and conversely, conservation for many years. Located south side of Elk Island National Park, approximately 40 kilometres east of Edmonton, the area was used by numerous tribes as a hunting ground for several thousand years. The fur-trade years, however, led to exploitation of the beaver and bison in the area. Bison did not reappear until they were reintroduced into Elk Island National Park. The beaver gradually re-established themselves without help from man.

Settlers began to arrive in large numbers late in the 1800s. The area was used for grazing and

Alberta. The dichotomy of catering to large numbers of visitors while protecting the environment is one that, until recently, park agencies were poorly organized to deal with. Park staff had to learn by experience; there were few opportunities for formal education.

In the early years, outdoor-recreation and tourism in the mountain parks focused almost exclusively on the scenery. The first provincial parks, such as Aspen Beach and Park Lake, were set aside because of their importance as recreational sites for local residents, little attempt was made to incorporate areas of the natural landscape that required significant protection.

The boom in outdoor-recreation and tourism of the 50s and 60s, however, brought this dichotomy into sharp focus.

Visitors flocked to the national parks in unprecedented numbers. Guides and outfitters could no longer cater to the wants and needs of the majority of tourists. Although Canada's national parks embodied a philosophy of protecting the environment, they were unprepared to cope with the influx of visitors. The private sector responded by providing artificial attractions such as golf courses, ski hills, furrier stores, luxury hotels and souvenir shops. Visitors, often preoccupied with these commercial attractions,

hunting, and supplied firewood and building materials for settlers in the surrounding area. At that time, much of the area was covered with extensive spruce forest. Numerous fires caused by railway activity, brush clearing and other activities resulted in the destruction of most of the spruce forest. Regrowth was mainly aspen and shrubs, and even today only scattered remnants of the spruce remain.

Due to the heavy pressure on the forest, the area was declared Canada's first federal forestry reserve in 1899. The northern portion of the reserve was formed into Elk Island National Park in 1906 and the southern portion, which included the Cooking Lake-Blackfoot area, continued to be managed as a forest reserve.

In 1947, the Blackfoot Grazing Association, formed by local farmers, acquired a grazing lease on the land. Over the years, however, the quality of the grazing area decreased due to tree growth. In the late-70s, the provincial government was asked to set up a grazing reserve on the site.

lacked the chance to experience the true value of parks. Few opportunities existed for the average visitor to engage in activities related to the natural environment.

Between 1951 and 1971, with provincial parks in Alberta in the midst of the greatest period of park establishment, the debate over expanded facility development versus protection of park resources gained momentum. Although many new parks were selected on a recreation basis and were facility-oriented, there were notable exceptions. Areas such as Dinosaur, Sir Winston Churchill, Writing-On-Stone, William A. Switzer, Bow Valley, Lesser Slave Lake and Dry Island

Buffalo Jump included significant natural resources — special landscapes that deserved protection.

By the early-70s, there was a growing realization that the dichotomy of recreation and preservation needed to be addressed. The conflict between protection of park resources and development of recreational facilities took centre stage in the House of Commons with the debate over the development of Village Lake Louise in Banff National Park. Armed with an awakening environmental consciousness, the public demanded increased protection of park resources, provincial and national. They wanted greater access to opportunities where they could

Marsh marigolds surround a beaver pond in Blackfoot Recreation Area. *(AV and Exhibit Services)*

After extensive discussions between the Grazing Association, Public Lands, Fish and Wildlife, and Recreation and Parks, an agreement to develop a multiple-use area was reached. A part of the area was cleared, broken and seeded with a mixture of forage plants; the remainder was left forested. The perimeter of the entire area was fenced with a high ungulate fence to prevent moose, elk and deer from leaving the area. Studies had estimated that the elk would disappear, and moose and mule deer would be greatly reduced without the fence. The fencing has proved to be successful as all species of ungulates are present in numbers equal to or greater than before the fence was erected. Recreational trails for use by hikers, equestrian users, bicyclists, and snowmobilers were constructed and in 1988, the Cooking Lake-Blackfoot Grazing, Wildlife and Provincial Recreation Area was officially opened. — *Ed Whitelock, John Nesbitt, Dave Vetra, Bob Stevenson, Jack Grey & Wes Lawson*

experience first hand the landscapes of Alberta and learn more about their natural heritage. People wanted to participate in the widest possible spectrum of outdoor activities and demanded facilities and developments to cater to their needs. At the same time, the public began to realize that parks could not be all things to all people.

Given the increase in public interest and concern, it is not surprising that Alberta's academic institutions began to offer diplomas and degrees in topics related to resource management, recreation administration and parks in general. Park agencies responded by hiring more specialists, experts with an understanding of the natural and social sciences and who had new ideas to cope with growing concerns. Visitor management and resource protection began to be recognized as different facets of the same challenge.

Planners working within Alberta's diverse network of parks started to acknowledge that some areas were best set aside for preservation purposes. These areas, it was reasoned, could be established as ecological reserves or wildlife sanctuaries where the emphasis was on protection and scientific research, not recreation. Other parks, it was thought, should be devoted almost

Parkland

Yellow warblers commonly nest in provincial parks such as Hasse Lake.
(Tom Webb)

Dillberry Lake Provincial Park

Dillberry Lake Provincial Park has a long history as a municipal park and recreational area for local people. In 1930, the Municipal District of Sifton responded to the lake's growing popularity by taking out a lease for park purposes. After the province gained control of the natural resources, the land was reserved for a provincial park. In the case of Dillberry Lake Park, cottages built before the park was established were allowed to stay and over the years, more were built. Facilities such as toilets, diving boards and change houses were built by volunteers. After World War II, interest in the park, which had been almost non-existent for a number of years, increased. In 1956, the Provincial Parks Board recommended that the park — which was in great disrepair — be treated as a new park as far as development was concerned.

Dillberry Lake Provincial Park, situated in a ranching district south of Chauvin, protects 955 hectares of aspen parkland. The lake has sandy beaches, and unlike most bodies of water in the area, the water is clear. Its fish population consists of darters, yellow perch and rainbow trout, the latter having been stocked. The land around the lake, aspen parkland, is generally grassland with scattered willow and poplar bluffs. Sandy soil, low precipitation and hot dry winds, characteristic of the region, limit tree growth. Mule deer and white-tailed deer are common. Numerous sloughs and lakes nearby provide nesting sites and staging areas for waterfowl. — *Bob Romanyshyn*

Dry Island Buffalo Jump

Deep in Alberta's east-central countryside lies a true gem. Situated in the 200-metre deep Red Deer River valley, northeast of Trochu, is Dry Island Buffalo Jump, a park rich in wildlife and vegetation species. This bounty also extends to the cultural resource base and provides the history for the park's rather unusual name. From the scenic lookout near the park entrance, you gaze out to the north where a flat-topped mesa called a 'dry island' sits in splendid isolation from the rest of the prairie. Cast your eye to the south and far off in the distance you can pick out the grassy slopes of an ancient buffalo jump, almost 3,000-years old.

Wild raspberry (*Kåre Hellum*)

entirely to recreation with emphasis placed on facilities and maintaining pleasant surroundings.

In larger parks, zoning schemes segregated uses. Some zones focused on protection, others on visitor use. Even where recreation was the focus, various activities were located in different places to avoid conflicts between different user groups. New developments in parks started to focus on the user experience, not just campsites or picnic areas. Trails and interpretive facilities were expanded and viewpoints and vistas became important considerations in road design. Facilities enabled the visitor to experience protected landscapes. Perhaps nowhere are these new philosophies better exemplified than in Kananaskis Country – philosophies clearly articulated in the statements of intent when Kananaskis Country was officially announced.

"We hope that by providing large-scale recreational opportunities in Kananaskis Country, the area will be used by people from all parts of the province, thus easing much of the pressure currently experienced by Banff and Jasper National Parks." — *Premier Peter Lougheed (October 7, 1977)*

"The Policy for Recreation Development of Kananaskis Country ... is intended to direct orderly development in such a manner as to

Parkland

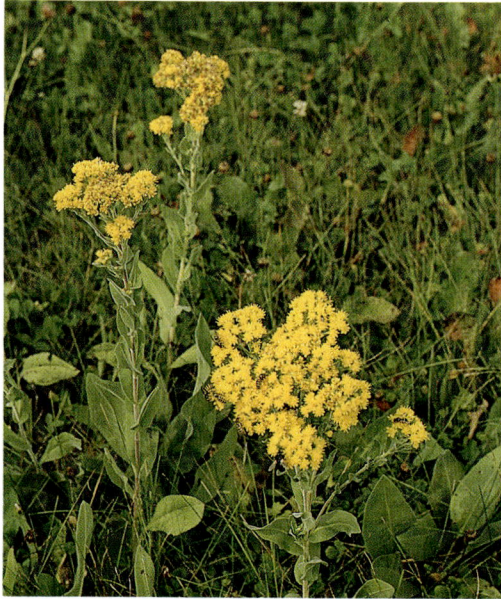
Bunchberries carpet a forest floor. (Kathleen S. Wark)

Floral meadows add a splash of spring color. (Kathleen S. Wark)

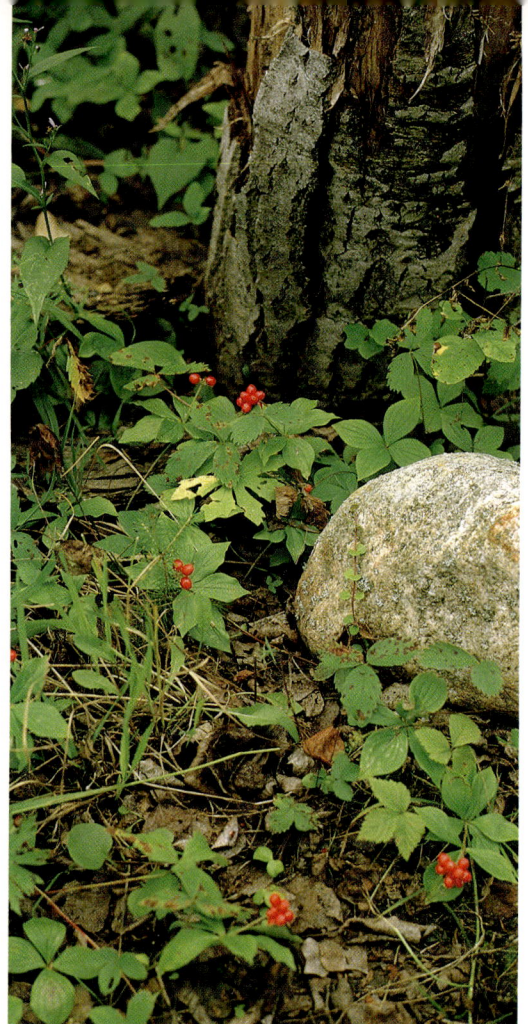

The area surrounding the park was among the last to be settled in central Alberta. Not until the railway reached Huxley, in 1910, did the area see an influx of people. The descendants of those early pioneers were the first supporters for the establishment of a park to protect the valley and its beauty. Local residents acted through community organizations such as the Huxley Fish and Game Association, the Trenville Elks Lodge and the Trochu Chamber of Commerce. Starting in 1962, these groups made representations to various government officials through the decade. Their efforts were rewarded with the official establishment of the park on December 15, 1970.

The strategic location of the park in the transition zone between the aspen parklands to the north and the short grass prairie to the south is the basis for its biological diversity. Several overlapping ranges of organisms enable visitors to see plants as different as prickly pear cactus and white spruce growing within a few hundred metres of each other. The life list of the park is impressive. Within an area of less than 1200 hectares, 400 plants, 150 birds and 35 mammal species have been

Wagner Natural Area provides opportunities to learn about nature. (Archie Landals)

allow the integration of the widest possible range of recreation opportunities while ensuring the preservation of this valuable resource for present and future generations." — *J. Allen Adair, Minister, Recreation, Parks and Wildlife (October 7, 1977)*

recorded. The river valley provides an important flyway for the turkey vulture and prairie falcon.

The steep valley walls that have kept most of modern man's impact on the prairie level have also played a role in aboriginal people's successful use of the jump method in hunting bison. This jump is the second highest in Alberta with a drop of 45 metres. Used rather infrequently between 700 and 2,800 years ago, this site is the second most northerly jump in the province. It is an important landmark in determining the geographical range of this hunting technique.

The sheer cliffs of the park echo, not only from stampeding bison and excited hunters, but of more ancient stories about life and death. These cliffs — originally deposited as river and lagoon sediment at the end of the Cretaceous Period — contain fossilized bones from the creatures that inhabited this semitropical coastal plain. Recent excavations have yielded dinosaur skeletons dating back 65 million years, the time when the very last of these creatures walked the earth. Part of the answer to the question of their extinction may yet be found in the colorful bands of mudstone and sandstone found at Dry Island Buffalo Jump. — *R. Fred Hammer*

Gooseberry Lake Provincial Park

Gooseberry Lake Provincial Park lies on the south side of the Neutral Hills where the fescue grasslands and parkland meet. The natural life of this 52-hectare park is highly diverse.

A local settler, J.J. Hilstob, purchased the land, which now comprises the park, from the Hudson Bay Company in 1919 and arranged to stretch the payment over ten years. Hilstob built a dance hall and concession booth on the park site as well as a cottage to serve as his family's residence. The dance hall drew crowds from the surrounding area, and for a number of years, the United Farmers of Alberta held their annual convention and campout at Gooseberry Lake. These conventions, with Premier Brownlee in attendance, attracted between two and three thousand people to the lake for the three-day event. When Hilstob was unable to meet his payments to the Hudson's Bay Company, the provincial government assumed ownership of the land. Gooseberry Lake became a provincial park on November 21, 1932. Financial restraints during the Depression and World War II, however,

Thistle *(Kåre Hellum)*

Continuing the Legacy

Alberta's park system involves the private and public sectors. All three levels of government are involved. Various provincial agencies are responsible for provincial parks, natural areas, ecological reserves and recreation areas. The federal government manages the five national parks and the four national wildlife areas. Local governments operate municipal and urban parks. Private land-owners and public-interest groups are involved in the setting aside of areas for preservation purposes. While sometimes these players work in close cooperation and at other times in looser associations, their success relies on interdependency.

prevented any significant developments. In 1947, a peninsula extending into the lake was subdivided, and nine cottages were constructed.

Numerous species of birds and animals can be seen in the park and surrounding area. Waterfowl make heavy use of the lake during spring and fall migrations. Antelope are occasionally seen near the park, but mule deer are the most frequently seen large mammal. — *Mitch Senger*

Hasse Lake Provincial Park

Hasse Lake Provincial Park, a popular spot west of Edmonton, originated as a game fishery. Its considerable depth in relation to its small surface area made it ideal for development as a recreational fishery. In 1953, the lake was stocked with 25,000 rainbow trout, and between 1955 and 1959, additional trout, perch and some walleye were planted.

A local man named H.P. Kulak began a recreational development on his land adjacent to the lake. He set up a public dock and started a boat rental concession. By the spring of 1986 it was decided that better public access to the lake was required if it was to be restocked. Kulak's operation was purchased for $18,000 – and shortly thereafter, the lake was restocked resulting in a fine rainbow trout fishery.

Concerned about creating a recreational fishery without supporting facilities, the province requested proposals for commercial development of the lake. Local opposition quickly surfaced to the idea of private development, and as a result, the province created Hasse Lake Provincial Park in 1970. Trout are stocked on an ongoing basis providing many hours of angling pleasure.

The Little Park that Could

Hommy Park, located alongside the Beaverlodge River north of Grande Prairie, may well be the "best little park in Alberta." The irony of this story is that it took 60 years to accomplish what Hans O. Hommy intended when he donated the land to the government for a provincial park back in 1931.

Painted lady *(Tom Webb)*

Alberta Provincial Parks

From the storm-swept beaches of Lesser Slave Lake, to the badlands of Dinosaur, to the snow-capped mountains of Peter Lougheed, to the bubbling springs with rare plants in Bow Valley, beautiful and diverse landscapes are protected as part of our legacy of provincial parks. These are places where family and friends can get together to relax and escape the hustle and bustle of everyday life. They offer visitors opportunities to explore, experience and learn about Alberta's natural heritage.

Provincial parks vary in terms of their natural resources, and thus, the outdoor

Cross-country skier. Vermilion Provincial Park *(Provincial Parks Service)*

Mule deer frequent Dillberry Lake Provincial Park. *(Archie Landals)*

Why didn't Hommy Provincial Park ever get developed? The original piece of donated land was small and a long way from the Parks Board in Edmonton. The Board had very little in the way of staff and resources in those early days. There were lots of letters from members of the Hommy family to the government over the years. Each letter would start a brief flurry of activity but little in the way of concrete action. Other than fencing, facilities were never developed — unless you count the picnic tables and toilets that were installed in the spring of 1971 — and were removed in 1972. The land was eventually decommissioned as a provincial park in the mid-70s.

The Hans O. Hommy Memorial Park Society, incorporated in January 1986, has developed this 6.65-hectare parcel of land into a high quality recreational area using Municipal Recreation/ Tourism Areas funding. The campsite, picnic area, ball field, playground and walking trail are, today, much the way Hans thought it should be all those years ago. The history of Hommy Park is much like the story of the little red train that kept saying, "I think I can, I think I can . . . ." —*Milton Hommy & Tom Cameron*

recreational opportunities they offer. Ma-Me-O Beach simply provides sand, sun and access to the water of Pigeon Lake. Peter Lougheed, by contrast, caters to an array of interests and activities: fishing, boating, camping, interpretive programs and more. Even its trails provide something for everyone. Back-country trails that climb to the high-country target the physically-fit wilderness enthusiast. Pleasant strolls through the forest and along the lakes permit visitors to enjoy nature at a leisurely pace or learn from interpretive signs and brochures. Bicycle trails challenge those who are so inclined. Here, the province's best system of cross-country ski trails

Parkland

Yellow lady slipper orchid *(Tom Webb)*

Ma-Me-O Beach Provincial Park

In 1929, the provincial government, in recognition of public enthusiasm about the recreational potential of Pigeon Lake, reserved the southeastern corner of it for public use. Ten years later, the Ma-Me-O Beach village council established a small picnic ground on this site. When the council requested financial assistance with the development of the facility in 1949, the Parks Board declared its intention to make the beach area a provincial park. This finally occurred in 1957. Although the park is only 1.6 hectares, it is a popular day-use area.

Miquelon Provincial Park

Miquelon Provincial Park is located 65 kilometres southeast of Edmonton in the Beaver Hills. Scandinavian settlers, who farmed and raised livestock in the area, displaced the Metis in the late 1800s. Joseph Zoel Cyr-Miquelon — a pioneer who served as an immigration and land agent, postmaster, justice of the peace, registrar and sub-land agent during the early 1900s — was a worthy namesake for the waters of this park. Even then, the natural resources of the Beaver Hills were highly regarded and a number of sites received special protection: a forest reserve at Cooking Lake, Elk Island National Park and bird sanctuaries on Miquelon Lakes.

The three Miquelon lakes were a very popular recreation spot for the people of Camrose and surrounding towns. There was a clubhouse, dance hall, boathouse, a cottage subdivision and a fine beach. People travelled by train to Kingman and then hired a horse-drawn rig for the rest of the journey. Kingman soon became known as the gateway to the Miquelons.

A ditch to drain water from the southernmost Miquelon Lake into a reservoir to supply water for Camrose was excavated in 1928. But in 1931, the worst drought in years began and the ever lowering water levels forced recreational activities to move to the beaches of another Miquelon Lake. Over time, this new area became so popular that people pressed for establishing a public park.

In 1958, the Camrose Lion's Club acquired and donated the original parcel of land that became Miquelon Lake Provincial Park. Today, over 800 hectares are protected for their significant plant, animal and recreation resources. — *Henry Saley*

---

provides access to a winter wonderland.

Similarly, Alberta's provincial parks vary in the significance of the resources they protect. Some of the smaller, recreation-oriented sites are managed solely to provide pleasant natural surroundings for an enjoyable outdoor experience. Dinosaur Provincial Park, at the other extreme, is recognized by the international community as a UNESCO (United Nations Educational, Scientific & Cultural Organization) world heritage site, one of the natural wonders of the world.

Volunteers have always played an important role in the legacy of Alberta's parks.

Early provincial parks were run by volunteer boards, and dedicated citizens donated labor, materials and cash. Even during the Great Depression, community spirit was high. For example, in 1932 volunteers planted 4,500 trees in Park Lake. What was then a lake in an open field is now a stately stand of spruce and poplar.

Volunteer efforts continue to this day. Today's volunteers play important roles in park clean-up and special events. Volunteers are actively involved in increasing park visitors' knowledge of Alberta's natural and human history. In 1991, over 1,000 volunteers spent more than 14,000 hours helping in parks.

Pigeon Lake Provincial Park

In 1955, the Edmonton District Planning Commission attempted to arrange a transfer of lands from the Municipality of Leduc to the Department of Lands and Forests for development of a provincial park. The Parks Board, however, recommended the land in question, located only five kilometres from the present park, be developed as a municipal park. Interest lagged until 1959 when the Town and Rural Planning Board pointed out the inadequacy of park planning in areas proximate to urban centres. Subsequently, the Parks Board attempted to purchase various sites around Pigeon Lake but failed. Success came in 1964 and in 1967, Pigeon Lake Provincial Park was formally established. The 444-hectare park is located on one of the largest clean bodies of water in the Edmonton area.

Trail-riding is popular at Blackfoot Recreation Area. *(AV and Exhibit Services)*

Mounted Patrol. Queen Elizabeth Provincial Park *(Mel Kozan/ Provincial Parks Service)*

Queen Elizabeth Provincial Park

Queen Elizabeth Provincial Park lies in the Peace River country near Grimshaw and Berwyn. The early settlers used the area extensively for recreational purposes, and in 1912, Bear Lake formally became Lac Cardinal, named for a local homesteader, Louis Cardinal. The railroad played an important role in the arrival of many settlers and the establishment of Berwyn and Grimshaw. Between 1922 and 1925, Berwyn was the end of the line. Grimshaw reached village status in 1930 and in 1938, it became mile zero for the lonely Mackenzie Highway.

In 1942, an article in the Edmonton Journal reported the development of a first-class resort at Lac Cardinal. The project — sponsored by the Peace Municipal District and Grimshaw and Berwyn — included a campground, dance pavilion, racetrack and kitchen facilities. There was bathing, boating and a campground for school groups and organizations. In 1951, the Ratepayers Recreational Association, which administered the facilities, asked the Parks Board to take over. Lac Cardinal Provincial Park was established in 1956. A condition of the land transfer was that the association be allowed to lease back the grounds so that the stampede and sports events could continue. The 86-hectare park was officially renamed Queen Elizabeth Provincial Park on August 1, 1980. — *Leslie Sullivan*

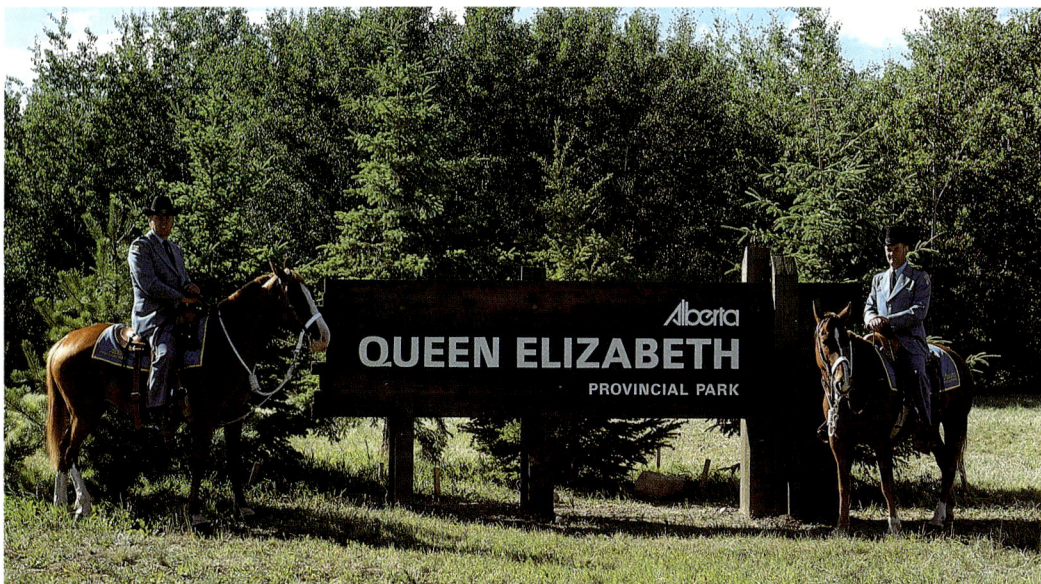

Parkland

Red Lodge Provincial Park

At one time, a huge red painted log house, styled after an English manor, stood in the area of the park. It was built in the beginning of the 1890s for Thomas Critchley, a son-in-law of Sir Sanford Fleming, the chief surveyor of the new Canadian railway. The Critchleys arrived, expecting to live like English gentry, but were sorely disappointed with the lack of mansions and palaces in the area. They subsequently sold out in 1898 and returned to England.

Soon after, the locals began to use the area as a picnic ground. In the 1920s, some locals formed a citizens' committee to finance and develop a sports field on the site. Some years later the committee heard that a buyer was interested in acquiring the land on which their development was situated and they appealed to the provincial government to reserve the land for park purposes. About 30 hectares were reserved in 1933 and the area became known as Little Red Deer Park. Local people continued to administer the park. In 1949, the Parks Board reserved the land in question for a provincial park. Upon the recommendation of the citizens' committee, swimming facilities became a priority. A small dam was built across the Little Red Deer River to raise the water level. But it was destroyed by high water more than once in the next few years, and in 1953, the Board decided to abandon the idea altogether.

The 129-hectare park, located southwest of Red Deer, provides opportunities for camping, canoeing, picnicking and hiking. In addition to the over 70 species of birds that have been spotted within the park, there are over 100 species of flowering plants.

Rochon Sands Provincial Park

Rochon Sands Provincial Park, located at Buffalo Lake, was among the many resorts put forward as candidates for provincial park status following the passage of the Provincial Parks and Protected Areas Act in 1930. Its chief proponents were residents of Erskine and Stettler. The government took no action at the time and the resort continued to be administered privately. It was quite popular as a swimming spot.

Cooking dinner at Red Lodge Provincial Park (H. Exell/Provincial Parks Service)

Partnerships with volunteers are worth strengthening.

In addition to expanded partnerships with volunteers, new associations are beginning to emerge — partnerships with private citizens, non-government organizations and industry. For example, the Amerada Trail at Crimson Lake Provincial Park was built through corporate support, volunteers in the Campground Host Program orient park visitors, and members of the Heritage Association of Cypress Hills Provincial Park help with the park's newspaper, host special events and run the recycling program.

Urban Parks and Recreation Areas

Parks in Alberta's 16 cities and over 800 recreation areas throughout the province bring parks to the people. They are selected more on the basis of their location than the significance of their resources. Close at hand, these parks can be used on an impromptu basis with little pre-planning. A sunny winter afternoon is all that is required to send thousands of people to our city parks to skate, ski, walk or simply enjoy the fresh air. Urban parks thus provide significant health and fitness benefits to home- and office-bound urbanites.

Municipal parks, highway waysides and private campgrounds are an important component of the province's tourism industry. They serve as short-term destinations where visitors can stop for a day or two as they explore Alberta's towns and surrounding countryside. Recreation areas on many of our lakes and throughout the forested areas provide campgrounds and other facilities that support fishing, boating, swimming and access to natural and cultural points of interest.

Parkland

While the lands were reserved for park purposes in 1954, it was 1957 before the government formally created Rochon Sands Provincial Park. The 119-hectare park continues to host thousands of birds, particularly during migration. Northern pike and burbot are found in the lake.

Saskatoon Island Provincial Park

Saskatoon Island Provincial Park lies in a blue lake surrounded by golden fields. Few visitors, though, are aware of its history. This small quiet spot is one of Alberta's oldest parks.

The early people of Alberta made good use of the island. The Cree picked the Saskatoon berries that grew here in abundance, then mixed them with other berries and meat to make pemmican. The word Saskatoon is an English version of the Cree word meaning "many flowers".

The first white settlers came to the area at the beginning of this century. Drawn by the fertility of the land, they soon became enamored with the island and its beauty. It became the focal point for picnics and celebrations. Games, races and baking competitions were the order of the day. Many local families spent a day or even a week relaxing on the island.

Time passed and the local residents began to worry about the fate of their island. More and more people were coming to the Peace Country. Concerned that the island could be homesteaded and this favorite spot lost forever, the settlers wrote to Ottawa to ensure that this treasured spot would not be available for homesteading.

All was well until 1919 when the lake level dropped making Saskatoon Island part of the mainland. As it was no longer an island, the land could be used for farming and in due time an application for homesteading was filed, causing quite a commotion amongst the locals. The protests convinced the Department of the Interior to reserve the land for park purposes.

In 1932, a 101-hectare area was established as Saskatoon Island Provincial Park. It is a preferred spot for picnics, camping and family reunions. Trumpeter swans are regularly sighted during the summer as are at least another 121 species of birds. The Canadian Wildlife Service ranks the area around Saskatoon Island an important waterfowl habitat. — *Marc Landry*

Oldtimers' picnic in 1935.
Saskatoon Island Provincial Park
(Provincial Archives of Alberta)

Wilderness Areas

Alberta's three wilderness areas, White Goat, Ghost River and Siffleur, protect slightly more than 1,000 square kilometres of the front ranges of the Rocky Mountains. These rugged alpine landscapes still retain their primeval character and are free from roads, human habitation and other development. The processes of nature continue, relatively unaffected by our use of the land. Visitors to these wilderness areas experience solitude and interact with nature on a personal level. Trails are unimproved and there are no campsites or other facilities.

Wilderness areas are the most stringently

Fall skies reflect in the waters of
Saskatoon Island Provincial Park.
(Dave Dodge)

Parkland

Strathcona Science Park

Strathcona Science Park has a unique history which is unknown to most park visitors. The 109-hectare park — located in Strathcona County on the east boundary of the City of Edmonton — has seen many different uses over the years. Early native people used part of the park for a tool-working site and likely hunted in the area. Later, when coal was discovered on the slopes above the river edge, numerous mines were established.

The Black Diamond Coal Mine, founded in 1911, was one of those mines. Individuals like Mr. A. Thompson, the surface manager, and Mr. A. Biamonte, the engineer, worked at the site for over 42 years. At one time, the operation employed 200 workers. Many came from Beverly, just across the river. From spring to fall, miners rowed across the North Saskatchewan or took the ferry. In winter, they walked across the ice. The underground pulley system of the slope mine was powered by horses. Small box cars of coal were hauled up to the tipple via the cable pulley and dumped into large C.N.R. box cars below.

When the use of natural gas became widespread, coal sales plummeted and the mines closed. Several years later, increased demand for land-fill space resulted in the area being used for an open dump. In the early-70s, a decision was made to reclaim the surface and develop it into a park.

Today, the Strathcona Science Park is linked to Rundle Park and the rest of the Capital City Park system by a foot and bicycle bridge across the North Saskatchewan River. A small ski-hill draws skiers from nearby communities. Numerous species of birds including hawks, waterfowl, Hungarian partridges, ruffed grouse, pheasants, crows and songbirds, and a surprising variety of wildlife including coyotes and small mammals are found in the park. The resident mule and whitetail deer, however, are rarely seen. — *Lynne Steele, Thelma Petruk, Maria Biamonte, Margaret Jenkinson & Ed Whitelock, John Nesbitt & David Vetra*

Male yellow warbler feeding a hungry brood. *(Tom Webb)*

Sylvan Lake and Jarvis Bay Provincial Parks

Although Sylvan Lake was one of the original provincial parks established in 1932, for a time it was turned over to the Town of Sylvan Lake. The 85-hectare provincial park was re-established in 1980. It draws huge crowds of weekend visitors for swimming, wind surfing, sailing and water-skiing.

The Red Deer Planning Commission initiated the development of Jarvis Bay Provincial Park in 1964 when it became aware that a choice piece of property on Sylvan Lake might be available for purchase. The Commission recommended that the Parks Board buy this land since nearby Sylvan Lake lacked public beach and campsite facilities. On July 8, 1965 Jarvis Bay Provincial Park, encompassing an additional 85 hectares, was established.

The park, surrounded by privately-owned cottages on the south and a church camp on the north, provides habitat for woodland birds and mammals including the white-tailed and mule deer.

protected of all of the elements in the province's system of parks. Travel is restricted to foot only, and consumptive pursuits such as hunting and fishing are precluded. The wilderness character is further enhanced by their location. On the west they abut back country areas of Jasper and Banff National Parks. To the east they are buffered by provincial crown lands where land uses are curtailed to protect watershed values.

A one-of-a-kind park, Willmore Wilderness, is an area of almost 4,600 square kilometres governed by its own legislation. Visitors experience rugged mountains, alpine lakes, rushing streams, forested valleys and grassy slopes. The diverse natural landscape provides a wide variety of habitats that are home to a host of plants and animals. Less restrictive than the three other wilderness areas, Willmore caters to a range of outdoor pursuits including horseback riding, hunting and fishing.

For many years, guides and outfitters have taken trophy hunters from around the world into Willmore. More recently, their services are in demand for eco-tourism. International clientele clamor to be escorted into the wilderness to paint, to photograph and to communicate with nature. Except for primitive campsites and trails, there are no facilities. Its wilderness character is

Parkland

Volunteers will always be important to Alberta's park system.

A Fistful of Weeds on Strawberry Creek

The land that surrounds Strawberry Creek in the Telfordville Natural Area is thick with mature aspen, peppered with balsam poplar and white spruce, and reinforced with diverse shrub and herb layers. We were responding to a call from a volunteer steward who had discovered an unwelcome addition to the site's vegetation. Scentless chamomile — pretty, flowery plants — were sprouting from seeds washed into the creek from upstream. Our plan was to unceremoniously yank them from the soil.

Natural areas are parcels of land set aside to preserve landscapes in as pristine a state as possible. Most are characterized by a unique aspect or are at least representative of a certain type of natural environment. The main attraction of this natural area is the creek that winds its way through the land leaving its influence behind in the shape of creek breaks and other fluvial features.

Albertans are key to the success of the province's natural areas. Since its inception in 1987, the Volunteer Steward Program, which enhances the management, public understanding and involvement of natural areas, has benefited tremendously from volunteers who observe, record and report on natural features, significant changes, disturbances and other possible problems. In this case, the outbreak of scentless chamomile was detected in time, by the volunteer steward, to control the invasion. Ultimately, parcels of land like Telfordville — cared for by individuals concerned about conservation — will guarantee a legacy for future generations. — *Paul Sparrow-Clarke*

Campground Hosts

The Campground Host Program is one of the most popular volunteer programs run by the Provincial Parks Service. Between May and September, volunteers commit to work three weeks, usually Wednesday to Sunday for four or five hours per day.

Hosts answer visitors' questions, help them with self-registration forms, explain the park facilities and discuss upcoming park events. Often these individuals volunteer for additional duties

Wild strawberries grow in Bragg Creek Provincial Park. *(Rosemary H.L. Calvert, FRPS/Focus/Tony Stone)*

preserved by the exclusion of roads, motorized vehicles and resource uses such as mining and timber harvesting.

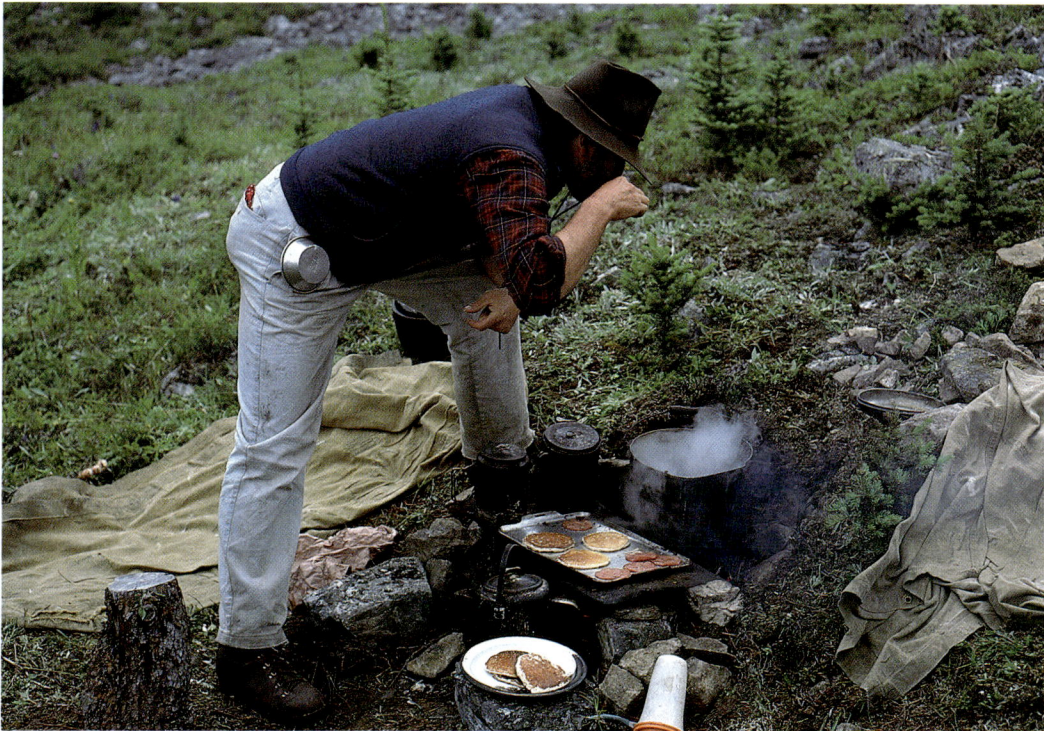

during special park events. Campground hosts operate from their camping site. They receive visual identification items — jackets, t-shirts, hats and such — so that visitors recognize the hosts as pseudo park staff. Some parks, like Aspen Beach, are so popular with volunteers that they have more than one host. Other parks have had the same campground hosts for a number of years. It's like welcoming back part of the family each spring! — *Brian J. Ogston*

Unfinished, Unsophisticated But Successful

Farmers are generous, trusting people. They hope for the best in weather, prices and people. But would they permit a hiking-trail over their land? That was the question pondered by an Edmonton Kiwanis

Ecological Reserves

Ecological reserves are the "new kid on the block" in Alberta's park system. The first reserves were proclaimed in 1987. To date, 13 reserves totalling almost 270 square kilometres have been established. They include representative examples of Alberta's natural landscapes and encompass special, rare and unique natural features. These areas of grassland, parkland, forest and mountains were set aside to contribute to a sustainable environment and economy for today and the future.

Ecological reserves, dedicated to scientific research, are places where we can study the structure, function and changes that occur within the natural environment. Plant communities are permitted to evolve, grow, die and decompose in an unregulated fashion. Soil-forming processes occur without interference. These reserves, which protect and maintain essential life-support systems, are a benchmark against which the effectiveness of resource management throughout the province can be measured. They provide knowledge essential to the integration of environmental protection with economic development.

Parkland

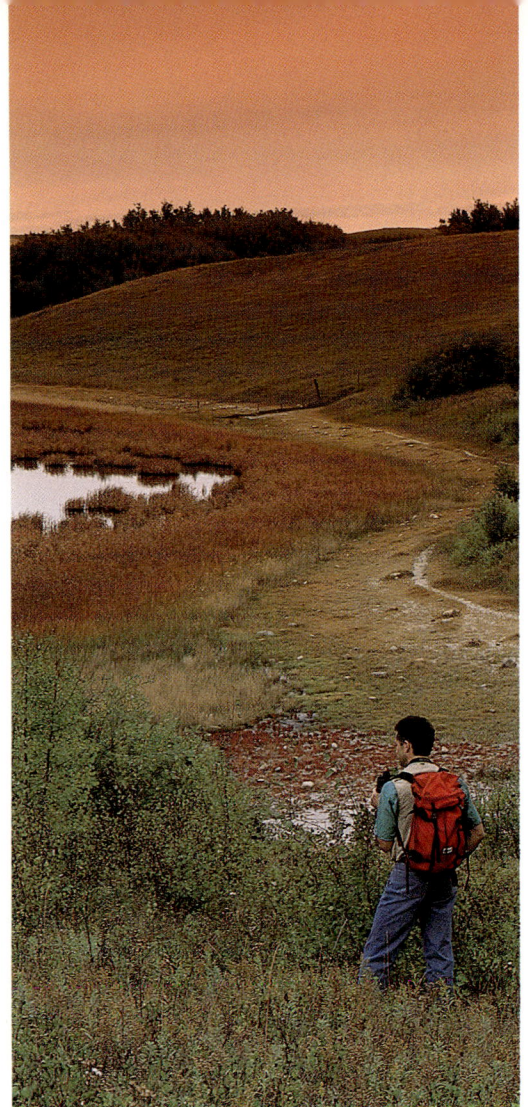

Local residents helped move the old C.N.R. railway station to Vermilion Provincial Park. *(Provincial Parks Service)*

The potholes of the parkland region are important for nesting waterfowl. *(AV and Exhibit Services)*

group back in 1967. The group decided it was worth a try and thus began the Waskahegan Trail.

The trail starts in Edmonton and is routed southeast to Gwynne following the scenic valleys of Blackmud Creek, Saunders Lake and Coal Lake; a side trail from Coal Lake leads to Wetaskiwin. From Gwynne, it runs east to Camrose via the Battle River Valley and the trail north of Miquelon Lake runs to Fort Saskatchewan via Ministik Lake, Wanisan Lake and Elk Island Park. Eventually, the trail will loop back to Edmonton by way of Gibbons and St. Albert and it will boast numerous campsites along the way.

Twenty-five years later, 200 kilometres of the planned 300 are finished. Waskahegan trail-blazers have become a valuable part of Alberta's evolving legacy through the establishment and preservation of this hiking trail.

Natural Areas

Natural areas are public lands set aside to protect natural landscapes primarily because of their interest to local citizens. Kimiwan Lake Natural Area, for example, is the pride of the residents of McLennan, who labored diligently to have the area protected and the lake water level raised so that bird life would return. McLennan now proudly boasts that they are the "Bird Capital of Canada".

Natural areas provide opportunities for non-facility pursuits including picnicking, bird-watching, berry-picking, hiking, cross-country skiing and nature-appreciation. Staging areas and trails have been developed in a few areas by local interest groups. A self-guiding interpretive trail through Wagner Natural Area, a few kilometres west of Edmonton, enables school groups and individuals to experience the marl ponds, orchids and abundant wildlife of this unique area. Natural areas are important as outdoor classrooms — places that local schools can depend on as a vital part of their environmental education programs.

Alberta's 118 natural areas (an additional 21 are pending) are managed by 150 individuals and representatives from 50 groups. These volunteers help with site monitoring, the

Vermilion Provincial Park

Vermilion, once home to the Beaver Indians, a small prairie town and a thriving trade centre, owes much to the coming of the railroad in 1905. A C.N.R. station was built, freight shipped and received, passengers serviced, telegrams sent and tickets sold for near and distant destinations.

A reservoir, created when the C.N.R. built a weir to impound water for its steam engines, made the Vermilion River a focal point for the town folks' recreation in the 1920s. The local residents swam on the north side of the river valley at a small beach. In 1930, the town approached the Provincial Parks Board to establish a dam to create a larger waterbody but the proposal was declined due to the cost. Two decades later, however, the proposal was reactivated and in 1952, a dam was built with funding from Canadian Utilities, the Department of Highways and Ducks Unlimited.

In 1979, the C.N.R. — which had played a significant role in both the park's and Vermilion's history — ceased full service and made plans to demolish the old station building. Rallying together, the town fought to save the historical landmark. An agreement with Alberta Recreation and Parks for a site was reached, and after lengthy negotiations, the 79-year-old station was moved to Vermilion Provincial Park. The wooden caboose, located in front of the station in the park, was dedicated to Mr. Bryon Moore the town's retired C.N.R. agent. The C.N.R. station was officially opened on September 20, 1987 as a historical resource within the park.

The natural resources of this 752-hectare park are representative of the central parkland natural region. The east-west Vermilion valley was both a pre-glacial river valley and a glacial meltwater channel. The valley is about 650 metres wide and the river meanders across its bottom until it flows into the reservoir. There are three topographical zones in the park: flat to gently rolling plateau, steep valley sides and flat valley bottom. The difference between the grassy south-facing slopes and the forested north-facing slopes is critical to the character of the park. Two archaeological sites (tipi rings) have been identified on the north side of the Vermilion River near the west end of the park. — *Gary Walsh, Lorraine Robinson, Charles Lychuk & Kelly Meynberg*

Although not a typical parkland resident, moose are frequently seen at Miquelon Lake Provincial Park. *(Rosemary H.L. Calvert, FRPS)*

Parkland

A New Lake for Future Parkland

Gaping holes in the ground, earth ripping machines, high bumpy piles of rocky debris, heavy dragline booms swinging across the sky and multi-ton trucks hauling away earth — hardly images that one associates with the quiet, natural scenes of a park. Yet these scenes — common to open-pit, coal-strip mines in Alberta — not only reflect the activities surrounding coal extraction, but they also signal an opportunity for new parkland.

Less than an hour west of Edmonton lies potential parkland, created totally anew. The place is the Whitewood Coal Mine lying to the north of Lake Wabamun, about two kilometres northwest of Wabamun Provincial Park. This open-pit mine, owned by TransAlta Utilities Corporation, has slowly eaten its way across the land in a westward progression along the north side of Highway 16. Woodlands, open fields, sloughs and lakes were seemingly gobbled up by machines, relentlessly searching for coal. For many individuals, their first reaction to the churned up landscape is, "What a waste." But a more realistic perspective is: "What a great opportunity for future land planning!"

Government regulations require mining operators to undertake "progressive reclamation" for the purpose of returning the land to its pre-mining capability. Hence, the tale of the demise of two lakes and their rebirth as a new, redesigned lake in the post-mining landscape.

At one time, two lakes lay west of where the coal was being extracted. One was a small, shallow slough that primarily attracted waterfowl. The second, Whitewood Lake, was larger (almost two kilometres long). It was a picturesque, recreational lake surrounded by poplar trees and a few cottages. The lake's quiet waters attracted small boats, fishermen and occasionally drew regional water-ski meets. When the westward shift of the mining resulted in the draining of both lakes, a plan for their reclamation was required. However, since lakes were involved, the goal

became the restoration of the lakes, not the usual targets of agricultural or forested land. Replacement of a lake as part of a reclamation program had never been attempted in such a major way in Alberta.

Saskatoon Island Provincial Park is popular with bird-watchers because of its rare trumpeter swans. *(Dave Dodge)*

The coal company moved steep piles of mine debris, left from earlier mining activities in the northeastern part of the old mine, so that this low area could be reshaped into the new lake's basin. For months during 1987 and 1988, bulldozers, scrapers and a huge mining dragline moved laboriously around the three-kilometre shoreline of the new lake, reshaping over a million cubic metres of earth material. What resulted was a rolling landscape with lots of variation in its surface. Flatter areas were smoothed out for future development of a day-use picnicking site or a small campground. On a broad, newly formed, gentle slope of the lake, a future beach was envisioned, allowance was made for a boat launch. The lake itself has an irregular shoreline with small embayments sheltered from wind and waves. The shallow, near-shore areas where fish and shorebirds can feed and that are also safe for wading are balanced with deep spots in the lake where fish can hide.

Vegetation has returned to the remolded land in the last couple of years. Poplar trees have naturally re-established themselves as well as planted evergreen trees and shrubs. Small minnows now swim in the lake and game fish will likely be planted. Waterfowl are beginning to use the new lake habitat and larger animals like deer are moving into area from nearby undisturbed woodlands.

Altogether, the new lake with 18.5 hectares of water area and a shoreline of more than one and half kilometres surrounded by another 107 hectares of new land surface will provide an attractive setting for numerous recreational activities. Lying so close to Wabamun Provincial Park and the Yellowhead Highway, this new parkland may very well play a satellite role in the future. — *Stuart Loomis*

Parkland

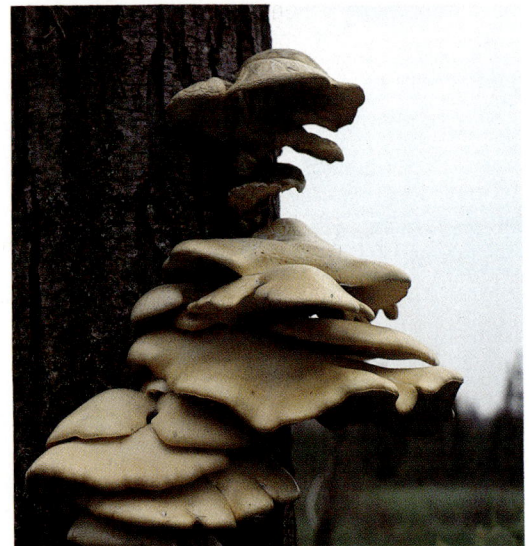

Young saw-whet owls *(Tom Webb)*

Mushrooms help break down forest debris. *(Rosemary H.L. Calvert, FRPS)*

Bracket fungi on balsam poplar in Garner Lake Provincial Park. *(Archie Landals)*

maintenance of fences and signs, and in some cases, preparation and delivery of interpretive programs. As guardians of our natural areas, Alberta's volunteer stewards are committed to caring for our legacy of parks.

Land Trusts

The Park Ventures Fund of the Alberta Recreation, Parks and Wildlife Foundation is actively engaged in the long-term protection of land through a land trust. The term "land trust" is used to describe a non-profit organization whose purpose is the protection and conservation of land for scenic, agricultural, recrea-tional or other purposes. Donors and other partners may designate special places where the natural environment can be protected and enjoyed.

One example is the bequest of Mary Louise Imrie of almost $1 million in land and

Owls, Orchids & Asphalt — Wagner Natural Area

Since the early-50s, numerous scientists, naturalists, photographers, school classes and local residents have focused their attention on the Wagner Natural Area. The wide range of habitats found there — calcium-rich marl ponds, peatlands, black spruce-tamarack forests, poplar and white spruce woods, grassy meadows and willow thickets — play host to an amazing diversity of plant and animal species. Its marl ponds and peatlands are supplied with spring water which flows continuously throughout the year at a temperature of four degrees Celsius.

This half-section of land, once called Wagner's Bog, has developed a reputation for its many owl boreal species, beautiful orchid displays and carnivorous plants. Fifteen of Alberta's 26 orchid species including two rare species have been found in this natural area which is located just a few kilometres west of Edmonton. The area is a remnant of a much larger peatland complex that has gradually diminished in size due to clearing for agricultural fields, logging, pipelines, seismic lines, acreage developments and roads. Its location near a metropolitan area of more than half a million people has meant relentless pressure from urban development.

The area, part of Alberta's Natural Areas Program, is managed by the Wagner Natural Area Society. This group of volunteers has, on several occasions, defended the area against the too near development of roads that would have destroyed important natural habitats. Owls and orchids were recognized to be more valuable than asphalt.

Scientific research, encouraged by the society, has discovered more than 310 vascular plants, 62 mosses, 10 liverworts, 78 lichens, 71 fungi and 97 species of birds in the area. Studies indicate that the peat is up to 236 centimetres deep and has been accumulating for almost 5,000 years. Zoologists are particularly interested in the disjunct (isolated) population of boreal toads and large population of northern water shrews.

The area is also home to a 330-year-old tamarack tree — Alberta's oldest. Additionally, the area is the first recorded site, in Canada, of a rare mushroom species. In entomological circles, the Wagner Natural Area is an internationally famous site. A survey of its terrestrial invertebrate fauna

funding. Through the efforts of volunteers, a beautiful park of 60 hectares at Devil's Lake — one of the parcels of land given to the people of Alberta by Mary Imrie — is being completed. Residents of the Onoway area, under the leadership of the local Fish and Game Association, are developing this park, balancing landscape protection, outdoor education and recreational use.

The Cross Conservation Area is a striking example of an existing new partnership. Ann and Sandy Cross donated 2,000 acres of prairie and aspen parkland to the people of Alberta on condition that it be used for conservation education and that the landscape be protected in perpetuity. Over 20 conservation-minded corporations along with the Park Ventures Fund have donated from $10,000 to $100,000 each. These contributions along with numerous smaller gifts have established an endowment in excess of $1-million that will ensure the ongoing legacy of this beautiful landscape. The Nature Conservancy of Canada, a non-profit organization, has been invited to manage the area.

Recognizing the importance of private land and cash donations and the value that the donor attaches to the gift, Dr. Stephen West, a former parks' minister concluded in 1991: "The

Parkland

was conducted in 1985 by the Provincial Museum of Alberta with a total of 2,195 species being identified. A self-guiding trail through a portion of the natural area allows organizations, individuals and school groups to enjoy this special outdoor laboratory. — *Alice Hendry*

An Outdoor Classroom

Getting my students really interested in learning was always a challenge. During my first year of teaching, I was introduced to a new concept — environmental education — teaching outside. We didn't go out everyday or every week, but when we did, the kids really tuned in.

It wasn't long before I discovered my local provincial park with its trails and beaches, places to get warm in the winter and all kinds of neat and natural stuff to look at and learn about. A social studies lesson on Alberta's pioneers took on new meaning when we sat outside and discussed the hardships they may have experienced. Watching a spider spin a web led to a skit about the life of a spider. A math lesson on estimation meant a whole lot more when we tried to count the number of leaves on a tree and then estimate the number in the park.

Environmental education can revolve around intensive study about a specific natural area or environmental problem. From mosquitoes to global warming to where to build a new park, provincial parks play an important role in educating our youth about the environment. — *Brian J. Ogston*

Watchable Wildlife

Fingers of fog curl gently across the bay, muting the sharp cries of gulls and terns. Shafts of sunlight break through, bronzing the marsh with rich, warm hues, turning the shoreline ripples to ribbons of liquid gold. A flock of sandpipers dart across the water, wings flashing brilliant white in the morning light. Glossy mallards doze, drifting with the gentle waves. Morning comes to Centre Bay. It is a place of intense vitality where the only thing constant is change. From mountain to prairie, from boreal forest to unglaciated plateaus, Alberta's landscape is rich and diverse. Enthusiasts from across the country and around the world recognize this province for its wildlife viewing opportunities. Residents

Balsam root is common in Upper Bob Creek Ecological Reserve. *(Rosemary H.L. Calvert, FRPS)*

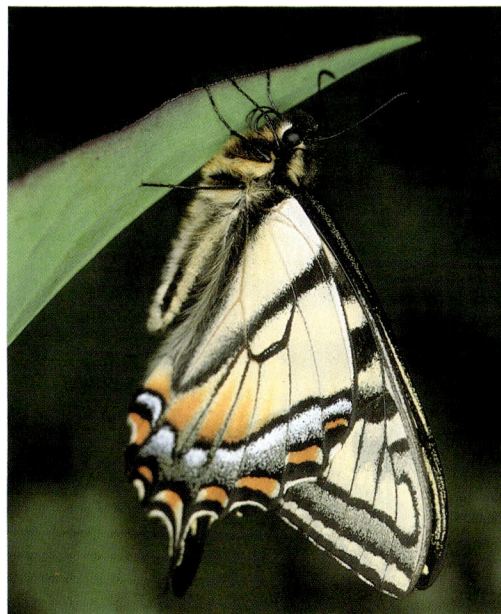

Bluebirds have declined across Alberta due to loss of nesting sites. (Tom Webb)

Short-eared owls nest frequently in the parkland especially in years when rodents are abundant. (Archie Landals)

Butterflies in Alberta's parks come in an endless variety of colors. (Rosemary H.L. Calvert, FRPS)

role of the Foundation is to facilitate the wishes of the public to protect and donate land for future generations."

Bird and Wildlife Sanctuaries

Bird and wildlife sanctuaries and habitat-development areas help to protect Alberta's wildlife. Migrating ducks and geese and other water-fowl and shore-birds are provided refuge on their northward or southbound trek. Habitat-enhancement projects, associated with programs such as the North American Waterfowl Management Plan, are restoring nesting cover to help stop the decline of duck populations across North America. Many of these are cooperative efforts involving organizations such as Ducks Unlimited and the Alberta Fish and Game Association.

Parkland

and visitors have unequalled opportunities for the close observation of wildlife which elsewhere may be accessible only in books and films.

Within Alberta's provincial parks, wilderness areas and ecological reserves are some of the most spectacular and attractive wildlife viewing areas in the province. In or near sites in the southern grasslands such as at Writing-on-Stone Provincial Park or Kennedy Coulee Ecological Reserve, the golden eagle and ferruginous hawk can be observed. Multitudes of breeding waterfowl including the majestic Canada goose gather on prairie wetlands and reservoirs. Dillberry Lake Provincial Park in the aspen parkland harbors a variety of hawks and owls, waterfowl, coyotes and sharptailed grouse. Scenic meandering rivers like the Milk, Bow, Red Deer and Vermilion beckon canoes to thread kilometres of wooded corridors past white-tailed deer, beaver and songbirds. Visit Wyndham-Carseland or Vermilion Provincial Parks by canoe to observe some of Alberta's wildlife.

In the vast wildland of the northern boreal forest at places like Notikewin Provincial Park, Whitemud Falls Ecological Reserve or Lesser Slave Provincial Park, the Canada lynx, moose, great grey owl, river otters, white pelicans and numerous warblers make their home. Along the highway corridor to the west of Nordegg, a visitor can experience some of the most rugged and spectacular alpine terrain in Alberta in the White Goat Wilderness Area. Here can be observed wildlife that is nearly unafraid of man including grizzly bear, woodland caribou, mule deer, wolverine and bighorn

sheep. In the nearby Kootenay Plains Ecological Reserve, elk and other species that prefer montane habitats can be viewed. Acquaint yourself with the colorful wood warblers at Sir Winston Churchill Provincial Park. Take a day-long canoe trip in William A. Switzer Provincial Park to observe beaver, mink, muskrats, loons and grebes. Sleep under the stars and listen to the coyotes and great horned owls at Dinosaur Provincial Park. Search for saxifrage and heather in the alpine meadows of Peter Lougheed Provincial Park.

The range of Alberta's watchable wildlife is beyond imagination. You won't see it all. No one ever has. But that which you discover will be with you for years to come. — *Wayne Nordstrom*

Outhouse. "Single combination vault pump-out toilet" in parks jargon. *(Archie Landals)*

Whitney Lakes Provincial Park

The first campers arrived at Whitney Lakes about 7,000 years ago. While the campsites weren't numbered and the shower building wasn't completed, those first inhabitants saw many of the same lakes and land formations sculpted 3,000 years before their arrival that we see today.

The land that is now Whitney Lakes Provincial Park has witnessed a progression of people passing near or over it. The first European passed through the area in 1754, just south of the park on the North Saskatchewan River. Such legendary figures as Anthony Henday, David Thompson and Peter Fiddler may have camped in the park on their way west, or passed through what is now the Ross Lake Campground. A hawk flying over Laurier Lake may have seen the smoke from Big Bear's camp on April 2, 1885, the day of the Frog Lake Massacre which historians mark as the end of an era in Alberta. As settlers arrived and agricultural communities were formed, the area was used for berry-picking and recreation. The beaches boomed with summer picnics, rodeos and a dance hall.

During the late-70s and early-80s, scientists working for Alberta Parks Service studied the great natural wealth of the land around the lakes. Their findings, coupled with the fact that the locale was a well-established recreational site, resulted in the area being designated as a provincial park. The development of this 1,489-hectare park in 1982 protects some of the province's spectacular landscapes. Whitney Lakes Provincial Park, a time capsule from the ice age, provides visitors with a window to Alberta's past. — *Kerry Hope*

Sanctuaries, like the Inglewood Bird Sanctuary in Calgary and the Gaetz Lake Sanctuary in Red Deer, attract wildlife to urban areas and are popular wildlife viewing areas. Alberta has 19 sanctuaries, many differing in focus, totalling 1,277 square kilometres.

National Parks

National Parks encourage public understanding and enjoyment of Canada's natural heritage while protecting, in perpetuity, landscapes of Canadian significance. Representative examples of the different natural regions of Canada are set aside to protect the landscape and associated plants and animals. Most of the land in national parks is devoted to protecting the environment. This precludes activities such as mining, forestry and agriculture. Relatively small areas are devoted to town sites, campgrounds, roads and facilities required for visitors.

ROCKY MOUNTAINS

The Rocky Mountains are Alberta's most rugged natural region, with peaks along the western border of the province reaching 3,500 metres. Valley bottoms average 1,200 to 1,500 metres. Exposed bedrock is common at higher elevations and icefields are not uncommon. As a result of the rugged terrain and elevation differences, the Rocky Mountains support the most diverse assemblage of vegetation in Alberta, ranging from dry grasslands and deciduous woodlands to lush coniferous forests to alpine tundra. The Rockies contain a rich collection of wildlife including elk, bighorn sheep, mountain goats and grizzly bear. Most of Alberta's major rivers originate from the glaciers and snow-capped peaks of the Rocky Mountains.

Alberta's parks are world-famous for their mountain scenery.
(Rosemary H.L. Calvert, FRPS)

Tips on Trout

Sixty years ago and sixty years from now, fishing will still drive people crazy! Sport fishing in Alberta's provincial parks, especially in the southwest region, offers some of the best trout steam fishing in North America. Provincial park lakes such as Beauvais, Park, Little Bow, Chain and Police each possess a variety of fish species.

There's no great mystery to fishing in a lake. Trout are creatures of habit, and when you understand their feeding habits you increase the chance of hooking a big one! Rainbow and brown trout are not native to lakes, rather they've been planted. Their food supply includes predominantly insect larvae as well as freshwater clams, snails, leeches and insects. Most of these organisms live in the shallow reed beds that skirt the lake. Insects lay their eggs in shallow water. It can be between one and three years before the larvae mature and hatch out. Many insects in the lake, dragon flies, damselflies and mosquitoes, follow this reproductive cycle. When an insect hatches, it makes its way to the surface. It is at this time — when the wings of the insect are too soft to fly — that it is most likely to be eaten by the trout. The small veins in the insect's wings, however, soon fill with blood and give the wing the needed stiffness for the insect to fly.

We've all seen insects flying over water or bunched together skimming the surface. To capture these insects, the trout makes its appearance at the surface. That's when we hear a splash

Buttercup *(Kåre Hellum)*

Rocky Mountains

Saturday Morning Woes — Bow Valley Provincial Park

Saturday morning and goodness me,
*   here they come!*
Now the week-end has really begun.
Well who is getting that favorite site?
I would like to scream but must be polite.
Someone tells me they will sleep in the car,
So I give them a site most secluded by far
But back they come with an embarrassed face
And ask me to put them some other place.
Oh me, oh my! such a terrible day,
Things go wrong in such a funny way,
They trade tags with people here and there
And I'm the last to now just why or where.
Now a lady has lost her pussy cat,
She expects me to guess just where it's at!
And somebody fell in a big dog's (—) mess,
But of course the owner will never confess.
Someone asks to picnic for a little while,
"Oh certainly Sir," I reply with a smile,
"But please don't go in a numbered site
And everything will be alright."
But saying these words didn't help at all
Because down they go and park in a stall!

And off they go for a nice long hike
As someone requests that particular site.
So I'm on the phone as I mutter and cuss,
"Ranger please come over and settle this fuss."
Now here comes a group that asks for a number
And counting heads I begin to wonder:
When he hands me just a dollar and a half,
I ask for more but he starts to laugh,
"Why there's just Mom and Dad and a few more."
But I swear I counted about twenty-four.
"We are all staying in just one stall,
I'll pay $1.50 and that is all!"
Well I doodle a bit as I think to myself,
Then "Sir, I'll give you number 10, 11, and 12."
He looks kind of funny but begins to dig
And that is the end of that little jig.
Now people that act like this are very few,
Most are extremely kind and thoughtful of you.
It would take pages and pages to list all the good
Of campers you meet in every kind of mood,
And remembering these people over all the years
I think of them fondly and sometimes with tears.

— Freida E. Hass (1909 - 1983)

Peter Lougheed Provincial Park is a cross-country skier's paradise.
(Rosemary H.L. Calvert, FRPS)

Kananaskis Country includes luxury hotels as well as rustic camp-grounds. *(Kananaskis Country)*

Trails in Kananaskis Country are wheelchair accessible. *(Mike Vassel/ Provincial Parks Service)*

or see the silvery side of a trout as it rises, leaving behind concentric ripples as a telltale sign of its presence. Larger trout slurp the insects off the top of the water leaving behind small ripples and a bubble from when they close their mouth. When fishing for trout in one of the rivers, remember that it is the large fish that reproduce. Removing them depletes the stock. Large fish should always be released, and that if you want to keep your catch, fish in a stocked lake. — *Jim Foley*

Kananaskis Country

The full story of Kananaskis Country will never be written. That 400,000-hectare chunk of mountains, rivers, lakes and trees between Calgary and Banff National Park means something different to each of the millions of visitors who cross its boundaries every year. Many come for the activities: downhill skiing, hiking, camping, mountain-biking, four-wheel driving, fishing, climbing, hunting, golfing, horse-riding, paddling, cross-country skiing, photographing, resort-hostelling, driving, sightseeing, wildlife-watching or picnicking. Ranges of the Rocky Mountains march

Canada's national parks are a very special part of Alberta's legacy of parks. Jasper, Banff and Waterton National Parks protect over 18,000 square kilometres of Alberta's rocky mountains. With their spectacular alpine scenery, these parks are the cornerstone of Alberta's tourism industry, attracting about 6 million visitors a year.

Wood Buffalo National Park, straddling the border between Alberta and the Northwest Territories, encompasses 44,807 square kilometres of the boreal forest making it one of the largest parks in the world. The wilderness, muskeg and wetlands of Wood Buffalo are the nesting area of the whooping crane. In 1941 there were only 20 whooping cranes recorded as living in the wild. Their nesting location remained a mystery until 1954 when forestry officer, G.M. Wilson, and a helicopter pilot, J.D. Landells spotted a family group containing a flightless young crane, in the remote wilderness of Wood Buffalo National Park. The following day Canadian Wildlife Service biologist W.A. Fuller confirmed the sighting, near the Sass River just west of Fort Smith. By the summer of 1991 there were 33 nesting pairs in the park and a population of 143 cranes. The gradual coaxing of the endangered whooping crane back from

Rocky Mountains

down most of Kananaskis Country like 3,000-metre-high soldiers blocked here and there by spectacular lakes. In the Country's eastern section — the gentle and verdant eastern foothills, with their abundant wildlife, are split by crystalline rivers like the Sheep, Highwood and Elbow.

Kananaskis Country is the result of a series of coincidences and a vision. Alberta's economy and population were booming in the 1970s and everyone was looking for recreational activities and outlets. The province had saved a few billion dollars in the Heritage Savings Trust Fund from natural gas and oil royalties, so meeting these demands was a possibility. Moreover, the land was available. The Eastern Slopes Management Policy was a type of zoning exercise in which the best use for the province's land base in the Rockies and Foothills was also being decided. A spectacular chunk of real estate between Banff National Park and the ranchland of the most westerly prairies presented itself. Most of it was Crown land with a history of varied recreational use such as hiking, camping, fishing and hunting.

Nothing, however, had ever been attempted on this kind of a scale. This wasn't a campground; it was 60 campgrounds. This wasn't a hiking trail; it was hundreds of kilometres of hiking-trails, horse-trails, snowmobile-trails and cross-country ski trails. It wasn't just building access to some lakes and backcountry; it was a year-round highway to mountain valleys and to lakeside facilities, boat launches, canoe launches and nature walks around the shorelines. A third provincial park, Kananaskis, later renamed Peter Lougheed Provincial Park, was created as were more than 90 recreational areas within the Kananaskis Country boundaries, joining the already established Bow Valley Provincial Park and Bragg Creek Provincial Park.

Information centres were built so every visitor could get the most enjoyment out of their visit safely. Service centres were built in case you forgot the hot-dog buns, or the transmission fell out of the Winnebago. Private developers chipped in as well with such facilities as the hotels at Kananaskis Village, the Southern Alberta Hostelling Association hostel at Ribbon Creek and Mt. Engadine Lodge. Some of the developments were contracted out to private operators.

Wheelchair accessible fish ponds are popular in Kananaskis Country. *(Kananaskis Country)*

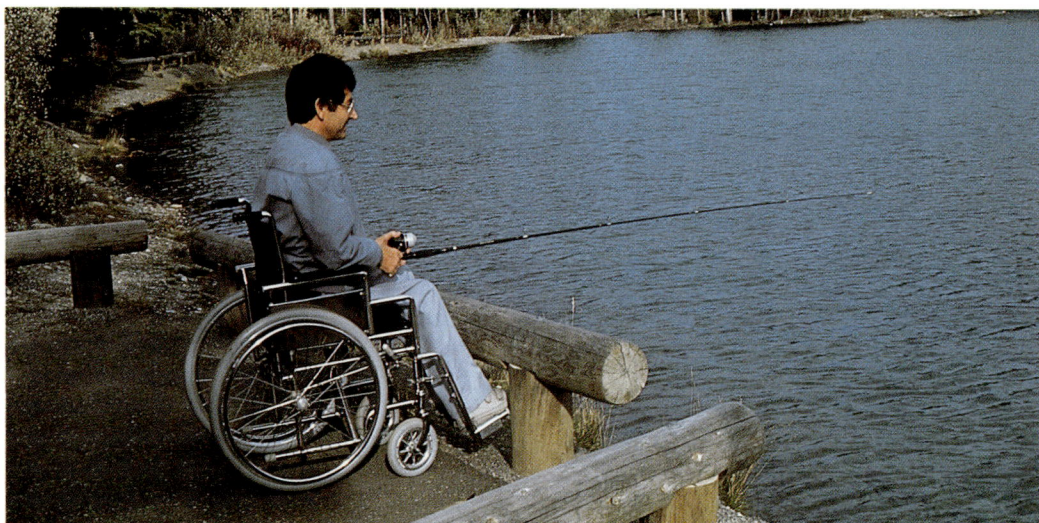

Winter is a magical time in Kananaskis Country. *(Kananaskis Country)*

the brink of extinction is a story of public concern, international cooperation and the protection afforded by parks.

Elk Island National Park, located east of Edmonton, is the smallest of the national parks in Alberta. Although it is small in size, there are numerous tales about the local citizens who lobbied and worked for its creation. The greatest story, of course, is the rescue of the plains bison from extinction, something of which all Albertans can be proud.

International Programs

Canada is signatory to three international conventions that play significant roles in the preservation of our natural heritage. Alberta is a key player in these initiatives with sites designated under all three programs.

The Man and the Biosphere program (M.A.B.) was launched in 1970 by the 16th General Conference of the United Nations Educational, Scientific and Cultural Organization (U.N.E.S.C.O.). Although primarily concerned with natural heritage, M.A.B. has adopted an integrated approach to the analysis of human interactions with different types of ecosystems.

135

Rocky Mountains

Over 18,000 people attended the 1981 Scout Jamboree in Bow Valley Provincial Park. *(Archie Landals)*

In addition to designating representative ecosystems of international significance, M.A.B. also recognizes landscapes resulting from traditional patterns of land use and degraded ecosystems capable of being restored.

In the Alberta context, Waterton Lakes National Park was designated a Biosphere Reserve in 1979. The reserve consists of two components. Waterton Lakes National Park in Alberta and Glacier National Park in Montana are officially designated as the "core area" of the biosphere reserve. The core area is essentially undisturbed and is afforded a high degree of protection within these national parks. A "zone of cooperation" surrounds the core and is made up of those lands, people and agencies which voluntarily become part of the program.

Technical and management committees made up of scientists, academics, landowners and concerned citizens are collectively working to prepare management plans to retain the overall integrity of the region, its ecosystems, and associated plants and animals. These management plans will also benefit cultural-heritage conservation because they will help to preserve the landscape created by traditional ranching in Alberta.

In 1972, the convention concerning the

Kananaskis Country is an area of Canada's majestic Rocky Mountains set aside for Albertans to enjoy. It was and is theirs to enjoy as they see fit whether they climb the highest peaks or drive through in hopes of seeing a Rocky Mountain bighorn sheep or majestic elk. When the Country was dedicated on January 1, 1979, a news release called it a mega-park. In reality, much of it is not park at all; rather it is a pristine forest, part of the larger Bow-Crow Forest Reserve. An operating agreement allows some of the traditional land uses such as grazing, small scale logging and natural gas extraction to be carried out provided it is not detrimental to the area.

The Albertans who use William Watson Lodge, Kananaskis Country's facility to allow people with disabilities the same access to the outdoors as the physically fit, would tell still other stories. Think of the accounts which could be told by users of Kananaskis Country facilities like the Canmore Nordic Centre, Boundary Stables, Nakiska At Mount Allan, McLean Creek Off Highway Vehicle Zone, Fortress Mountain, Sheep River Wildlife Sanctuary or Canoe Meadows whitewater kayak course. The stories are endless.

Future visitors will be able to write their own histories of Kananaskis Country. Then as now, the Country will mean something different to each one of them. That's the way it is supposed to be.
— *Don Morberg, Ron Chamney, Ron Henderson & Paul Durant*

The 10th Largest City in Alberta

Twice in its short history, Kananaskis Country has played host to Baden Powell followers. Both the 1981 Canadian Jamboree, the biggest jamboree ever held in Canada, and the XV World Jamboree, which welcomed over 13,000 Scouts and volunteers from 87 countries, were held in the Country's Bow Valley Provincial Park.

By the time the Canadian Jamboree started, the number of Scouts, Venturers and leaders totalled 17,986. Additionally – 1,425 adult volunteers, 255 specially trained Hikemaster Venturers and 107 Armed Forces staff – lent their support to the Canadian youth. In total, almost 20,000 people lived on the 500-hectare site for ten days making it the tenth largest city in Alberta.

Viewing platform. Peter Lougheed Provincial Park. *(Archie Landals)*

Alberta Parks performed organizational miracles during the Jamboree. They supplied 2,500 picnic tables, back-country rescue and garbage removal. Parks Service arranged for Fish and Wildlife to provide bear patrol, the R.C.M.P. to offer site security, Forest Service took care of fire protection, Cardinal Coach furnished a fleet of buses, General Motors made vehicles available to ferry volunteers, and Canadian Forces provided staffers and a 60-bed field-hospital and field-kitchen which fed 1,700 staffers three times a day.

By the time tents were being pitched for the XV World Jamboree in July 1983, the temporary water system from the Canadian event was a permanent installation. While the event was smaller in size, it required more hands-on management because of its international flavor. Scouts from around the world participated in river rafting, trap shooting, an assault course, moto-cross races, mountain hiking, and trips to Banff and the Calgary Stampede. Volunteers — 2,380 people from all walks of life — helped to strengthen the spirit of scouting. In 1993, the Canadian Jamboree returns to Kananaskis once again to experience Alberta's parks at their best! — *Donn E. Cline*

protection of "World Cultural and Natural Heritage" was adopted by U.N.E.S.C.O. The objective of the World Heritage Convention is to ensure the identification, protection, preservation and interpretation of the world's most significant cultural- and natural-heritage sites. Jasper, Banff and Wood Buffalo National Parks are World Heritage Sites under federal jurisdiction in the province of Alberta.

In 1979, cooperative efforts between the governments of Canada and Alberta resulted in Dinosaur Provincial Park becoming the first provincial park to be accepted to this prestigious international program. In addition to its badlands and rare riverside (riparian) eco-systems, Dinosaur Provincial Park is recognized as having the best assemblage of Cretaceous dinosaur fossils in the world. Additionally, in 1981, Head-Smashed-In Buffalo Jump was declared a World Heritage Site because it is one of the oldest, largest, longest used and best-preserved buffalo jumps in North America.

In agreeing to have these two sites added to the World Heritage Site list, Alberta made a commitment to the world that it would protect the integrity of the sites, preserve the fossils and artifacts found there, and present them to the people of the world through programs of

Trail-rides are popular in Alberta's Rocky Mountains. *(AV and Exhibit Services)*

White Goat - Where Wilderness Lives

White Goat Wilderness. Even the name conjures up images of the wild. My partner, Len Knapik and I entered White Goat by fording the Brazeau River. At this point, the river is braided into a number of channels all fairly shallow but flowing rapidly and not far removed from the melting glacier that gave them birth. It was mid-August and this was one of the first really hot days of the summer. We decided to stay dry and cross the river in our bare feet, a foolish stunt in rocky, rapidly flowing rivers at the best of times.

It took several hours to bushwack the steep slopes to Cline Pass after which we called it a day. Dropping our packs, Len and I climbed a nearby mountain peak simply to admire the scenery. On our scramble up and down the mountain, we saw numerous fresh grizzly diggings. That night we prepared a supper of freeze-dried food. It was clear and calm and there were few bugs. Len and I decided that we were going to sleep out under the stars, something that is not recommended in bear country. We witnessed a meteorite shower that night. The clear mountain air made the stars seem

---

interpretation and education. The Royal Tyrrell Museum of Palaeontology in Midland Provincial Park, the Field Station in Dinosaur Provincial Park and the Head-Smashed-In Buffalo Jump Interpretive Centre are major components of this commitment. The commitment is not Alberta's alone, but it is made on behalf of the Government of Canada, a signatory to the World Heritage Convention. For its part, the Government of Canada provides international publicity for the sites, but it has no direct control over them.

There are a number of benefits to having these two sites included on the World Heritage list. Alberta and Canada both receive political recognition of their commitment to conservation, and the prestige associated with designation results in international media attention to both parties. With the growing importance of global tourism, World Heritage sites effectively become an international calling-card, attracting visitors to Canada and Alberta.

At the invitation of the Iranian government, in 1971, international organizations and countries from around the world met in the town of Ramsar to discuss the alarming global loss of wetlands. This gathering drafted the Convention on Wetlands of International

Rocky Mountains

Immature Swainson's hawks sometime wander into the mountains. *(Tom Webb)*

The Eagles Soar

On rising air
The eagles soar;
Lifting spires,
Beyond earth's floor;
To heights where man's
A threat no more.
Beyond rattle of trains
And highway's roar,
Amidst solace of clouds
May his spirit restore,
His own private sanctum
Beside heaven's own door.

— James Robert Butler
(From an observation in the Sheep River Wildlife Sanctuary, west of Turner Valley)

close enough to touch. Many looked as if they would collide with the mountains. The purple, green and yellow display of the dancing northern lights added awe to the evening.

We hiked along Cataract Creek to its junction with the Cline River during the second day. As the afternoon wore on, clouds once more engulfed the mountain peaks and descended into the valleys. In the twilight, bats flitted in and out of the forest clearings pursuing mosquitoes that were now out in droves in the wet valley bottom. As darkness set in, we were forced into the sanctuary of our nylon hiking tents by an approaching storm — the most violent and spectacular thunderstorm I can ever remember. Brilliant flashes of lightning lit up the sky followed by the deafening roar of thunder. The sound was magnified by the confining valley walls. Since we were

White mountain avens *(Kåre Hellum)*

Importance, now known as the Ramsar Convention. This convention came into force in 1975 with Canada joining in 1981. Four major wetlands in Alberta have been designated under this program: Beaverhill Lake, the Peace-Athabasca Delta, Hay-Zama Lakes and the Whooping Crane nesting area in Wood Buffalo National Park.

Beaverhill Lake, east of Edmonton, protects over 18,000 hectares of shallow lakes, small sloughs and rolling uplands. Beaverhill Lake is an extremely popular birding area, especially during fall migrations when over 200,000 ducks, geese and swans have been

recorded at one time. In 1987 the town of Tofield opened the Beaverhill Lake Nature Centre in recognition of the growing interest in wildlife viewing as a tourist attraction.

Continuing to Evolve

Over the past 100 or so years, the landscape of much of Alberta has been significantly altered to meet the needs of a growing population. Today, fields of grain blanket a landscape where former prairie grasslands stretched to the horizon.

Reflecting on the passing of the open-range ranching era that was all but gone by 1900, pioneer rancher Frederick Ings writes: "Gradually, the range had been closed out. Each year more and more land had been taken up by farmers and more fences built. Wheat took the place of cattle on the plains. The roundup wagons no longer came this way... In all, the heyday of ranching was of short duration, a scarce 25 years bridged the span between vast, open, unsettled stretches of unsurveyed country and the small fenced-in holdings of the wheat farmer. Those were the halcyon days of Alberta; in the march of progress much of her loveliness, her lure and romance has been lost... In the natural course of events such a country could not have been kept unexploited, or given over for long to one great industry. Each year more and more people poured in. The great leases were cut up into farms and smaller ranches. The cattle were

Colorful mountains surround White Goat Wilderness Area. *(Maureen Landals)*

Ice Formations hang from a cave entrance. *(Rosemary H.L. Calvert, FRPS)*

Mountain goats are highly visible in summer. *(Rosemary H.L. Calvert, FRPS)*

141

Rocky Mountains

camped at the confluence of three valleys, the echoes rolled up one valley and then the next. Each volley of thunder set off rockslides from the surrounding cliffs and avalanches from the glaciers at the head of the valleys. Separated from the raw power of nature by only a thin nylon tent, we could easily forget that civilization existed. Sleep was impossible.

On the third day, we decided that a long to trek would take us past Pinto Lake, over Sunset Pass and out to the Jasper-Banff Highway. Such was not the case. Somewhere along an ill-defined trail we took a wrong turn and ended up in a side valley eventually running out of trail altogether. We wanted to go west so we headed that way — across country. Bushwhacking along a valley slope, I managed to get some distance ahead of Len. I broke through a dense thicket of alders and willows into the active centre of an avalanche tract and there, not 20 metres in front of me, was a sow grizzly with two half-grown cubs. They were digging at something in a remnant snow patch, perhaps a mountain goat that had been killed in last winter's avalanche. Fortunately, I was down-wind and they had not detected my presence. Cautiously, I backed into the cover of the thicket and climbed up the slope where I could watch the bears and alert Len before he stumbled into this potentially dangerous situation.

Observing the bears in their natural surroundings was an experience never to be forgotten. All were magnificent creatures, the sow a reddish color, one cub a silver tip, the other a creamy white except for the black tip of its nose. After we watched through our binoculars for perhaps 20 minutes, the breeze shifted and the bears caught our scent. Standing on their hind legs, they sniffed and then wandered off through thickets of dwarf fir. Occasionally they stood up to make sure we were not following.

White Goat Wilderness and the surrounding area is as close to pristine wilderness as can be found anywhere in Alberta. The lucky adventurer can still spot grizzly bear, wolverine, caribou, mountain goat, cougar, wolf and other species associated with wilderness. Even for those not so fortunate — the spectacular, unspoiled scenery, wildflowers and smaller creatures — will provide memories to be cherished forever. — *Archie Landals*

Gentian *(Kåre Hellum)*
Willmore Wilderness allows the adventurous to hike and trail-ride. *(Fred Vermeulen)*

From Willmore Wilderness to Kananaskis Country, Alberta's mountain parks contain many challenging peaks. *(Glen Crawford/ Provincial Parks Service)*

Mountains to Climb — Rivers to Cross

"This is your first lesson", I told my three-year-old grey mare as I tried to entice her to cross a water-puddle. Seconds later I was flat on my back in the puddle and my boots were full of water.

Despite the hazards of trail-riding, and they are numerous, I am drawn back during all seasons of the year to Willmore Wilderness Park. Up on a slope of the Permission Range with a cold mountain creek only 30 metres away, Camp 52 presents a panoramic view across the valley to the Starlight Range with its uniquely shaped reddish slopes. With the horses grazing within sight, their bells jingling, all activities are geared toward relaxation. As we sit around the campfire, the conversation usually revolves around recent trails, the horses, improvements to gear, or other areas to be explored.

restricted in their wanderings by the home fence. The open range was gone."

Gone are the free-roaming herds of bison and the plains grizzly and prairie wolves that depended on them. A part of Alberta's heritage has been lost forever. Changes to the landscape are proceeding at an accelerating rate. With each passing day we make new commitments to the land — forestry agreements, new roads and pipelines and more land cleared for agriculture. The future may leave room for minor shuffling — slight boundary adjustments to existing parks and other land-use commitments, or there may be room for changes in resource management practices — but before long, options for new park designations will no longer exist.

Lupine *(Kåre Hellum)*

143

Cow and calf elk *(Archie Landals)*

Trail-riding is more than just enjoying the alpine landscape. It's seeing the carpet-like cover of delicate alpine flowers in June and July, a double rainbow against the backdrop of the multi-colored slopes, the fulfilment of childhood dreams. Alone in the wilderness, you are forced to be self-sufficient and to reconcile your needs with those of Mother Nature. — *Werner Jappsen*

Nature's Way — Elk, Wolves and Habitat

The Athabasca River runs clear and blue between golden poplar groves, a rich contrast with the dark mantle of spruce that covers the steep mountain slopes on either side. A herd of two dozen elk graze peacefully on a river island. Suddenly, the animals come to attention. Three cows accompanied by calves are the first to run. The rest follow, splashing through the braided river, entering the trees on the opposite bank. Wolves!

Such exciting observations are possible for lucky visitors to Jasper National Park, but that was not always the case. Prior to 1965 there was no lack of elk in Jasper. Wolves, however, were very scarce. The not-so-natural history of the park's large mammal fauna began many years ago, even before the first Europeans arrived on the scene.

On a steep slope overlooking the site where the wolves chased the elk, there is a cave — the Pocahontas Cave — in which archaeologists have found evidence of *homo sapiens* dating back 4,000 years. While these stone-age people probably had little bearing on the abundance of wildlife in the valley, a major change occurred in the 1700s with the arrival of bands of Iroquois and Cree. Pushed out of traditional homelands in Ontario by the "white man's" conquest of eastern Canada, and armed with rifles obtained from the fur traders, the immigrant Indians had a great impact on local game.

Willmore Wilderness Park *(Fred Vermeulen)*

Bighorn sheep *(Rosemary H.L. Calvert, FRPS)*

Rocky Mountains

There is evidence that elk were very scarce in present-day Jasper Park by the time David Thompson, an explorer for the North West Company, arrived. Two years later, in 1813, the Company built a fur-trading post called Jasper House. The diaries of the early postmasters make frequent reference to the scarcity of game and to starving Indians. Towards the end of the 1800s, elk were practically exterminated in all of western Alberta.

A slow improvement began in the early 1900s after protective measures were taken. Jasper National Park was established in 1907 and elk, from Yellowstone Park, were reintroduced in 1920. They multiplied rapidly and reached high densities by the late-30s when they were considered too numerous in the park. The winter ranges in the lower Athabasca Valley, which the elk share with bighorn sheep and deer, became overgrazed. To reduce competition, park wardens embarked on a program of elk reduction; up to 300 cows were shot each winter from 1945 to 1970.

Where, however, were the elk's natural predators? Ironically, while it was evident that the prey species were far too numerous for their own good, the occurrence of large predators was seen with concern and even downright hatred. Park wardens shot all wolves on sight — dens and pups were destroyed. An all-out war on wolves raged in Alberta from 1952 to 1956, during which the province conducted a poisoning campaign to halt the spread of rabies. In 1953 strychnine baits were also set out in Jasper National Park. The shooting of wolves continued until 1959. On adjacent provincial wilderness lands, routine poisoning of wolves lasted to 1966. At that time, a new understanding and even appreciation of wolves began to emerge among wildlife biologists as well as the Canadian public.

At present, the number of elk in Jasper National Park is estimated to be 1,000 animals, down from a high of 2,500 in the 1960s. The decline began quite suddenly in the early-70s, after several severe winters with deep snow. Since then, the combined effect of the park's predators — wolves as well as bears and cougars — have kept the park's elk population quite stable. Wolf numbers, as high as 80 to 100 from 1975 to 1983, are now between 40 and 50 animals.

Majestic bull elk are a traffic stopper in Jasper National Park. *(Archie Landals)*

The relationship between elk and wolves, between prey and predators, is a dynamic one which may show fluctuations from year to year. Overall, predation has been shown to work as a check on elk numbers, preventing them from becoming too numerous for their food supply. To the long-term observer, it is clear that the meadows along the great blue river have recovered from the disastrous chain of events set in motion long ago. There is now plenty of grass and browse for elk, sheep and deer in one of Canada's finest natural treasures, Jasper National Park. — *Dick Dekker*

Tracking the Trends

During the 1980s, one of the most significant societal trends to emerge was the increased personal awareness of health, well-being and self-fulfilment. Albertans are becoming increasingly involved in activities and opportunities that encourage participation, promote personal improvement and ongoing education, and that result in fulfilling experiences. This trend will likely continue as Albertans are expected to maintain active lifestyles into their later years. Population forecasts indicate that the number of Albertans over age 65 will increase from 220,500 (8.9%) in 1990 to 471,500 (14.6%) by 2016.

Alberta's families are also changing. Single parent families are increasing and the number of children per family is decreasing. At the same time, there are more families in which both parents work outside the home, often with different days off. These changes in age and family structure are resulting in a well-defined trend toward more frequent but shorter pleasure trips and to more vacations during non-summer months.

In 1991, speaking to the joint government and industry conference "Making Tourism Your Business," June Markwart, Provincial Parks Service District Manager for Lesser Slave Lake District,

BEARS, BOMBERS

A collection of stories from past and present Provincial Parks Service rangers.

Blueberry Bombers

A bear sow, with three cubs, had been hanging around the residences, and after she charged at me, a decision was made to trap and relocate the family. Early the next morning, we trapped the sow only to have the cubs scramble up nearby trees. Since the mother couldn't be moved without her cubs, our work was cut out for us.

We decided to fall the tree where the cubs were perched, grab the furry little creatures and stuff 'em into gunny sacks. The cubs, however, had other plans. As the tree fell to the ground, the cubs jumped and scurried up other trees. Over and over, we cut and the bears jumped. Eventually we decided the only way to capture the cubs was for one of us to climb up the tree, grab'em and drop'em into a waiting gunny sack.

Like most bears, these cubs were partial to blueberries, a fact which became abundantly clear as I climbed up under the first youngster. The frightened cub climbed higher and began to bomb me. It wasn't long before I was perched at the tip of the tree under the cub, still out of reach and covered in "muck."

A fish and wildlife officer suggested that a snare on a long pole might work. The challenge was not in snaring the cub but in stuffing 15 kilograms of fighting muscle into the gunny sack, a feat which fully engaged five men. An off-duty police constable who was camping in the park and who had offered to help jumped into the group, adrenaline pumping and fists swinging like he was apprehending an armed bandit. One of his swings went astray and whacked the supervisor, Andy McCracken, on his bald head. A red lump rose through the muck. The constable was asked to take a backbencher's role.

Bears are attracted to people by poor food handling practices. *(Archie Landals)*

By four o'clock only two cubs were sacked. We had been at it since ten in the morning and we were stinky, tired and injured both physically and egotistically. Andy went up after the last cub, this time getting closer and closer. The cub, however, reversed direction and climbed down the opposite side of the tree, pausing for a moment to stare at Andy. The cub, still out of reach, jumped. I swung my snare and the lasso gripped the last of the trio in mid-air. Presumably, the bears, which were relocated into the wilderness, have lived happily ever after.

Bear Facts

In 1984 a park ranger on patrol in Lesser Slave Lake Provincial Park witnessed a strange and baffling sight. He was alone and far from help when he caught sight of a woman in the distance. "She was behaving very peculiarly and seemed to be acting out some sort of primitive ritualistic dance," reported the ranger. "I decided to investigate and radioed my intentions to the permit booth."

The ranger drove closer and observed the woman. She was holding two sticks in a cross-like formation and hitting them rhythmically together as she approached a Saskatoon berry bush. "I was going to drive on, but my sense of curiosity was too great to resist," added the ranger. Getting out of his vehicle, he walked cautiously towards the lady. "Good afternoon," he said. "Could I ask you what you're doing?"

The lady replied: "I'm picking berries." Continuing to hit the sticks together, the woman explained that she remembered hearing that banging two sticks together would scare the bears away from a berry patch . . . .

Who's treed? *(John Wilson)*

In their natural habitat, bears thrive on berries and plants. *(Rosemary H.L. Calvert, FRPS)*

Bears, Bombers

Sunshine with a Collar

Highways pose a threat of injury to wildlife. In one such incident, a bear was hit on the highway. It was so stunned that it also stumbled into the side of a bus. The call to the park office said: "Bear bleeding badly. It's crawled off into the woods." At the scene of the accident, there was enough blood to pick up the trail.

A few years ago, it would have been: "Wounded bear, track it and put it down." But we now know that there are few bears and each one is a precious resource. By following the trail of blood, we found the black bear lying down at the edge of the forest. It had a small tag in its right ear (our code for handled females), and we figured it must be "Sunshine," one of our research bears whose collar had been removed the previous summer.

Rather than put the bear down, we opted to tranquillize her. Sure enough, it was 13-year-old Sunshine, a mother to a yearling cub. A close examination showed that her right front leg was broken, she had a long laceration on her rear leg and she was bleeding from one ear. Severe injuries by anyone's standards. Bears, however, are extremely resilient and if she could make it through to hibernation, she would possibly heal over the winter.

We radioed the office for a suture kit and proceeded to administer more tranquillizers, preparing to operate. After an hour of using black thread with a miniature needle to stitch a black furry bear, the worst wounds were pulled back together. We put our new super radio-collar on the bear to monitor her recovery. By the end of the day, Sunshine had her head up but was still lying down on the moss operating table. Sometime during the night, our patient shook off the effects of the drugs and left. The next afternoon, we found bright red buffalo berries scattered at the operation site, the collar, however, indicated the bear was at least a kilometre away. The next day there was no radio signal.

The collar that we put on Sunshine had an on-board computer to transmit a signal to indicate how much the animal was moving, and a built-in tranquillizer dart that could be remotely detonated. Although Sunshine was left to recover within shouting distance of a hiking trail, she was not a threat

Heart-leaved arnica *(Kåre Hellum)*

summarized the trends and challenges facing Alberta's parks: "There is a growing awareness and concern about our environment. We're concerned with our own personal health, well-being and need for self-fulfillment. At the same time, society's awakening political consciousness is demanding greater accountability of government and citizen involvement in decision-making at all levels. Albertans, when faced with issues they believe important, will expend considerable effort to become informed. It's important for all agencies involved in the delivery of Alberta's park system to provide reliable, up-to-date information to the public. Involving them, as well as non-government organizations, in ongoing decision-making processes, will help build community support for park programs. Park personnel will need to return to being 'Jacks and Jills of all trades.' Smiles, quality service and clean facilities, not enforcement, will become the priorities for rangers. Our future legacy of parks will be, in a very real way, molded by the support park managers do or do not get from Alberta's citizens.

"Indicators tell us that there is a growing preference for more frequent but shorter pleasure trips, day trips, group-outings and vacationing during non-summer months. The public is also telling us that they want 'creature

Mule deer are common to Bow Valley Provincial Park. *(Rosemary H.L. Calvert, FRPS)*

comforts' like full service campgrounds with flush toilets, showers and electricity — all the comforts of home. Tourism is a major economic force in our province. Visitors want heritage-appreciation opportunities complete with interpretation of our natural, prehistoric and historic resources as part of their travel itinerary. The public is demanding more, larger, nature-oriented parks and better protection of existing parks. Nature-appreciation activities such as bird-watching and photography are on the increase; consumptive activities such as hunting are declining. Eco-tourism and adventure tourism are booming."

Benefits from Alberta's Parks

Collectively, the components of Alberta's park system provide countless benefits – recreation and health, ecological, scientific, economic, cultural and spiritual, and educational. These benefits, direct and indirect, accrue to Albertans today and in the future. While many of these benefits are not readily measured in economic terms, they nevertheless are important in reflecting who we are as a society.

Pileated woodpeckers dependant on old-growth forests can be found in parks such as Notikewin and Sir Winston Churchill. *(Tom Webb)*

Recreation and Health

Alberta's parks provide opportunities for friends and families to get together and enjoy a multitude of outdoor-recreation experiences. Outdoor recreation plays an important role in developing our social fabric and it is vital to the mental and physical well-being of Albertans. This is a long-recognized role of parks. Speaking to the need for a chain of parks along Alberta highways, J.D. Robertson, Chairman of the Provincial Parks Board stated in the 1930/31 Annual Report: "Perhaps the greatest benefit will accrue from the fact that the leisure hours of our people will be guided into avenues that will

impart a clearer view of life's true value; inspire them with love of beauty; quicken their interest in the lives of their fellow-men; and send them back to their duties strengthened in body and mind."

There is a need to ensure that the opportunities, programs, facilities and services provided by the parks system are distributed as widely and as equitably as possible. For example, recreation-oriented parks throughout the province with quality beaches, trails or opportunities for heritage appreciation, in addition to more stop-over sites along our highways, may very well be what tourists want in the future.

While in the past, people were kept away

to the numerous hikers in the area. Ten days later we immobilized Sunshine, checked her progress and wished her a happy hibernation.

Bombs Away!

AAIIEE! WOWOO! AAIIEE! We knew to run for cover. Park visitors were out of range, but park staff, well . . .

I work in Sir Winston Churchill Provincial Park. A fire plan had been developed for the park with the cooperation of the Alberta Forest Service. A fire plan, though, is no good without practice.

Park staff were briefed. The island maintenance staff greeted the idea with restrained enthusiasm. It was, however, a great opportunity for Alberta Forest Service to give their CL-215 water bomber, affectionately known as a "duck," flying practice. Park visitors were also briefed. They were asked to go to the nearest beach when the fire alarm sounded. Soon we had a large black plume of smoke billowing into the sky from the practice fire. The wail of the fire alarm stirred up squirrels, visitors, maintenance staff and rangers alike.

The "bird dog," which always flies ahead of the "ducks" on the bombing run, warned everyone with its siren to clear the area as it passed overhead. Two "ducks" flew over, bombing the fire. Their accuracy was amazing.

My attention was grabbed by the wailing of the bird-dog siren once again. It should be noted that the CL-215 has two doors to two tanks which each hold roughly 1,200 gallons of water. I was positive the bombers had dropped two loads and therefore were out of water. I walked out of the bushes, stood beside the practice fire, looked up and got ready to take a photograph when to my surprise, the belly of bomber opened once again . . . .

Dam Busters

On a cool day in 1968, the Department of Highways foreman from Elkwater asked the park manager responsible for Cypress Hills Provincial Park to assist with the removal of a problematic beaver dam near Highway 48. Two young rangers, somewhat familiar with the use of dynamite, were assigned to the project.

The industrious beaver occasionally floods park facilities causing problems for managers. (*Archie Landals*)

from fragile park attractions, they are now encouraged to get as close as safely possible. Location, layout and design of facilities are now being improved to maximize visitor use and minimize impact on the landscape. Boardwalks, viewing platforms, asphalt trails and handrails are being used to guide visitors while protecting the environment. Use of private automobiles is being minimized; campgrounds in most lake parks are now within walking distance of the beach. Regardless of the level of their physical ability or interest, visitors will be able to access the diversity of experiences afforded by Alberta's parklands.

Bears, Bombers

Although the Highway foreman suggested that too much dynamite was being planted, the two rangers, full of confidence, proceeded to set the charge. The blast was substantial, the dam was gone. Its remains, however, hung from nearby power lines and a grader was needed to remove the rest of the dam debris off the highway. . . .

Emergencies — Park Style

Emergencies are regular occurrences for parks staff. They crop up in irregular intervals, sometimes in bunches. Most of them are routine — sprained ankles, burned hands and missing kids that turn up in 15 minutes. Incidents like this are soon forgotten in the blur of a busy summer, but once in a while . . . .

I was a ranger at Crimson Lake when a man came running out of his campsite. He flagged me down and told me his son had cut his head badly. Grabbing my first-aid kit, I followed him and found a 10-year-old boy with a large laceration on the top of his head. I asked how he had received the injury. He said he had been chopping wood with a double-bit axe when he snagged a clothesline string between two trees. The line pulled the axe out of his hands and the axe dropped dead-centre on his head . . . .

The R.C.M.P. contacted us at 0400 to help look for a teenager who had walked over a cliff into the Bow River near Bow Valley Provincial Park. He had been looking for a school party that was being held in the area. We searched along the banks and in the water by foot. Boats and helicopters were brought in to assist in the search. At 1030 a dive team from the Calgary Fire Department arrived. They located the body on their first sweep, 6 metres downstream from the last seen point in 2 metres of water. . . .

A climber had fallen at Mt. Yamnuska near Bow Valley Provincial Park and sustained numerous fractures. The required equipment and people were moved up to the top of the mountain. The injured climber, who had two neck fractures, two skull fractures and a broken right elbow, was brought down without incident. . . .

Public demand for outdoor recreation is continuing to evolve. Parks will need to track the trends and meet these changing demands. Today's communities are benefiting from the foot and bicycle trails that weave through new subdivisions, linking them with nearby urban and municipal parks.

Some outdoor recreational activities, however, are not compatible. Power boating and water skiing, for example, may be in direct conflict with visitors trying to observe wildlife or experience a quiet canoe ride. If these activities are spatially separated, visitors will be able to enjoy quality experiences. Segregation of recreational activities, as well as restrictions on the type and level of use are some of the effective management tools that are being used. Areas in Kananaskis Country are designated for use by all-terrain vehicles in summer and by snowmobiles in winter. These zones provide safe, enjoyable opportunities for pursuits in environments that are not easily damaged and that are away from other visitors where conflicts would arise.

Conversely, restricted areas have been designated in Dinosaur Provincial Park to protect the fossils and in Writing-on-Stone to preserve the petroglyphs. Visitors entering these restricted

The 1959 fire at the Pembina River Provincial Park was, in fact, caused by a wedding. The friends of a local boy, who had just married, wanted to celebrate with the nuptial couple. When they couldn't find the pair, they headed down to the park to celebrate. The group stoked up a fire in an open firepit close to an old shelter and had a grand time. A wind picked up and the fire, which the group had left burning, blazed out of control. Before it could be extinguished, the shelter and much of the underbrush were destroyed. . . .

I was in charge of Cross Lake Provincial Park when a forest fire started on May 19, 1968. The fire, thought to have originated from a farmer burning stumps, surrounded Cross Lake on three sides and was burning completely out of control by the afternoon of May 23.

Forestry hired 350 men as ground crew and two water bombers. Fifty caterpillar tractors with dozers built fire guards, and two helicopters transferred men and supplies to and from the fire. It took six weeks to bring the fire, which destroyed 2,500 hectares, under control. — *Richard Huseby, Raymond Lavoie, Frank Fraser, Karen Stroebel, Chris Bruntlet, Rick Knuelius, Dave Chabillon, Shirley Sullivan & Wilton Allers*

Rock climbing clinics are held in Kananaskis Country. *(Provincial Parks Service)*

U R B A N P A R K S

Since the mid-70s, large areas of open space within Alberta's cities have been turned into urban parks. These parks, which contain beautiful natural environments, areas or buildings where historical events have taken place, supply a wide variety of outdoor recreation activities. They have become the heart of many cities . . . .

Each urban park contains a large natural area which provides a wide variety of landscapes, plants and animals for visitors to experience. Natural areas such as Police Point Park in Medicine Hat, Alexander Wilderness Park in Lethbridge and Gaetz Lakes Sanctuary in Red Deer beckon city dwellers away from the noise and pressure of living in a city. These parks are designed to provide a wide variety of recreational activities including trail systems for jogging, hiking, cross-country skiing, snowshoeing and bicycling, horseshoe pits, softball diamonds, tennis courts, golf courses and lawn bowling greens.

Urban parks let us see how people and groups have contributed to the development of Alberta. At Fort Normandeau in Red Deer and Fort Whoop-Up in Lethbridge, visitors can discover how the traders and settlers brought about change to the native people's lifestyle and how the natives affected the lifestyles of the traders and settlers.

Festivals such as the Heritage Day Festival in Lloydminster and the Dinosaur Festival in Grande Prairie are now staged in urban parks. In outdoor amphitheatres, the development of our culture, past and present, comes alive through theatre, music and dance. Friends and family can talk and enjoy each other's company in a beautiful natural setting.

Urban parks are also of significant economic value. In addition to the materials and labour required to build and operate them, they serve as beacons for tourists and people moving into Alberta's cities.

The Jewel in Edmonton's Crown

Capital City Recreation Park — several major parks connected by an extensive trail system along the banks of the North Saskatchewan River — is the jewel in Edmonton's crown. The history of European-type planning for the North Saskatchewan River Valley can be traced back to the time of

Saskatoon (*Kåre Hellum*)

Alberta's inception in 1905. One of the most important publications of the era, Frederick G. Todd's 1907 report on open space and parks, encouraged environmental protection and land acquisition.

The river valley has played an important role in Edmonton's development. At first it was the northern boundary for the sometimes fierce Blackfoot tribe. Later, the river became an important transportation and trade route, and the fur-trade brought with it settlement of the river valley. As more and more people settled in the Edmonton area, the river valley's resources were increasingly utilized. Trees were cut for lumber, clay was extracted from the terraces for brickmaking, gravel was used for street construction, coal mines dotted the banks, gold was panned and sluiced from the gravel bars, and ice was cut to be stored and sold.

areas are accompanied by interpretive naturalists who provide an educational and entertaining first-hand look. These fragile resources and the experiences they provide would have long since disappeared without this restrictive zoning. Rather than interfering with visitor opportunities these tours are often the highlight for tourists.

Ecological Benefits

Parks protect undisturbed ecosystems, leaving them to evolve in a natural way. They also permit the continued evolution of wild species of plants and animals without human interference. Parks help to maintain essential ecological processes and life-support systems such as soil regeneration, recycling of nutrients and the cleansing of waters. These are processes upon which we depend for survival and economic prosperity. Parks are vital to preserving the biological diversity that occurs within Alberta. They are paramount to ensuring that a full range of ecological options are

Edmonton's river valley is part of Capital City Recreation Park. *(AV and Exhibit Services)*

Several events shaped the future of the river valley. The railway decreased the importance of the river for transportation. Instead, it was used more for recreation. Ice-skating and horse-racing became popular in winter, and excursions on the steamer, *City of Edmonton*, were enjoyed in summer. A boat ride between Big Island and Fort Saskatchewan was considered the thing to do on a Sunday afternoon. Finally, when numerous homes and business were washed away by the 1915 flood, many people decided it would be safer to live and work on higher ground — especially since a number of bridges, such as the High Level, now existed. The focus of the river valley began to change from industrial/residential to recreational/natural.

It was about this time that the first efforts were made to preserve the river valley for future

available for future generations.

Albertans are fortunate in that we still have opportunities to set aside representative examples of most of the different landscapes in the province. Securing the land base required to represent all of Alberta's natural landscapes challenges everyone involved in Alberta's network of parks to be innovative, futuristic and perhaps, to some extent, risk-taking. Development as a prerequisite in park establishment is being questioned more and more. Banking representative parklands is a concept that is gaining acceptance. Undisturbed stretches in northern Alberta's boreal forest and Canadian shield have untapped potential as future parklands. Those landscapes that cannot be adequately protected within provincial or national parks can be designated as ecological reserves or similar mechanisms. Landscape-oriented parks will allow present-day visitors to experience, appreciate and understand the diverse natural landscape of Alberta while ensuring that future generations will have the chance to see and understand what the province was like prior to its development and industrialization.

Park boundaries seldom reflect ecological realities or encompass definable ecosystems.

Urban Parks

Alberta's urban parks provide opportunities for active pursuits or quiet relaxation. *(AV and Exhibit Services)*

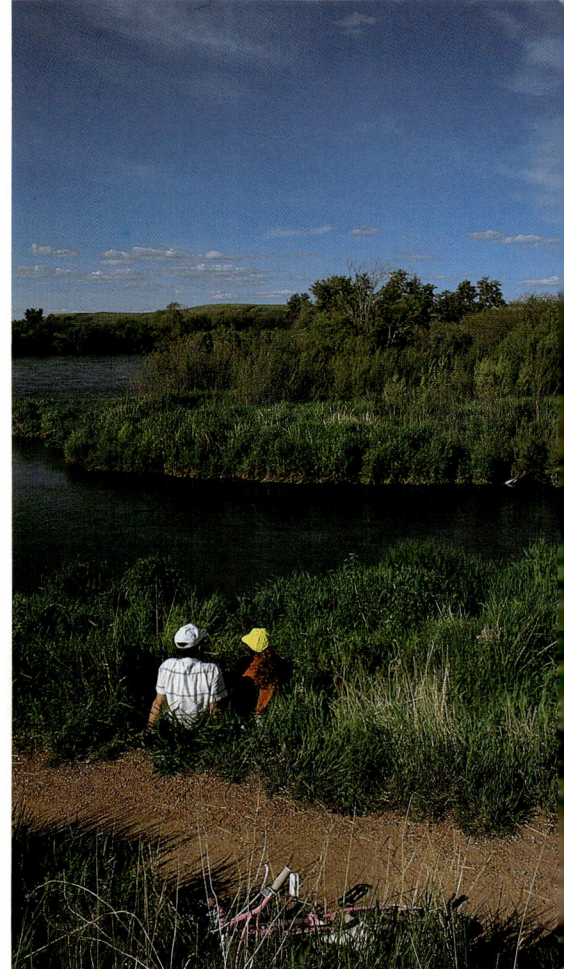

Many species of wildlife that are protected in parks require ranges beyond park boundaries. Even species of plants that are totally within parks are susceptible to external influences. Air pollution from nearby industrial sources, accidental toxic spills along roads and rail-lines or pipeline ruptures all pose threats to parks. Effective management of our parks includes coordination with those responsible for the stewardship of surrounding lands. By working together in partnerships, local communities, private landowners, commercial interests and industry, we will protect significant natural resources within Alberta's parks.

Boundary adjustments are one way of guaranteeing the integrity of significant park resources. Perhaps in the future, the expansion of some existing parks will come about as a result of acquisition and donations by private citizens and non-government organizations. Some of these parcels will most likely include natural and cultural resources, resulting in the consolidation of park boundaries and overall improvement in protection of park landscapes. For example, including an entire wetland instead of only part will ensure the long-term viability of its flora and fauna. Natural corridors for wildlife to move between parklands will be important.

generations. By 1950, the Edmonton District (now Metropolitan Regional) Planning Commission was formed to develop a truly metropolitan vision for the river valley. This vision included not only the City of Edmonton but also the surrounding rural locale which was annexed to the city as rapid growth became the accepted standard for the next 40 years. Municipal, regional and provincial authorities have continually tried to protect the valley's natural open space from urban development and to provide for a distinctive park system for the enjoyment of the urban population. This culminated in the joint venture between the province and the city to begin developing Capital City Recreation Park in the early-70s. Edmontonians have a river valley park system which is unrivalled in any other river city in North America.

Waskasoo Park

The 1,000-hectare park sprawls along the river valley and is tied together with paved bike-trails and gravel walking-paths. Parts of this park system existed long before they became part of an interconnected system. Gaetz Park was given to Red Deer by the Gaetz family in 1909. The Gaetz Lakes were designated a Dominion Bird Sanctuary in 1924. Rotary Park has been a popular camping and picnicking ground for many years, and Bower Ponds started off as the mill ponds for the Bawtinheimer and Great West Lumber Company sawmills.

People have long fought to protect and preserve Red Deer's parks. When a forest fire threatened to destroy the Gaetz Lakes Sanctuary in 1950, volunteers worked through the night to contain the fire. And when the Government of Alberta wanted to log the heavily forested escarpment, local citizens put a stop to it.

Red Deer is fortunate indeed. As late as the 1950s, barely 5,000 people lived in the city. Being small for so long meant that much of the land in the river valley was not developed or lost. When Waskasoo Park was being created, some of the river's meander loops — which had been gravel-mined or used as garbage dumps — were reclaimed for parkland. Three Mile Bend, Heritage Ranch and McKenzie Trail are excellent combinations of wildlife habitat and well-used recreational areas. Lower Heritage Ranch has fishing ponds, equestrian trails, a picnic area/playground and prime

Blazing star (Kåre Hellum)

Oil refineries overlook Capital City Park in Edmonton. (Maureen Landals)

161

wildlife habitat. Even the barren, dusty waste of a cement plant has become one of Alberta's most beautiful and popular campgrounds!

Planners recognized the high priority that people placed on undisturbed natural areas, and emphasized the protection of the Gaetz Lakes Sanctuary. The Kerry Wood Nature Centre, built at its entrance, uses education as the tool to protect this fragile environment. The heart of the Sanctuary lies between the two lakes, unvisited and undisturbed. Waskasoo Park is truly a gift to future generations.

Fish Creek Provincial Park

Sixty years ago, Fish Creek Valley was a place of sprawling ranches, picnic grounds and campgrounds. There was a small store, the Midnapore Stampede Grounds, a cable car crossing and even Paradise Grove, a dance hall where some say illicit liquid could be had. Thirty years ago, plans to turn this area into a park were tossed out. One city alderman went so far as to state that Calgary's city limits would never stretch this far south. Now, of course, city limits extend beyond the Fish Creek Valley, beyond what was once the small town of Midnapore and still further south.

A group of far-sighted Calgarians realized the city would soon engulf this valley. Not only was there many centuries of native history to protect, but also southern Alberta's early settlement and business history as well as the wildlife and plant life, much of it unique to this riverine environment.

Today, Fish Creek is a small stream in a wide valley and that makes it somewhat unique. It wasn't always this way. The valley was once filled, from wall to wall, with the raging Fish River, where torrents of glacial meltwater escaped down the path of least resistance. As the glaciers receded and the river level dropped, terraces were formed. It was on these flat lands that Indian winter camps were set up, cattle grazed and settlers grew their crops. It's also where John Glenn dug the first irrigation ditch and where the Shaw family set up the first industry in Alberta — a woollen mill.

Urban parks are close at hand for a family picnic. *(AV and Exhibit Services)*

As along most creeks in southern Alberta, a poplar forest sprung up. Its shade gave shelter to animals and birds. It also supplied wood for fires, tepee poles, drying racks and fence posts. Many shrubs and flowers grew in the shade of the forest, some of which were needed for the food, medicines and dye. In the open grasslands of the valley, important plants were found. One was the sage plant, vital in native culture. Protection from the elements was provided by the often steep valley walls. These walls were sometimes used as buffalo jumps and corral sites. Although the Blackfoot, who inhabited the valley in more recent history, would only eat fish as starvation food, the creek provided many an aquatic meal to later settlers and ranchers.

Fish Creek Provincial Park, located within the City of Calgary's southern boundaries, is steeped in history. Many of southern Alberta's most colorful and trend-setting characters resided within this 1,159-hectare park. There was James Votier, a French expatriate who once studied for the priesthood. He fought hard against the ranchers for settlers' rights. Nelson Bebo, another French settler, was nearly burned at the stake by local natives convinced that this cantankerous man was the devil. Addison Horne brought horses and polo to the newly formed province of Alberta, formerly a part of the Northwest Territories.

There were also families with lifestyles far removed from each other. John and Adelaide Glenn brought in everything they owned on a mule, opened a road-house and trading-post and went on to dig the first irrigation ditch in the area. John Glenn was born in Ireland and travelled around North America trying his hand at almost everything before finally becoming the first white settler in this area. Conversely, Samuel and Helen Shaw lived in a grand house in England with their nine children. They had servants and all the niceties of a wealthy life but they too decided to try their hand at living in the west. Unlike many of their monied contemporaries, they did not ranch but decided to settle. They arrived with over 30 tonnes of household effects including a woollen mill.

There were others that made the Fish Creek/Midnapore area special. One man, though, is often overlooked. He came to the area in the 1880s and stayed for almost 40 years. His real name we may never know, for he was the Chinese cook at the Bow Valley Ranch House. He was simply called "Charlie".

Sky-diver lands in an urban park.
(Dave Dodge)

Scientific Benefits

As protected areas, parks preserve the genetic diversity of plants and animals so that we continue to possess the potential for new foods, medicines or other products. Over 50 per cent of modern medicines rely on materials derived from wild plant and animal species. Parks protect genetic materials in trees, grasses and other plants that presently may appear to have little value, but that possibly have resistance to diseases. These traits may be required by future Albertans to improve forest production, rangelands or agricultural crops.

Undisturbed areas in parks function as

Charlie

The initial purchase of land for Fish Creek Provincial Park, established in 1975, was from the Burns Ranching Company. The purchase included over 500 hectares, the ranch site containing several buildings and the stately old brick house built by William H. Hull in 1896. As the first Chief Ranger of the new park, I moved my family into the main portion of the house. I used the single-story wing for office space. Before we moved into the house, however, the occupants invited us to tour the site to learn about maintenance requirements, quirks of the old house and to meet Charlie. . . .

Charlie, we were informed, was a ghost who considered this house his home. The name Charlie was selected because a housekeeper by the name of Charlie Yuen had once lived in the house for many years. Charlie, we were told, was friendly and should be considered a part of the family. He had his own place at the table for each meal and was always treated with respect. My family accepted this information as good character for the old house, but not to be taken seriously.

Soon after we moved in, the kitchen tap turned itself on full blast. Five minutes later, it happened again. It took us a full year to realize that Charlie was indeed a full-time resident. Those stairs that squeaked a few steps ahead of you once in a while and the little gust of wind in the hallway that would make you shiver began to have meaning. Even one of our first overnight guests met Charlie. He apparently stood in the hallway and talked to our guest about the ranch for 15 minutes in the wee hours of the morning. After that, we had few overnight guests.

The kids blamed Charlie for anything and everything. I think Charlie was a bit of a kid himself and toys were his favorite item. He especially liked our son's battery-operated helicopter. We removed the batteries when the kids were not playing with it — otherwise it would mysteriously turn on and run by itself.

Charlie, it seems, was attached to the past. By the summer of 1979, Burns Ranching was closing down operations and selling their remaining ranching equipment. We were told by a local in most definite terms that when the sale of the ranch was finished, Charlie would leave. We thought very little of the comment at the time, but the night the sale was done, Charlie nailed packing crates together in the basement of the old house for over two hours. The next day he was gone.

Yellow toad flax (*Kåre Hellum*)

natural laboratories in which to conduct scientific research on the structure and function of naturally occurring ecosystems. Parks render secure sites for both short- and long-term monitoring of environmental changes and they serve as benchmarks against which to measure changes, resulting from human use. Our protected areas in parks are areas against which to measure the effectiveness of resource-management strategies. Knowledge gained from scientific research in our parks is vital to our ability to manage Alberta's resources on a sustained basis. Integrating environmental and economic decisions is fundamental if we are to ensure a sustainable future for present and future generations of Albertans.

Timber Tom

One man from the Bow Valley Ranch was neither a cowboy nor a ranch hand. His name was Tom Ward and he was the very first interpreter hired at Fish Creek Provincial Park. He was a historian by choosing and fell into the role of interpreter by virtue of being grandfatherly and knowledgeable. He was also a big hit with the public and left a lasting impression on many a young person.

But Tom was more than just an interpreter. He was also an accomplished artist. There are over 1,000 of his carvings in existence. They were created from burls, usually from the white spruce tree. Rather than imposing his own form on to them, Timber Tom, as he was known, would allow the spirit of the wood to come alive under his carved and calloused hands. Today his carvings can be found throughout the province. — *Dennis LaFreniere, Bill Porter, Barry Manchak, Margie Peers, Wes Shannon, Jim Robertson, Leslie Pringle & Bob Hutchison*

Cyclists get away from traffic on urban park trails. *(AV and Exhibit Services)*

CELEBRATING PARKS

When editor Donna von Hauff asked me to write 1,200 words on the value of wilderness, I hesitated. So much to say, so few words. I thought first of my two young daughters, Terra and Teal, bending to scoop their first drink from a mountain stream. I thought of Judy and Del Whitford — rough hewn, wildlife-loving horse outfitters whose summers are spent guiding people through the Bighorn-Ram Wilderness. May everyone come to know a Del and Judy and the joys of the Bighorn. I thought of Jim Butler, conservationist and poet, and Monte Hummel, president of the Canadian chapter of the World Wildlife Fund. Both men dream that a portion of each of Alberta's different 17 ecological regions will be set aside so that future generations might experience a native grassland, an untrammelled alpine meadow, an aspen parkland in its natural state.

I thought of two carriers of their dream, artist Adeline Rockett and photographer Charles Truscott. Fifty-some years old, Adeline endured three days of rain, sleet and aching muscles only to be dragged by me through cold creeks so that she could paint an unnamed waterfall at the head of Hummingbird Creek. Young and wiry, Charles carried 35 kilograms of camera equipment up mountains and across tundra to capture images of each of the ecological regions. View Adeline's paintings, look at Charles' photographs, read Jim's poems. Learn from them the value of wilderness.

I was once told that those who believe in protecting lands from motorized travel are selfish — wanting to keep these areas for a few elite backpackers. I see it differently. I know that those working to protect wilderness will not personally benefit. In this generation, we can never exhaust the opportunities that our lands provide for adventure and spiritual enhancement. I suggested, in reply, that if we fail to protect some of these wild spaces, our children's children will live in a world of limited opportunity. Wilderness isn't the kind of thing that hangs around for the next generation — it's on the run.

Many dedicated people work quietly behind the scenes to help shape our parks system. Some of them you will find in this book. If not here, in organizations like the Alberta Wilderness Association, the Canadian Parks and Wilderness Society, the World Wildlife Fund of Canada, the Alpine Club, the

Landscapes protected in Alberta's parks are a cause to celebrate. *(Rosemary H.L. Calvert, FRPS)*

Yellow columbine *(Kåre Hellum)*

Celebrating Parks

Federation of Alberta Naturalists, the Recreation, Parks and Wildlife Foundation and Alberta's Department of Tourism, Parks and Recreation. I wonder if those who contributed to this book, like me, felt some awkwardness in their attempt to put their feelings to pen. I urge you to read carefully their words, to search with them the mantle of responsibility for a future that we will not ourselves see.

Donna asked me to write of wilderness values, but I thought also of a different kind of park, one wherein three generations of my family have bicycled, swum, boated and hunted (the fierce leopard frog). I remember the winds whispering us into a barbecue-sated sleep on the porch of my in-law's lakeside cottage. May many more generations enjoy these places set aside for human convenience.

I thought also of the needs, not convenience, of the other species of the earth — those that are struggling to survive what seems to be limitless human expansion — that we should provide for them simply because they are here and should always be here, or at least should not be removed by our careless hands. And, I thought of a time sitting with friends on a wildflower covered ridge

watching 31 mountain goats, large and small, pick their way across the rugged head wall of Persimmon Basin. When a yearling stumbled and was nudged back to safety by its mother, I was reminded of my own children. I wished that my grandchildren would one day be able to see the goat's grandchildren. That night, our campsite was visited by a pair of owls — many species of which are dependent on old-growth forests that only wilderness provides. My friend, Tom Jacklin, hooted so expertly, with such enthusiasm, that I wasn't able to tell whether the hoot was the owls' or Tom's. What value should we place on Tom's mad midnight dance with the owls?

I thought of the boreal forest of northern Alberta, perhaps as valued a set of earth-lungs as those of the Amazonian rainforests. We southern Albertans imagine only an expanse of forest and bog, but our indigenous peoples can speak directly of the particular beauty and of the many species inhabiting the boreal lands. I worry that the few remaining woodland caribou that dwell in these lands will soon expire.

The Wild Rose, Alberta's floral emblem is found throughout the province. *(Rosemary H.L. Calvert, FRPS)*

Economic Benefits

Parks are becoming increasingly important components of Alberta's growing tourism industry. One of the major reasons for foreign visitors coming to Alberta is the rich variety of natural landscapes and beautiful scenery protected by our parks. As activities such as birdwatching and eco-tourism continue to grow in popularity, so does the contribution of parks to the economy. Provincial parks such as Crimson Lake, William A. Switzer and Saskatoon Island are important focal points for watchable wildlife — places where wildlife can be viewed in its natural habitat.

Alberta, with its scenic rivers, is blessed with abundant opportunities for new initiatives that could greatly enhance our tourism. Rivers such as the Athabasca, Clearwater and Peace are historically linked to the fur-trade and early exploration of western Canada. Today, the Wabasca and Christina rivers provide opportunities for canoeing in a wildland setting while the Bow and North Saskatchewan rivers offer exciting recreational corridors near Edmonton and Calgary. Historic trails and multiple-use recreational corridors offer untapped opportunities. The Athabasca Landing Trail from Edmonton to Athabasca has been the focus of

And, I thought of the settlement of Canada, first by the aboriginal people who wandered across the Bering land bridge and later by the displaced peoples of Europe who arrived by boat. Their character was forged by a frontier wilderness. We inheritors still envision Canada as limitless wilderness. What a shame if, ensnared by this illusion, we let all of our wild lands fall to the relentless plough of development. Bow Valley naturalist, Mike McIvor suggests that we need to protect some portions of our lands just to demonstrate to ourselves that we humans, as a species, are capable of restraint. Monty Hummel put it to us this way: "We are the last generation, in one of the last countries on the planet, that still has any choice in the matter."

Finally, I remembered that special day, that day of all days when I walked for what seemed endless hours in a sky filled with light along the top of the Starlight Range in Willmore Wilderness. What value was that walk? I don't know, but may each of you be blessed with such a day! I recalled with gratitude that it was the value placed on wilderness by an Alberta Minister of Lands and Forests named Norman Willmore and in whose honor the park was named that made my walk possible. My wish for this book is that it will serve in the spirit of Norman Willmore to celebrate what we have already set aside and to renew our commitment to the task of making wilderness walks possible for our children and their children. — *Ray Rasmussen*

Benefactors to Alberta — Ann and Sandy Cross

Conquering the land has been the occupation of generations. Across Alberta, rivers have been stilled and fences have gone up, transforming wilderness into quarter sections for farmers and cattle ranchers. Every year Calgary's subdivisions swallow more and more of the Rocky Mountain foothills — the price of prosperity. Ann and Sandy Cross have watched the city's sprawl with trepidation. Living on their farm, 20 kilometres outside the city, they have always felt close to the land, and believed their land was safe from the city's appetite, but they felt Calgary's rapid approach. On clear days from their farm, they now see a yellow, chemical smog hanging over the skyline. Something had to be done to save some of the land so future generations could remember the foothills as nature intended.

some interest over past years. Built in 1875 by the Hudson's Bay Company and surveyed in 1879 by the legendary George Mercer Dawson, after whom Dawson City in the Yukon is named, the route has a wealth of possibilities to explore and interpret the early history of Alberta. As a scenic corridor through the boreal forest and rural countryside, it offers opportunities for hiking, horseback riding, bicycling and other activities. Moreover, the development of trails such as these would allow communities along the routes to develop facilities and services to benefit trail users, further enhancing Alberta's tourism appeal. According to Don Sparrow,

Alberta's Minister of Tourism, Parks and Recreation: "There is substantial and growing public and municipal support in Alberta to convert abandoned rail rights-of-way to recreation, tourism and wildlife uses. These rights-of-ways present a unique, once only opportunity to maintain linear open-space corridors linking communities, natural and man-made attractions, and historic resources."

It is commonly recognized that parks also have significant economic spin-offs in terms of their impact on real estate values. The most expensive properties in Alberta's cities are generally those that overlook, or are in close

Great spangled fritillary (Tom Webb)

Alberta's mountain landscapes regenerate the spirit. *(Fred Vermeulen)*

proximity to, parks. Similarly, land near rural parks is beginning to increase in value. Cottage and rural residential subdivisions near parks are regarded as more desirable than those without access to park resources and facilities. Commercial tourist developments in areas such as the Canmore Corridor, outside of Banff National Park, are starting to capitalize on locations near parks.

Tourism is expected to play a very important role in the economy of Alberta with parks as one of the cornerstones of the industry. The parks system, with convenient, clean and accessible rest stops and overnight accommo-

dation, and programs and opportunities to encourage visitors to stay longer, can complement and strengthen the industry. Albertans and visitors seeking opportunities to explore, experience and enjoy the many diverse natural, cultural and historical landscapes of the province will contribute to our economic growth and diversification.

In 1987, Ann and Sandy made the largest land donation in Canadian history for the purpose of conservation. In a selfless example of environmental philanthropy, the couple deeded over 800 hectares to the people of Alberta. Known as the Ann and Sandy Cross Conservation Area, the $3 million package of land represents an oasis of wilderness that will be preserved in perpetuity. "I wanted it kept the way it is," is how Sandy describes the couple's simple vision. It appears they may have acted just in time. From the Cross Conservation area today, the outline of the Calgary skyline is visible in the northeast. In 1987, the city was several kilometres away. Today it is less than two kilometres and getting closer.

Turning one's back to the city and looking south and west, a breathtaking panorama unfolds. From here, this northernmost extension of the Porcupine Hills rolls gently away until the hills blend into the distance and become the Rocky Mountains. The conservation area bridges the transition between the foothills and grasslands, a tranquil spot, interspersed with aspen groves. It is also a cornucopia of Alberta's mountain and prairie wildlife.

It is here that Pine Creek originates, an unpolluted brook that is home to waterfowl, beaver, muskrat and tiger salamanders, just some of the hundreds of species that make this island part of their range. A day at the Cross Conservation Area can result in sighting Baltimore orioles, bald and golden eagles, red-tailed hawks, ruffed grouse, Richardson's ground squirrels, coyote, bear, squirrels, badgers and mice. At dawn or dusk, a visitor is virtually guaranteed an encounter with ungulates such as the mule or white-tailed deer, elk and the occasional moose. Even threatened species, animals dying off as their habitat disappears, find refuge here. This legacy is a shining example of how industry, government and individuals can save vital ecological systems through cooperation. Its genesis is a lesson on getting people united behind a worthy project.

When Sandy and Ann first decided to take on this project, they began consulting with friends and neighbors. George Crawford, neighbor and lawyer, converted the concept into reality. As the architect of the transfer of the land to the people of Alberta, he conceived the idea for a broadly-based management authority.

Educational Benefits

Parks function as outdoor classrooms, special places where school children come in direct contact with nature, are something that is important at any age. Such direct contact is increasingly difficult for the majority of Albertans as our cities continue to grow. Park landscapes, plants, animals and other natural wonders help awaken the keen interest of our youth to the environment. They help mold our environmental ethic and build support for pollution abatement, waste reduction, habitat retention and other environmental concerns throughout the province.

Birds of prey (raptors) are common in Alberta's parks. *(Tom Webb)*

Celebrating Parks

Another neighbor of Ann and Sandy, rancher-biologist Ray Glasrud, recommended the Nature Conservancy of Canada as the custodian. This was subsequently accomplished by a 99-year lease from the Province of Alberta, the title-holders designated by Ann and Sandy. The Nature Conservancy of Canada is a national organization dedicated to the protection of ecologically significant natural areas and places of special beauty and educational interest.

The first major initiative of the Nature Conservancy was to build consensus for the conservation area. The municipality where the land is located agreed to permanent closure of the undeveloped road allowances within the conservation area, something vital to managing the ecosystem. All landowners within an eight-kilometre radius were invited to an open house to discuss the project. Considerable support was garnered, and as a result, the first link was formed with the educational community. A team of graduate students from the Faculty of Environmental Design, University of Calgary was commissioned to prepare a strategic management plan.

This document also occasioned the first fund-raising, and donations by Norcen Energy and Husky Oil primed the pump for additional donations from more than 50 individuals, corporations and foundations. Chevron Canada Resources and Amoco Canada played a leading role in establishment of an endowment fund. The fund, which presently stands at close to $1 million, will ensure the area's operation and help generations of Albertans understand the intimacy the Cross family felt toward the foothills.

As recipients of the prestigious Bighorn Award, Dr. and Mrs. Cross were formally recognized by Alberta in 1988. The Cross Conservation Area isn't finished. Efforts continue toward building the endowment fund. There will be outdoor education and conservation programs, thus fulfilling the vision of Ann and Sandy Cross as benefactors to Alberta and Canada. — *Tom Beck*

Aster *(Kåre Hellum)*

A charred forest soon turns into a natural flower garden. *(Fred Vermeulen)*

Alberta's Badlands — How and Why?

It was mid-afternoon on one of those blistering hot days in the late June of 1968. The sort of day when the shimmering heat haze combines with a light breeze to make the southern Alberta prairies really look as if the surface of the land was rolling waves. We had just crossed the Red Deer river on the old Steveville Ferry — now replaced by a modern concrete bridge. There's nothing to prepare you for that first sight of Dinosaur Provincial Park's badlands. "Nearest thing to the Grand Canyon in Alberta," said my companion, Bruce Rains, a geographer at the University of Alberta. We got out of the car and tried to gauge the size of that astonishing landscape which forms such a stark, dramatic contrast to the gentle, undulating plains.

How and why were the badlands formed? I've been trying to answer these questions ever since that first visit back in 1968. In the process, I've used a wide variety of research techniques, taken ideas and help from many people and expended a great deal of hard labour. I've also had a lot of fun!

While most people who visit the park know that it is famous for its dinosaur fossils, the enormous, sub-tropical river delta in which these fascinating creatures lived and died was far removed in time and scenery from what we see today. Yet, those forested, swampy conditions 80 or 90 million years ago were critically important in the story of the badlands. In these huge, sluggish rivers that drained the ancient delta were carried the sand and mud that would eventually harden into sandstone and shale. These are the building blocks for the badlands. They form an easily erodible medium for Nature's handiwork. Running water, rain, wind, ice, snow and other agents have been at work carving the badlands. But why are the badlands so spectacular here? There are badlands elsewhere in Alberta but only in Dinosaur do they occupy such an extensive area.

Extensive badlands occur along the Red Deer and Milk Rivers in Alberta. *(Archie Landals)*

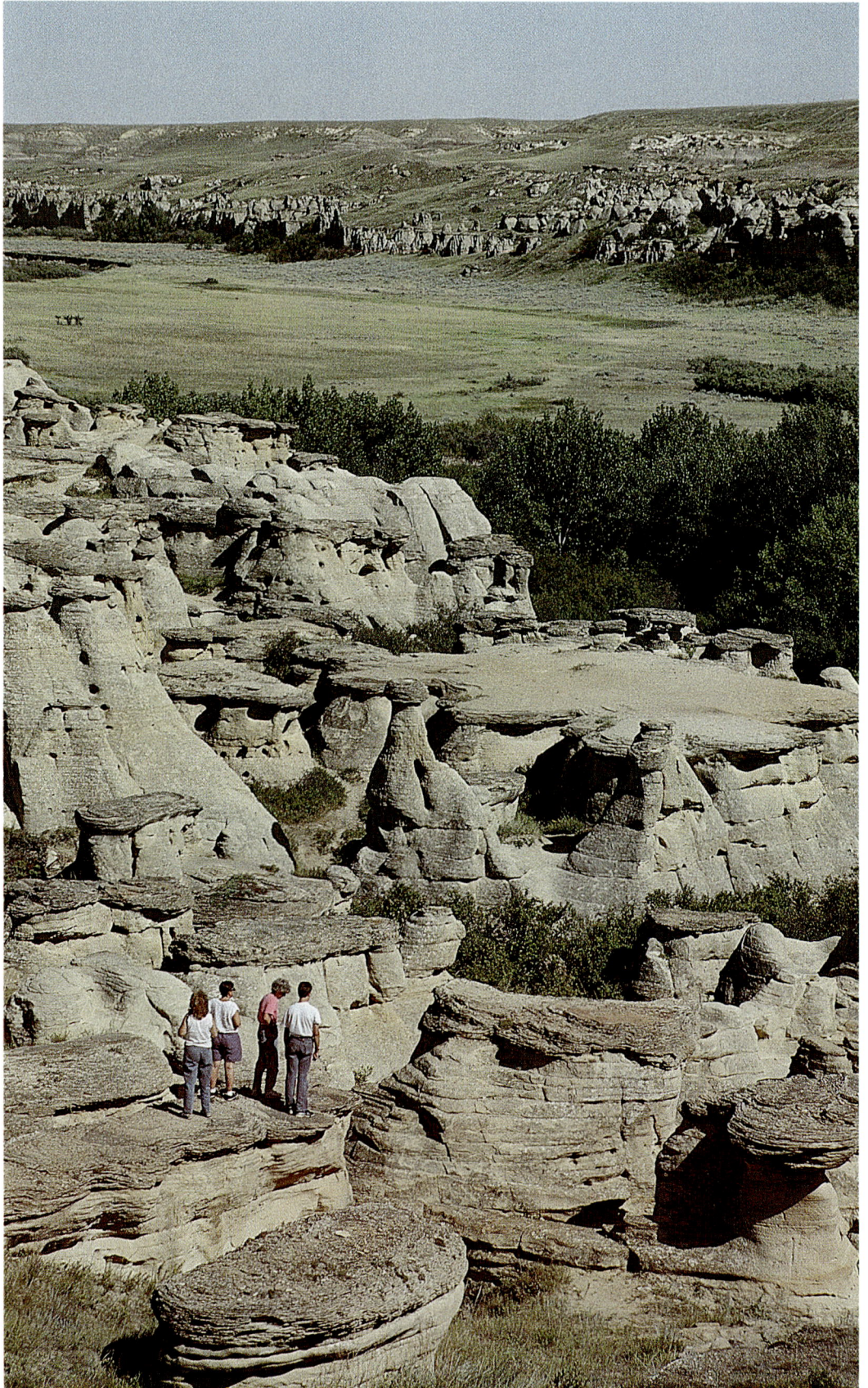

Writing-on-Stone Provincial Park enable the visitor to experience the badlands. *(Archie Landals)*

The badlands owe their initial creation to vast quantities of glacial meltwater that surged across this and much of Alberta as the great ice sheets retreated some 15,000 years ago. We can get some idea of the sheer size and power of these events only if we view the park from a great distance. And what better way than to do this from space!

The satellite image shows the obvious network of roads and scattered farmsteads. It also reveals extraordinary landforms never before seen on the surface of the Alberta prairies. "These features are as subtle on the ground as they are spectacular from a height of 700 kilometres", says Bob Skoye, a remote-sensing analyst at the University of Alberta. They also provide some clues as to what happened here thousands of years ago.

The ice sheet did not retreat in a continuous fashion. At times it underwent minor, but probably rapid readvances of several kilometres. These 'surges' were often accompanied by the release of prodigious amounts of meltwater, perhaps tens or even hundreds of cubic kilometres from beneath the melting ice. Great lakes formed in front of the ice. Two of these lakes are involved in our story.

We can call them Glacial Lake Bassano and Glacial Lake Patricia from the names of the two places that lie close to the centre of the lakes. Glacial Lake Bassano filled and emptied its waters eastward into Glacial Lake Patricia. The satellite image reveals numerous drainage channels entering from the west. These were the routes the water followed. Finally, Lake Patricia filled and the rising waters cut through what may have been an ice dam or, more likely, simply the ridge of higher land made of glacial deposits that lies just a little east of the park. The lake waters then drained east, into Saskatchewan, and the tremendous quantities of water that were released scoured out the valley of the Red Deer River. Because most of this erosion was concentrated in the area of the park, the badlands are best developed there.

Since then, the soft rocks have been rapidly eroded, and sand and mud are now once again being carried in a river just as they were 80 million years ago. Each year the Red Deer moves about 3 million tonnes of sediment downstream.

Environmental-education initiatives are proving to be very useful. Parks are used by all levels of our education system from elementary to post-secondary, as outdoor classrooms, support services including teacher training and self-guided field-study manuals are becoming more readily available.

Our parks have evolved to become much more than playgrounds that satisfy our recreational needs. They include many special places that serve as living examples of our commitment to sustainable development. There is an ever-increasing need to enhance the understanding by both Albertans and visitors of the value of parks. Society and individuals derive benefits in terms of health, recreation, environment, science, economy, education and culture. These benefits will increase. Parks will serve as important role models for integration of environment and economy as we strive for a sustainable future for Alberta.

In 1990, the Federal Provincial Parks Council of Ministers endorsed the numerous benefits of parks – preservation, conservation, economic development, land-use planning, and public participation, information and education – as key roles for parks in promoting sustainable development.

Celebrating Parks

The photograph is a satellite image of Dinosaur Provincial Park and its surrounding countryside. The image covers about 60 kilometres from east to west, and about 40 kilometres from north to south. The park, with its badlands, is near the centre, adjacent to the Red Deer River. The Town of Brooks and part of the Trans-Canada Highway are in the lower left (southwest) corner. This image was acquired by the Landsat 5 satellite in January 1985. The snow cover and the shadows created by even very gentle slopes from the low angle winter sun combine to produce an almost three-dimensional quality.

Badlands along the Red Deer River. *(Archie Landals)*

So, while the badland rocks are quite old, in a geological sense the badlands are brand new. We can speculate that the badlands will, almost imperceptibly, gnaw their way back into the prairie, but perhaps, massive, continental-sized glaciers will come again obliterating everything in their path, finally retreating to create conditions for another new valley and other badlands. After all, it's all happened before. — *Ian Campbell*

China-Canada-Alberta-Ex Terra

Dinosaur Provincial Park has long been known as one of the richest sites for articulated dinosaur skeletons. More than 35 institutions around the world display original specimens from Dinosaur Park. Palaeontological work carried out in the park has moved away from the traditional approach of collecting only articulated skeletons. Skeletons such as a virtually complete *Albertosaurus*, found in 1991, are still being excavated but other palaeontological resources can provide more information on dinosaur biology.

The condition in southern Alberta during the late Cretaceous favored the fossilization of large dinosaur skeletons. Although these have made Dinosaur Provincial Park famous, the remains of smaller animals are rare. Rivers that once flowed through the area were large and powerful and constantly worked their way back and forth across the coastal plains. The bones of large skeletons were heavy and held together by strong connective tissues they could withstand the action of flowing water long enough to be buried. The skeletons of small animals, however, were far more likely to be torn apart by carnivores, scavengers, bacterial action and fast flowing water. Thus they were seldom preserved intact. The systematic collection of bonebeds, microvertebrate sites and even scattered, isolated bones led to the identification of many dinosaurs and other animals not previously found in this park.

It has long been known that Late Cretaceous dinosaurs of North America and Asia are closely related. But one consequence of the new work in Dinosaur Provincial Park was the recognition that many of the smaller species of dinosaurs may be the same genera, and possibly the same species as their closest relative in Asia.

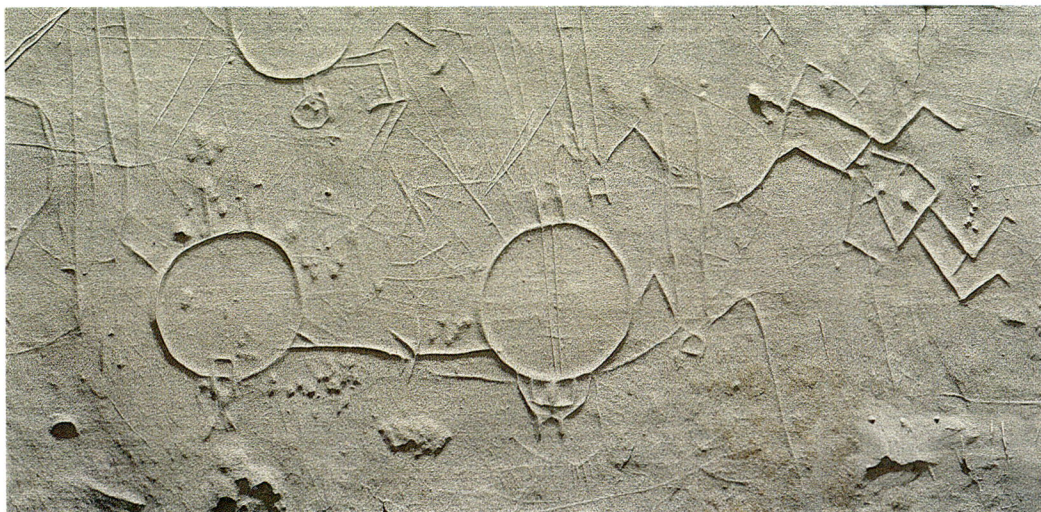

Alberta's parks include places of special significance to Canada's plains people. *(Blaine Landals)*

Celebrating Parks

In 1982, Brian Noble, at one time a naturalist at Dinosaur Park and then the public relations officer during the development of the Royal Tyrrell Museum of Palaeontology, asked me what I would like to do once the museum opened and I had time to become involved in other projects. Without any hesitation I responded that it would be wonderful to work in central Asia to make direct comparisons between our dinosaurs. Brian proceeded to set up an international exchange. In 1983, the Ex Terra Foundation was established and by 1985, an agreement had been signed on behalf of the Chinese Academy of Sciences. The agreement was a major victory over competing proposals from the United States, France and Britain. The Chinese were aware of the well-balanced research programs in Dinosaur Provincial Park.

The project involves fieldwork in China, Alberta and the Canadian arctic, preparation and research on material collected in these areas, and ultimately, the largest travelling display of dinosaurs. The project participants include staff of the Royal Tyrrell Museum of Palaeontology (Drumheller), the Canadian Museum of Nature (Ottawa), the Institute of Vertebrate Palaeontology and Palaeoanthropology (Beijing) and the Ex Terra Foundation (Edmonton).

The first combined expedition of Chinese and Canadian palaeontologists worked in Dinosaur Provincial Park in 1986. Six Chinese colleagues participated including the two leading dinosaur authorities from the People's Republic of China, Dong Zhiming and Zhao Xijin. These scientists were amazed by the richness of fossils. Under the leadership of Dr. Dale Russell, a smaller group of Canadian and Chinese went north in July (1986) to Axel Heiberg and Ellesmere Islands.

Thousands of specimens were collected, including the beautiful *Centrosaurus* skull on display in the field station in Dinosaur Provincial Park and a braincase of *Troodon*. The latter was particularly significant because it was found by the most experienced Chinese preparator, Tang Zhilu, and because troodontids are known from both Asia and North America. An arctic expedition in 1989 saw the collection of dinosaur and bird bones from the Cretaceous exposures on Bylot Island. The 1990 joint expedition collected dinosaur footprints near Grande Cache. Some are very similar to those in China.

Giant goldenrod *(Kåre Hellum)*

Part of the Alberta-China Dinosaur team *(Phil Currie)*

Dinosaurs skeletons *(Royal Tyrrell Museum of Palaeontology)*

Dinosaur egg *(Ex Terra Foundation)*

The 1988 and 1990 expeditions worked mostly at Bayan Mandahu in China. One excavation revealed twelve juveniles of the armored dinosaur Pinacossaurus, each 1.5 metres long. While we have never found baby ankylosaurs in Dinosaur Provincial Park, we have a better chance of identifying their remains now that we know what to look for. — *Phillip J. Currie*

The Peaceful Valley Day Lodge

The Peaceful Valley Day Lodge originated in an unsuccessful search for an antique bathtub for use in the cottage my sister, Kathleen, and I owned at Ma-Me-O Beach. We had hoped to find it in a place about three kilometres south of Westerose near the ridge separating the Pigeon and Battle River valley. While our quest for the tub was futile, the drive turned into a future legacy for Albertans.

A sign and map for a new subdivision near the Battle River suggested that some lots might have a view. The road into the division looked inviting. We pushed through the deep band of poplar, spruce and birch and were rewarded by a broad, rolling meadow carpeted with wild flowers that commanded a spectacular view to the southwest. We bought the property. My sister began planting little native spruce and pine and I put up a simple bench of two-by-fours at the prime viewpoint.

Some years later we bought the adjoining lot. Having both lots, however, made us think about the long-range use of the property.

My sister, a volunteer at St. Joseph's Auxiliary Hospital in Edmonton, was aware that patients were taken out once or twice during the summer to Pigeon Lake where they could enjoy a few hours in the country. We encountered the group, in their blue caps and wheelchairs, and decided, right then, our acreage would make an ideal setting for a park for the disabled. We acquired the third view lot by 1985.

The property is an area of a little over five hectares with a rich variety of meadow, woodland, views, flowers, two small streams, a little pond and even a waterfall. There are many little hills and dales to enliven the place further.

Our dream is now a reality. Since the end of 1987, the Recreation, Parks and Wildlife Foundation has worked with us to devise concept plans and bring administrators from lodges, nursing homes and auxiliary hospitals to survey the property. All of this was accomplished despite the fact that I live in southern California and my sister in Edmonton.

On August 21, 1991, we signed an agreement whereby we gave the property to the

Parks like Saskatoon Island Provincial Park provide refuge for wildlife amid an agricultural landscape. *(AV and Exhibit Services)*

Celebrating Parks

Foundation, a start for the initial construction and a pledge of long-range support for maintenance. The facility will be constructed and maintained by the Foundation and the Alberta Provincial Parks Service. When finished, the project will include a lodge building, a road and parking area that will permit small buses to drop off and pick up passengers at the lodge building. Work on the first phase of the project — compacted surfaces, walking trails, a shelter, washrooms and a service road — is underway. Its first guests will arrive sometime before the mid-ninties.

The foregoing is only the first chapter of a land trust, and my sister and I are only the initial donors. Peaceful Valley Day Lodge is part of Alberta's evolving legacy of parks. — *Kathleen & Robert Wark*

Wetlands — The Surveyor's Role

Surveyors have been identifying and recording data on Alberta's wetland areas for over 100 years — an indication that water and the adjacent lands have always been highly valued in our society. Public awareness and conservation concerns are not a new concept. Our forefathers assured this part of our heritage by insisting that the ownership of waters be held in public trust.

Wetlands add an unparalleled quality of richness to our lives. Without wetlands, opportunities for recreation, tourism, wildlife, fisheries, agriculture and water sources would be severely limited. Unfortunately, 60 per cent of the wetlands in Alberta's settled areas have been lost to agriculture, transportation, urban growth and climactic changes — their disappearance is occurring at such a rate that we must act to slow the process.

Wetland boundaries often involve two ownerships, private uplands and public wetlands. In Alberta's settled areas, 70 per cent of the lands around wetlands is owned by individuals. The remaining 30 per cent is owned by the provincial government and municipalities. Surprisingly, there is no provincial legislation that specifically covers the management of wetlands. There are, however, a variety of laws managed by a number of different provincial departments. Fortunately, environmental protection and enhancement legislation is being developed. In 1991, the Alberta Water Resources Commission moved toward developing a policy for the management of wetlands in these settled areas.

Wetlands are vital component of Alberta's landscape. *(Archie Landals)*

184

Alder catkins *(Rosemary H.L. Calvert, FRPS)*

Alberta land surveyors are often requested to determine the boundaries of wetlands for municipal and environmental reserves, as well as bank locations. Municipal and environmental reserves are governed by provincial legislation and preserve natural and delicate areas of the environment.

The determination of the bank and its origin in law extends back to the earliest of land grants. It also acknowledges the importance of water. Unfortunately, the bank as a legal boundary (the position controlled by the action of the water) and the bank as a physical feature (the position witnessed by severe elevation changes) causes confusion. This confusion is further magnified when conflicts of use arise between Crown agencies and private land owners — or when the Crown wishes to enhance its ownership through wetland developments for fish, plants or wildlife. There is no guesswork involved in bank establishment, it is the spot where the land has been "...covered so long by water as to wrest it from vegetation or as to mark a distinct character on the vegetation where it extends into the water or on the soil itself." [Alberta Surveys Act, Sec. 17(2)(3)]. Wetlands can no longer be regarded as cheap land to be filled and developed. — *Gordon Haggerty*

Windsurfing *(Rosemary H.L. Calvert, FRPS)*

Man-made lakes provide hours of quiet fishing in Kananaskis Country. *(Archie Landals)*

Cultural and Spiritual Benefits

Parks are very much a reflection of who we are: they help to strengthen our cultural identity. One could say, Alberta's parks are the "crown jewels" of the province. Certainly, they are a source of pride for all Albertans. Parks help to ensure the survival of species — the bighorn sheep, great horned owl and wild rose – that symbolize the province. They deepen our understanding of the relationship between humanity and the environment, helping us to better appreciate the interconnectedness of our natural and cultural world.

Our parks provide us with a sense of identity, place and well-being. They also help us to understand our relationship to the land as a society, as well as our past values and decisions that affected land use. Parks enhance our ability, both as society and individuals, to make informed decisions concerning the environment and economy. As places of spiritual renewal and moral regeneration, parks continue to be a source of inspiration for artists, poets, musicians, writers and sculptors. Moreover, parks inspire Albertans in their everyday life — they are symbols of hope for the future.

Visionary Albertans

Elk Island National Park is set in the Beaver Hills, a glacial moraine that rises above the surrounding land. The vegetation is a remnant of boreal mixed-wood forest and aspen parkland. Only 35 kilometres east of Edmonton, the park contains one of the highest concentrations of big game animals in the world including both plains and wood bison, elk, moose, and white-tailed and mule deer. The importance of Elk Island in the survival of some of these species is a story of dedicated and determined Albertans.

A large part of the Beaver Hills was set aside as a Dominion Forest Reserve in 1899. This act of conservation was in response to the need to preserve some timber from the continuing threat of fires. A major blaze in the summer of 1895 had completely denuded the Hills. Soon after, the vegetation flourished and so did the native elk. This soon became the largest group of elk left on the settled part of the continent. Hunters from the region, particularly nearby Edmonton, came in droves, and huge kills were made just for sport and the odd trophy head.

Fortunately, a far-sighted game guardian, William H. Cooper, was deeply moved when he came upon evidence of several large kills with the meat left to rot. Cooper wrote his member of parliament, Frank Oliver, in 1903, describing the senseless slaughter and motherless calves wandering helplessly in the woods. He pressed Oliver to set aside and fence a small parcel of land as an elk preserve. Cooper went on to impress Oliver with the urgency of the matter as he had heard of parties being organized for another "shoot during the following winter, and the probable elimination of the entire herd." Four other men, William A.D. Lees and F.A. Walker of Fort Saskatchewan, and Johnson Carscadden and Ellsworth Simmons, local farmers, all members of a local rifle club, were enthusiastic about saving the elk. In February 1906, these five made an offer to Oliver, who had just been appointed Minister of the Interior. They agreed to post a $5000 bond guaranteeing delivery of at least 20 elk to a reserve around Astotin Lake if the Federal Government would pay for fencing the land. Oliver was delighted and an agreement was signed on March 28, 1906. Wheels were put in motion to construct the fence and the last major elk hunt was cancelled.

Peaceful Valley Day Lodge, a private donation to Albertans.
(Hiske Gerding)

Celebrating Parks

The establishment of this game preserve is said by some historians to mark the real beginning of Canada's game laws. Elk Island was the only national park in Canada formed to protect a native mammal, the elk, and was also the first large mammal sanctuary established in Canada. By the spring of 1906 the fence was finished and, as the Edmonton Bulletin (Frank Oliver's paper) stated, it was "horse high, bull-strong and pig-tight" and encircled 41 kilometres. Cooper and his friends found help and rounded up 24 very wild elk, and drove then into the new enclosure. These elk have never been crossed with other elk and hence the herd is probably one of the few pure herds anywhere, if not the only one.

Plains Bison, or Buffalo as they are commonly known had been nearly exterminated by the 1880s. One small group of calves was saved by an Indian, Walking Coyote, whose hunting party had wiped out the adults in the Sweetgrass Hills of Montana and southern Alberta. Walking Coyote took the calves home and released them to reproduce on his reserve. Several years later, two ranchers, Allard and Pablo, recognized that Walking Coyote's buffalo were the last small herd in existence and bought them. The herd continued to multiply on the Flathead Indian Reserve in Montana where the ranchers also ran their cattle. As the United States government continued to settle Indian lands, Allard and Pablo were told they must get rid of their buffalo herd and an agent was sent out to purchase the animals. It is rumored that a bribe or kickback was suggested to Pablo (by this time Allard was dead). Pablo was furious and stated he would rather kill the herd than sell it to a corrupt (U.S.) government.

Fortunately, Frank Oliver heard about the buffalo and immediately sent an emissary south. Canada purchased the 716 animals in 1907, and now had to find a place to house the last of the bison. Oliver sent word to the men who had recently created the elk reserve near Edmonton, to prepare to receive the first 400 buffalo. The animals arrived by train at Lamont, 10 kilometres north, and were herded down a specially constructed fenced road into the reserve. The next year more bison were shipped to the new Buffalo Park at Wainwright. In 1909 the Elk Island buffalo were rounded up and sent to Wainwright. The local wardens said they "could not find" 48 animals, and thus the nucleus of the present herd was started.

By 1936, there were 2,479 plains bison in Elk Island and the park was starting to show serious signs of overgrazing. To avoid further overgrazing and discontinue the need for supplemental feeding with hay, the herd was reduced to about 700 animals and is now maintained at that size.

Thanks to visionary Albertans such as Frank Oliver, the plains bison were saved from extinction. Thanks to Elk Island Park and the staff who prized the buffalo enough that they "looked the other way" while 48 fugitives escaped, the plains bison are no longer endangered. Today more than 100,000 plains bison live in parks, zoos and on private ranches across North America. Most are descendants of the 48 fugitives. — *Joy & Cam Finlay*

Protection and Conservation

Over the last 25 years conservation of the world's natural resources has become a movement of national and international concern. The *World Conservation Strategy,* published in 1980, argues that if society is to have a sustainable future, economic activity must be based on sound environmental management. Both the federal and provincial governments endorsed the World Conservation Strategy with the recommendation that provinces should prepare their own strategies. In 1985, the Public Advisory Committees to the Environmental Council of Alberta began working towards the preparation of a conservation strategy for Alberta.

The World Conservation Strategy has three major objectives: (1) to maintain essential ecological processes and life-support systems; (2) to preserve genetic diversity; and (3) to ensure the

Whitemud Falls Ecological Reserve
(Archie Landals)

Celebrating Parks

sustainable utilization of species and ecosystems. Three additional objectives were set out for an *Alberta Conservation Strategy*: (1) to provide for the recreational, spiritual, aesthetic and other non-material needs of Albertans; (2) to maintain and improve the quality of life in the urban environment; and (3) to use and manage non-renewable resources in the interest of developing a long-term sustainable economy for Albertans.

Conservation strategies advocate the need to integrate an environmental ethic and conservation practices into all aspects of land-use change and economic development. Parks and protected areas have an important role to play in conservation strategies because they provide a representative sample of a country's natural diversity of landscapes and plant and animal life.

For the most part, the application of the principles of the World Conservation Strategy and, specifically, the concept of sustainable development, has largely taken on an anthropocentric or people-oriented perspective. The designating of lands as protected areas is often justified for the benefits these areas provide to society. These benefits many be categorized as follows: spiritual benefits; recreation and aesthetic benefits; ecological benefits, including the preservation of genetic diversity; scientific and education benefits; economic benefits derived from recreation and tourism; and the *in absentia* benefits resulting from the contribution that natural areas make to society's culture and heritage through painting, music and literature.

However, a balanced parks system must also include a "biocentric" or nature-oriented perspective. Value must be placed on protecting lands for the inherent and intrinsic values of the ecosystems they represent. Ecosystems are systems formed by the interaction of all living things of a particular environment with one another and with themselves.

The Provincial Parks Service acknowledges that resource management practices must be sensitive to natural processes. In this regard, parks may serve as models of environmental management and stewardship and provide environmental standards to which other lands can be compared. Moreover, increasing attention has been focused in recent years on the need for park agencies to be sensitive to the ethical choices associated with determining appropriate activities in

Athabasca Dunes Ecological Reserve *(Archie Landals)*

Conclusion

Natural resources, ecological processes, and our use of species and ecosystems are all interconnected. Our continued prosperity, even our survival, is dependent upon striking a balance between the environment and economy. Parks play a vital role in this symmetry. They are the link.

Alberta's system of parks is a legacy that has evolved to reflect our changing values and concerns as a society. Parks are special places where we can learn to enjoy and appreciate nature, and better understand our role in the environment. Perhaps more importantly, our

parks and recreation areas. In the case of wilderness areas, ecological reserves and provincial parks, human use must be compatible with protecting the natural assets of the area.

Tension will inevitably occur within the existing parks system between heritage resource protection and the provision of outdoor recreation and tourism opportunities. The extent to which these tensions are reconciled within protected areas will provide a microcosm of the general well-being of society, its management of natural resources and its respect for the environment as a whole.
— *Guy & Noni Swinnerton*

Visitors learn about Alberta's natural heritage in William A. Switzer Provincial Park. *(Archie Landals)*

system of parks is a legacy that has been entrusted to our care and stewardship, its a legacy to be passed on, unspoiled, to future generations.

The lofty mountains of Kananaskis and White Goat Wilderness, the dark shady forests of Lakeland and Notikewin Provincial Parks, the waving grasslands of Hand Hills and Kennedy Coulee Ecological Reserves, the rugged foothills of Beauvais Lake and William A. Switzer Provincial Parks, the ghostly hoodoos and badlands of Writing-on-Stone and Dinosaur Provincial Parks, and the storm-swept beaches of Lesser Slave Lake Provincial Parks – are landscapes of

tremendous diversity and magnificent scenery. They are protected as parks, not only for our enjoyment, but also as refuges for the myriads of plants and animals that live there.

Alberta's parks — our legacy – are there to celebrate and pass on to future generations! — *Archie Landals*

Calypso *(Kåre Hellum)*

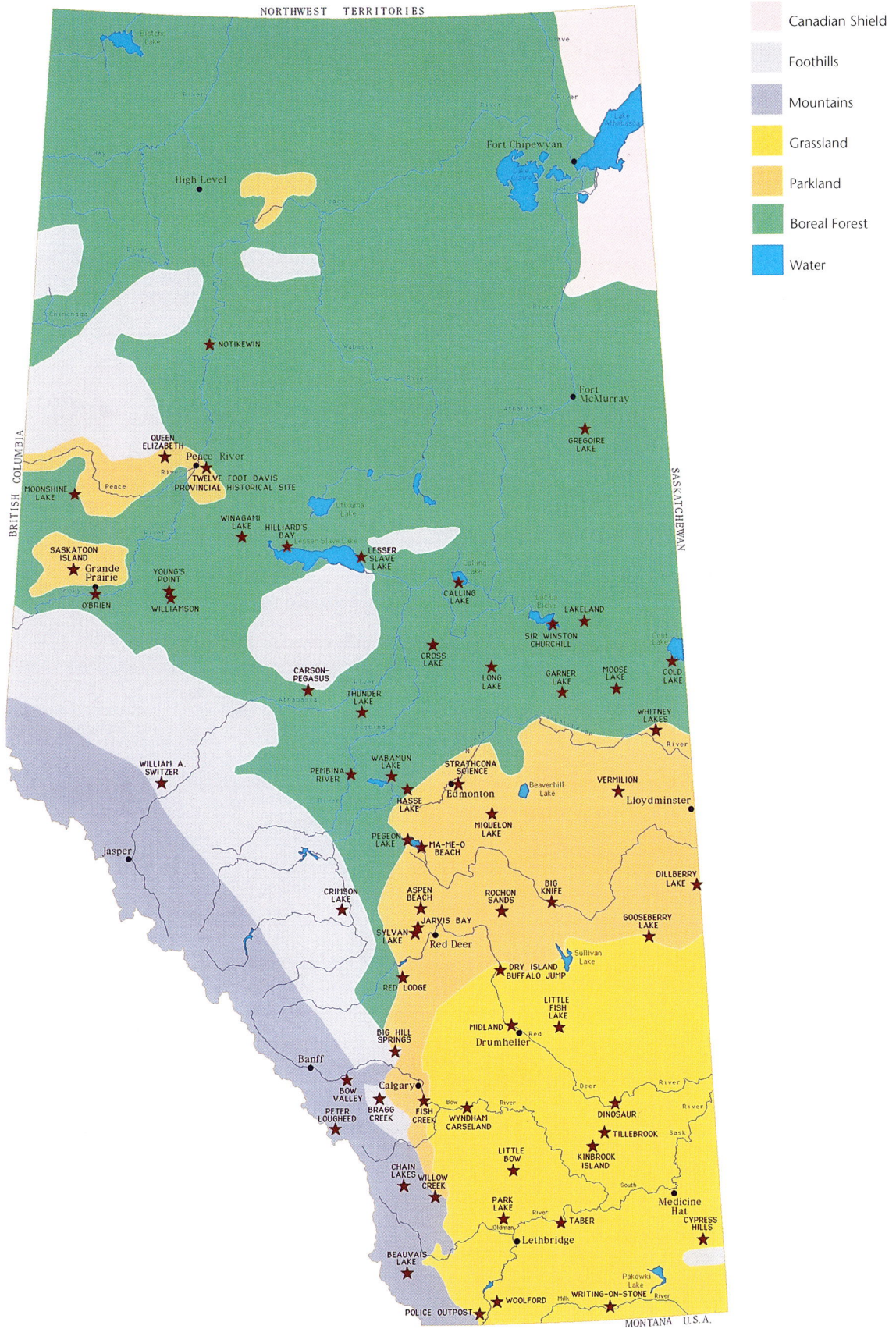

NORTHWEST TERRITORIES

Canadian Shield
Foothills
Mountains
Grassland
Parkland
Boreal Forest
Water

Bistcho Lake

Slave

Hay River

River

Lake Athabasca

Fort Chipewyan

High Level

Lake Claire

Peace River

Chinchaga

NOTIKEWIN

Wabasca

River

BRITISH COLUMBIA

Fort McMurray

Athabasca

GREGOIRE LAKE

QUEEN ELIZABETH
Peace River
TWELVE FOOT DAVIS
PROVINCIAL HISTORICAL SITE

MOONSHINE LAKE

Peace

River

Utikuma Lake

WINAGAMI LAKE

HILLIARD'S BAY
LESSER SLAVE LAKE
Lesser Slave Lake

Calling Lake

SASKATOON ISLAND
Grande Prairie
YOUNG'S POINT
O'BRIEN
WILLIAMSON

CALLING LAKE

Lac La Biche
LAKELAND

SASKATCHEWAN

Cold Lake

SIR WINSTON CHURCHILL

CROSS LAKE

LONG LAKE

GARNER LAKE

MOOSE LAKE

COLD LAKE

CARSON-PEGASUS

THUNDER LAKE

Athabasca

Pembina

River

WHITNEY LAKES

River

WILLIAM A. SWITZER

PEMBINA RIVER

WABAMUN LAKE

STRATHCONA SCIENCE

Beaverhill Lake

VERMILION

Lloydminster

River

Jasper

HASSE LAKE
Edmonton

PEGEON LAKE
MA-ME-O BEACH

MIQUELON LAKE

CRIMSON LAKE

ASPEN BEACH
JARVIS BAY
SYLVAN LAKE
Red Deer

ROCHON SANDS

BIG KNIFE

DILLBERRY LAKE

GOOSEBERRY LAKE

Sullivan Lake

DRY ISLAND BUFFALO JUMP

RED LODGE

LITTLE FISH LAKE

BIG HILL SPRINGS

MIDLAND
Drumheller

Red

Banff

BOW VALLEY
PETER LOUGHEED
BRAGG CREEK

Calgary

FISH CREEK

Bow

River

WYNDHAM CARSELAND

Deer

River

DINOSAUR

River

Sask

TILLEBROOK

CHAIN LAKES
WILLOW CREEK

LITTLE BOW

KINBROOK ISLAND

PARK LAKE

TABER

Oldman

River

South

Medicine Hat

CYPRESS HILLS

Lethbridge

BEAUVAIS LAKE

Pakowki Lake

WOOLFORD
WRITING-ON-STONE

Milk

River

POLICE OUTPOST

MONTANA   U.S.A.

Provincial Parks

Canadian Shield
Foothills
Mountains
Grassland
Parkland
Boreal Forest
Water

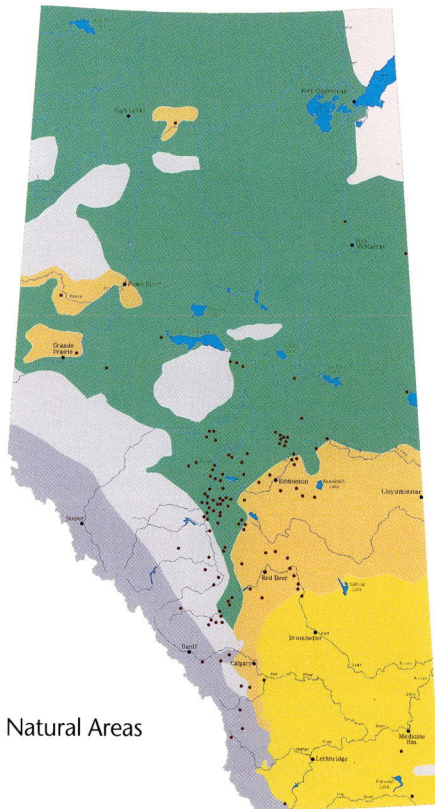

Natural Areas

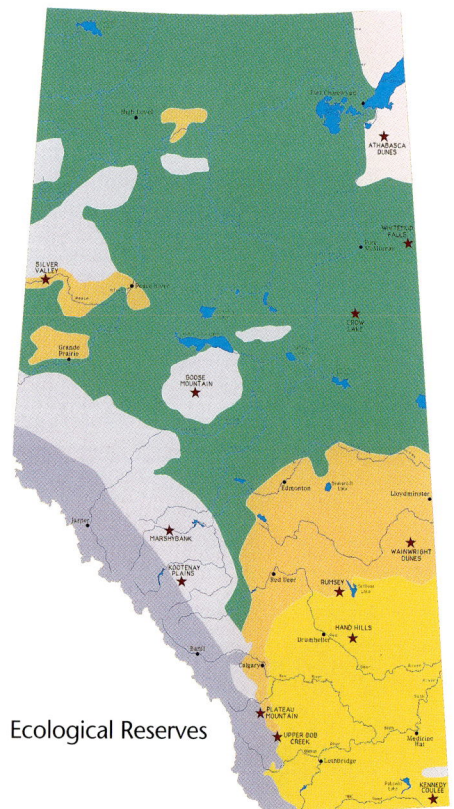

Ecological Reserves

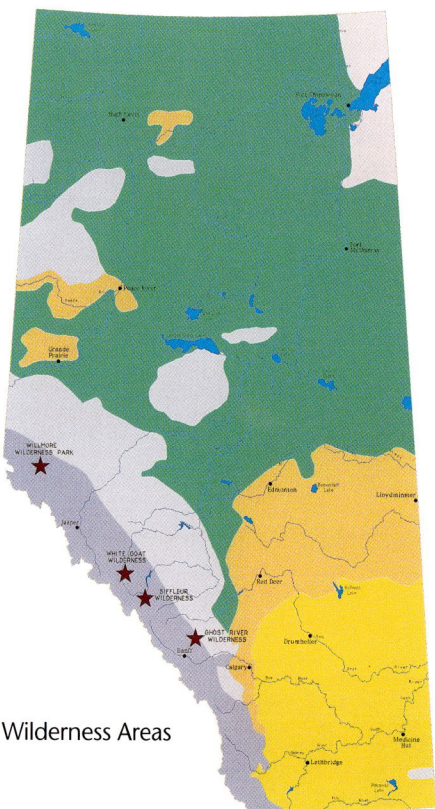

Wilderness Areas

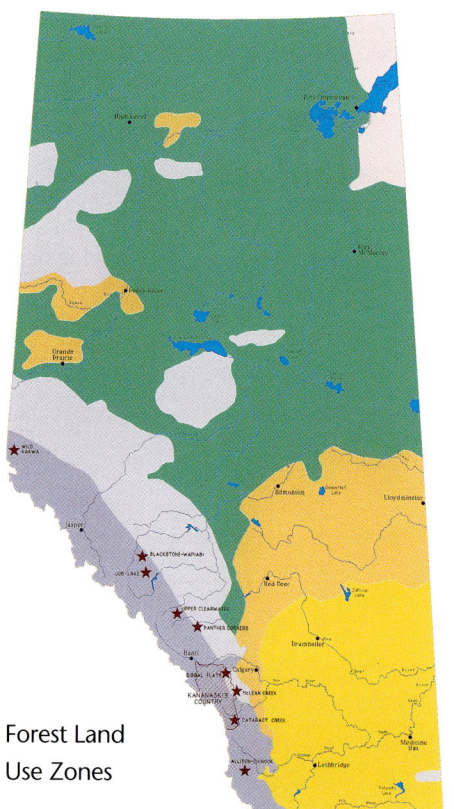

Forest Land
Use Zones

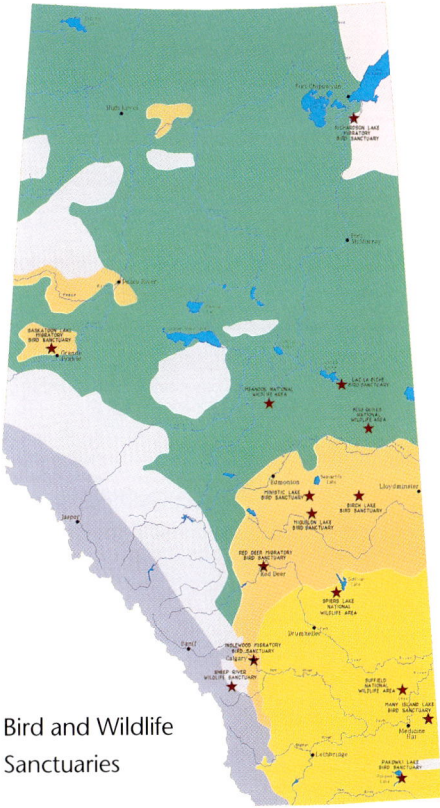

Bird and Wildlife
Sanctuaries

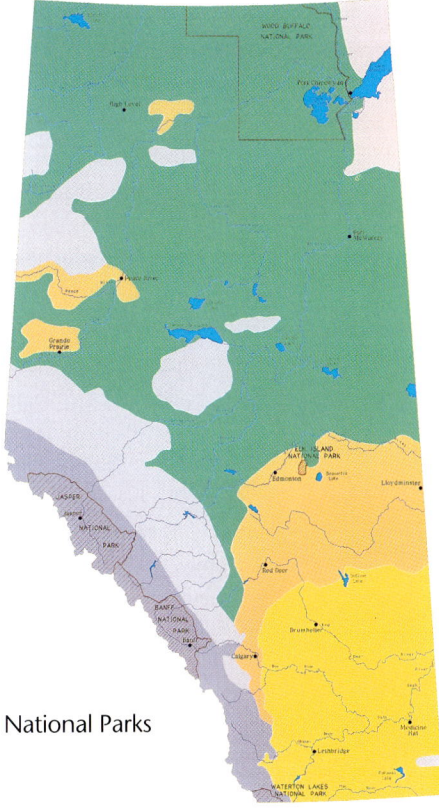

National Parks

International
Designations

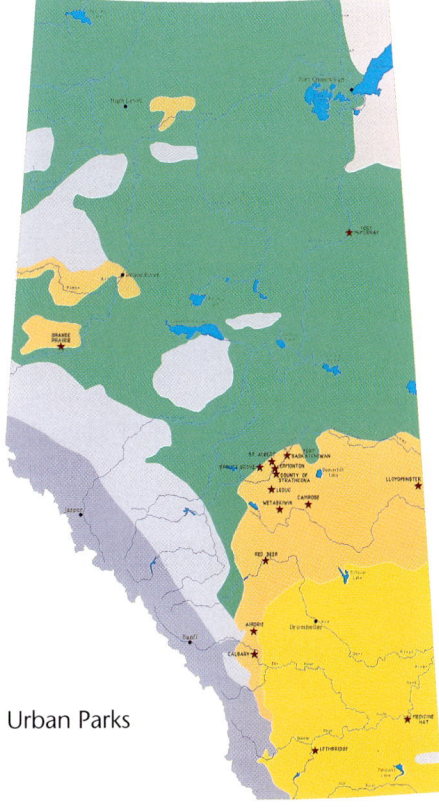

Urban Parks

Dates Relevant to the Establishment of Alberta Provincial Parks

1885   Banff Hot Springs set aside as a Crown reserve

1887   Rocky Mountains Park Act established Rocky Mountains Park (subsequently called Banff National Park)

1895   Waterton Lakes National Park established

1905   Alberta becomes a Province

1906   Alpine Club of Canada established

1906   Alberta Natural History Society founded

1907   Jasper National Park established

1910   Alberta Audubon Society established in Edmonton

1911   Ministik Bird Sanctuary established

1913   Elk Island National Park established

1922   Wood Buffalo National Park established

1922   Gaetz Lake Sanctuary established

1923   National Parks Association founded

1928   Act to Facilitate Town Planning and the Preservation of the National Beauties of the Province

1928   Alberta Fish and Game Association founded

1930   Transfer of Resources from Federal Government to Alberta

1930   Provincial Parks and Protected Areas Act

1932   First provincial parks established in Alberta - Aspen Beach, Gooseberry Lake, Park Lake and Saskatoon Island

1938   Ducks Unlimited Canada founded

1950   Alberta Recreation and Parks Association founded

1951   Provincial Parks transferred to Lands and Forests; Provincial Parks and Protected Areas Act revised; permanent staff hired

1953   Alberta Provincial Parks introduces fees and charges

1955   Alberta's Golden Jubilee

1957   Provincial park attendance exceeds 1 million

1959   Wilderness Provincial Park Act (renamed Willmore Wilderness Park 1965)

1961   White Goat/Siffleur Wilderness areas declared under the Forest Reserves Act

1961   Canadian Wildlife Federation founded

1963   National and Provincial Parks Association of Canada founded

1964   Provincial Parks Act amended

1965   Provincial park attendance exceeds 3 million

1966   Nature Conservancy of Canada incorporated

1967   Provincial Parks Policy Statement - stronger emphasis on conservation and preservation while providing for recreation

1967   Provincial park attendance exceeds 4 million

1967   Ghost River Wilderness Area established

1968   Edmonton Chapter, National and Provincial Parks Association of Canada founded

1968   Alberta Wilderness Association founded

1969   Sierra Club Canada founded

1970   Provincial park attendance exceeds 5 million

1970   Federation of Alberta Naturalists incorporated

1970   Public Lands Act included provision of setting aside of natural areas

1971   Wilderness Areas Act relating to the White Goat, Siffleur and Ghost River Wilderness Areas

1973   Provincial Parks Policy - Position Paper No. 13

1974   Capital City Park, Edmonton announced

1976   Recreation, Parks and Wildlife Foundation established

1977   Kananaskis Country Recreation Policy

1977   First natural area formally designated by Alberta Legislature

1979   Urban Parks Program announced

1979 Urban Parks Program announced

1979 Dinosaur Provincial Park designated as a World Heritage Site

1980 Campsite Reservation Program introduced in provincial parks

1980 Wilderness Areas, Ecological Reserves and Natural Areas Act

1981 Municipal Recreation Areas Program

1984 Campground Host Program introduced in provincial parks

1985 Centennial of Canada's national parks

1986 Municipal Recreation Tourism Areas Program initiated

1986 Bighorn Wildland Recreation Area Announced

1987 Establishment of first ecological reserves in Alberta

1988 Winter Olympics held in Kananaskis Country

1988 Park Ventures Fund established

1989 Cypress Hills Interprovincial Park becomes the first of its kind in Canada

1989 $1 million bequest to Recreation, Parks and Wildlife Foundation by M.L. Imrie

1989 Expansion of the Urban Parks Program

1991 Provincial park attendance exceeds 8.5 million

1991 Peaceful Valley Day Lodge donation to Recreation, Parks and Wildlife Foundation by Kathleen and Robert Wark

1991 Cross Conservation Area dedicated

1992 60th Anniversary of Alberta Provincial Parks

1992 Provincial Parks Service becomes part of Alberta Tourism, Parks and Recreation

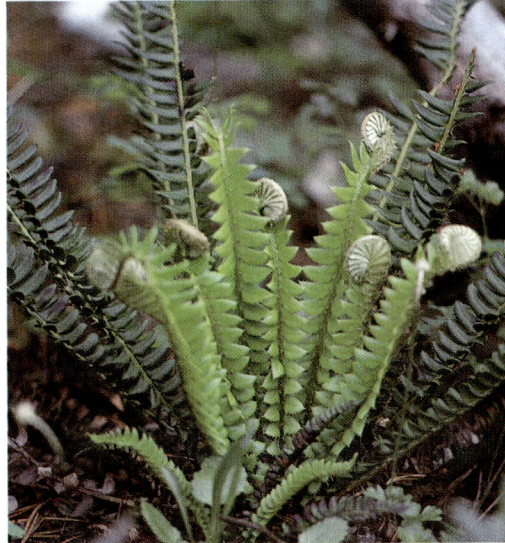

(Archie Landals)

Alberta's Parks

I remember the first time I went to an Alberta park. I loved it. I liked the wild animals, the fresh air, the mountains, the forest and also the sports I could do. I was surprised how there was a place, like an Alberta park, still left in the world. I thought everything nowdays was cities and factories. I felt great hiking, breathing the fresh air, looking at the trees around me and the quiet animals that were running everywhere.

Alberta parks are also good for camping, mountain climbing and all sorts of sports. I did all the sports, except one, mountain climbing. My family wanted to go but I was afraid that I would fall or be too tired to walk back — so instead, we went fishing. When we got ready to leave, I said: "I am sure I will come back next year!"

David Yang, Grade 6,
Westbrook Elementary School

Numerical & Percentage Distribution of Population by Rural & Urban, Alberta 1901 to 1991

Year	Total No.	Rural No.	Percent of Total	Urban No.	Percent of Total
1901	73,022	61,171	83.8	11,851	16.2
1911	374,295	264,359	70.6	109,936	29.4
1921	588,454	411,284	69.9	177,170	30.1
1931	731,605	503,723	68.9	227,882	31.1
1941	796,169	545,564	68.5	250,605	31.5
1951	939,501	509,413	54.2	430,088	45.8
1961	1,331,944	480,368	36.1	851,576	63.9
1966	1,463,203	455,796	31.2	1,007,407	68.8
1971	1,627,874	423.317	26.0	1,204,557	74.0
1981	2,237,725	510,179	22.8	1,727,545	77.2
1986	2,365,825	488,067	20.6	1,877,758	79.4
1991	2,521,300	not available	not available	not available	not available

Provincial Parks Statement of Capital Expenditures 1929/30 to 1934/35

Park	1929/30 $	1930/31 $	1931/32 $	1932/33 $	1933/34 $	1934/35 $	TOTAL $
Buffalo Lake					1,330.77		1,330.77
Canmore Village		191.89					191.89
Elkwater Lake	307.86			729.55			1,037.41
Ghost River	1,180.03						1,180.03
Gooseberry Lake	3,695.25	5,713.48	648.52				10,057.25
Gull Lake	9,230.58	5,758.56	1,188.13				16,177.27
Hommy Park			24.63				24.63
Lundbreck Falls		318.71					318.71
Oliver Mental Hospital	47.84						47.84
Park Lake			2,685.44				2,685.44
Pigeon Lake	28.22						28.22
Sylvan Lake	2,077.50		1,355.80				3,433.30
Sturgeon River	125.92						125.92
Turner Valley	572.88						572.88
Vermilion		1,206.43					1,206.43
Travelling Expense		1,131.80					1,131.80
Miscellaneous	4.20	57.19	249.90				311.29
	17,270.28	14,378.06	6,152.42	729.55	1,330.77	nil	39,861.08

Park Name / Total	Amount
Sylvan Lake	1,800.00
Kinbrook	3,000.00
Park Lake	3,000.00
Saskatoon Island & Mountain	2,000.00
Crimson Lake	1,500.00
Red Lodge	3,000.00
Gooseberry Lake	300.00
Beauvais	150.00
Taber	500.00
Chestermere Lake	400.00
Elkwater Lake	2,500.00
Pigeon Lake	350.00
Markerville	100.00
Woolford	800.00
Writing-on-Stone	300.00
General	300.00
	$20,000.00

Example of Park Expenses	
Red Lodge	
Roads, park areas	500.00
Park area	150.00
Diving raft, board, etc.	200.00
Slides, playground equipment	350.00
Sidewalk, railing, bench	8.00
Band stand	500.00
Pier and steps	200.00
Caretaking	200.00
Miscellaneous	100.00
Total	**$3,000.00**

1991/92 Provincial Parks
Selected Information

$40 million - Labor and capital expenditures

8,314,288 visitors
(1,446,944 campers 6,786,590 day-users)
350 permanent staff
340 person years available for seasonal staff
3 Wilderness Areas
13 Ecological Reserves
63 Provincial Parks
127 Provincial Recreation Areas
11,696 campsites
12,661 camp stoves
1,326 washrooms
1,150 kilometres of park roads
17,187 picnic tables
126 boat ramps
99 boat docks
3,121 kilometres trails
(hiking, cycling, cross-country skiing,
equestrian, snowmobiling)

Provincial parks
And other parks should be
Recognized for their natural beauty.
Kind and
Smart People should preserve them.

Eric Zhou, Grade 4,
Westbrook Elementary School

Alberta's Parklands - 1992

63   Provincial Parks
5   National Parks
16   Urban Parks (cities)
800 Recreation Areas (Forest, Provincial,
      Municipal, etc.)
13   Ecological Reserves
118 Natural Areas
4   Wilderness Areas (including Willmore)
20   Bird and Wildlife Sanctuaries
1   Biosphere Reserve
4   World Heritage Sites
4   Ramsar Sites

Total Area over 70,000 square kilometres

Parks Trivia

Name	Acres	Hectares	Name	Acres	Hectares
Aspen Beach	534.61	216.36	Moonshine Lake	2,092.83	846.93
Beauvais Lake	1,880.00	760.84	Moose Lake	1,816.98	735.33
Big Hill Springs	62.94	25.47	Notikewin	23,960.37	9,696.76
Big Knife	729.10	295.07	O'Brien	161.15	65.22
Bow Valley	3,116.53	1,261.26	Park Lake	553.36	223.93
Bragg Creek	316.36	128.03	Pembina River	413.15	167.20
Calling Lake	1,824.37	738.32	Peter Lougheed	123,900.00	50,142.33
Carson-Pegasus	2,988.97	1,209.64	Pigeon Lake	1,095.72	443.42
Chain Lakes	1,010.56	408.95	Police Outpost	550.61	222.82
Cold Lake	984.15	398.27	Queen Elizabeth	211.47	85.57
Crimson Lake	7,929.23	3,208.96	Red Lodge	318.97	129.08
Cross Lake	5,129.60	2,075.95	Rochon Sands	295.25	119.49
Cypress Hills	50,532.86	20,450.65	Saskatoon Island	250.61	101.41
Dillberry Lake	2,360.84	955.43	Sir Winston Churchill	591.40	239.33
Dinosaur	16,363.16	6,622.17	Strathcona Science	269.75	109.16
Dry Island Buffalo Jump	2,914.94	1,179.68	Sylvan Lake	210.75	85.29
Fish Creek	2,863.70	1,158.94	Taber	125.36	50.73
Garner Lake	182.08	73.68	Thunder Lake	514.22	208.11
Gooseberry Lake	128.00	51.79	Tillebrook	139.15	343.87
Gregoire Lake	1,720.28	696.20	Twelve Foot Davis Provincial Historical Site	2.10	.85
Hasse Lake	170.40	68.95	Vermilion	1,858.85	752.28
Hilliard's Bay	5,755.39	2,329.21	Wabamun Lake	566.28	229.17
Jarvis Bay	212.11	85.84	Whitney Lakes	3,678.74	1,488.77
Kinbrook Island	95.00	38.44	William A. Switzer	6,636.80	2,685.81
Lakeland	36,324.48	14,700.52	Williamson	42.88	17.35
Lesser Slave Lake	18,672.98	7,556.95	Willow Creek	268.60	108.69
Little Bow	271.57	109.90	Winagami Lake	2,992.39	1,210.97
Little Fish Lake	151.21	61.19	Woolford	86.51	35.00
Long Lake	1,887.47	768.83	Writing-on-Stone	4,254.19	1,721.67
Ma-Me-O Beach	4.00	1.61	Wyndham-Carseland	440.33	178.19
Midland	1,479.88	598.91	Young's Point	2,692.46	1,089.59
Miquelon Lake	2,064.95	835.69	**TOTALS**	**351,652.95**	**142,313.94**

GLOSSARY

Aeolian are deposits arranged by the wind, as the sands and other loose materials in dune fields.

Alien species refers to a species occurring in a particular country or area outside its historically known natural range, as a result of intentional or accidental dispersal by human intervention.

Alluvial pertains to deposits resulting from modern, flowing streams.

Arete refers to the acute and rugged crest of a mountain range, ridge between mountains, or mountain spur.

Beach ridge refers to a mound of beach material behind the present beach that has been heaped up by a wave or other action.

Biological diversity (biodiversity) refers to the variety of and variability among living organisms and the ecological complexes of which they are a part including diversity within and between species, and ecosystems.

Biosphere reserves are part of the UNESCO network which collectively represent the world's major ecological systems, different patterns of human use and adaptations. Each reserve includes a protected core of relatively undisturbed land and areas being managed to meet human needs. Waterton Lakes Biosphere Reserve is the only such designation in Alberta.

Biotechnology is the use of biological systems and organisms for scientific, industrial, agricultural, medical and environmental applications.

Bog refers to a nutrient-poor, organic wetland not influenced by mineral groundwater, developing an acidic peat forming on level, raised or sloping surface with raised hummocks and wet hollows, usually covered by a moss carpet dominated by sphagnum and supporting a layer of shrubs, with or without trees.

Boreal refers to the forest region that covers most of northern Alberta. Stands of spruce, poplar and pine trees are interspersed with muskegs and other wetlands.

Braided stream refers to a stream flowing in several dividing and reuniting channels, forming an interlacing pattern.

Brunisol refers to moderately developed soil intermediate in character between regosols and luvisols of podzols.

Chernozem refers to a mineral soil with an organic-rich, surface layer developed under grasslands or grassland-forest edges.

Cirque refers to a broad, cliff-walled basin in the mountains in which a glacier has originated.

Clastic rock refers to a consolidated sedimentary rock composed of the cemented fragments broken down from pre-existing rocks, e.g., conglomerate, sandstone, shale.

Col refers to a saddle or gap across a ridge or between two peaks.

Collapse sink refers to a cavern so enlarged by solution and erosion that it has locally collapsed, an example of karst topography.

Colluvium refers to a general term applied to loose deposits, typically along steeper slopes, and brought there chiefly by gravity.

Competent refers to rock strata able to withstand folding without flowage or change in original thickness.

Conglomerate refers to a cemented clastic rock containing gravel or pebbles.

Conservation of biological diversity means the preservation of, maintenance, sustainable use, recovery and enhancement of the components of biological diversity.

Country of origin of biodiversity means a country which is the source of indigenous biological resources, including genetic material.

Country providing biodiversity means the country supplying genetic material, organisms and parts thereof, or populations which may or may not have originated in that country.

Convention on the Conservation of Wetlands of International Importance see Ramsar Convention.

Glossary

Crag-and-tail refers to a streamlined hill or ridge, resulting from glaciation and consisting of a knob of resistant bedrock (the "crag"), with an elongated body (the "tail") of more erodible bedrock or till, on its lee side.

Crevasse filling refers to a relatively straight ridge of stratified sand and gravel, till or other sediments, formed by the filling of a crevasse in a stagnant glacier which later melted.

Cryosol refers to a soil with permafrost with one metre of the surface.

Disjunct refers to a species found in a locality which is widely separated from other areas of its distribution.

Domesticated or cultivated species means species in which the evolutionary process has been influenced by humans to meet their needs.

Drumlin refers to a streamlined hill or ridge of glacial drift with the long axis paralleling the direction of flow of a former glacier.

Dystrophic refers to a type of lake found in bogs, characteristically brown coloured from a high concentration of humic materials, low pH, low oxygen concentration in deeper areas, high CO_2 and low nutrient levels.

Ecological reserves are representative or special natural landscapes and features of the province and protected as examples of functioning ecosystems for research, education and heritage appreciation purposes.

Ecosystem refers to a dynamic complex of plant, animal and micro-organism communities and their non-living environment interacting as an ecological unit.

Extinct refers to any indigenous species of fauna or flora no longer known to exist anywhere.

Extirpated refers to any indigenous species of fauna or flora that is locally extinct.

Endangered species are a species in danger of extinction and whose survival is unlikely if the causal factors continue operating.

Threatened species are any indigenous species of fauna or flora that is likely to become endangered if the factors affecting its vulnerability are not reversed.

Vulnerable refers to any indigenous species of flora or fauna that is at risk because of low or declining numbers but is not yet threatened.

Endemic species are a species whose natural geographic distribution is restricted to a specific area or country.

Esker refers to a serpentine-shaped ridge composed of irregularly bedded gravel and sand, deposited by subglacial meltwaters flowing in tunnels near the bottom of glacial ice.

Eutrophic refers to a generally shallow lake, rich in nutrients, with an extensive zone of emergent and submergent plant growth.

Ex-situ conservation is the conservation of components of biological diversity (genetic material, organisms, populations) outside their natural surroundings, e.g., zoos, botanic gardens and gene banks.

Fan refers to a fan-shaped accumulation of debris deposited by a stream (fluvial fan) or by gravity (colluvial fan) usually where the slope changes from a steeper to a more gradual angle, as at the base of a valley wall or slop.

Fen refers to a nutrient-rich, organic wetland influenced by mineral-bearing groundwater, developing a poorly to moderately decomposed peat with a slightly alkaline pH. The surface is generally level and uniform, occasionally with subparallel ridges or slightly elevated islands, linear drainage features and dispersed small pools, usually covered predominantly with brown mosses, sedges, grasses and often scattered willow and birch shrubs or trees.

Fibrisol refers to an organic soil with relatively undecomposed organic matter which comprises at least 30 per cent by weight of the soil to a depth of at least 60 centimetres. These soils develop mainly in poorly drained peatlands.

Flora are plant species of an area.

Flowstone refers to deposits of calcium carbonate accumulated on a rock wall where water trickles from the rock.

Fluvial refers to deposits left by flowing water.

Forest is any area wooded with trees.

Genetic material is hereditary material found in living organisms or parts thereof. The characteristics of an organism are derived from this material.

Glacial erratic boulder train is a series of widely separated large rocks deposited over a long distance, indicative of former glacial action.

Glacial fluting are long parallel ridges formed by advancing continental glaciers. They may extend for many kilometres and be several hundred metres high.

Glaciofluvial pertains to deposits by streams flowing from glaciers.

Glaciolacustrine refers to materials deposited in a glacial lake.

Gleysol are soils developed where there is prolonged water saturation resulting in reducing conditions.

Ground moraine is a flat to undulating moraine of low relief, closed depressions and without pronounced topographical features.

Habitat is the place or type of site where an organism or population natural occurs.

Hanging valley refers to a tributary valley whose floor is higher than the floor of an adjoining trunk valley.

Hibernaculum is an overwintering den for snakes, often in cavities in badlands.

Hoodoo refers to the pillar-like formations in the badlands.

Horn refers to a high pyramidal peak with steep sides formed by the intersecting walls of three or more cirques.

Hummocky moraine refers to the strongly undulating knob and kettle topography produced by either active or stagnant glacial ice.

Ice contact stratified drift is a drift exhibiting both sorting and stratification, and making up forms such as kames and eskers deposited in contact with melting glacier ice.

Incompetent is the converse of competent. Incompetent and competent are relative terms. An incompetent bed is relatively weak.

Indigenous species are a species occurring in the wild in a particular area or country, within its known natural range.

In-situ conservation is the conservation of ecosystems and natural habitats and the maintenance and recovery of viable populations of species in their natural surroundings.

Kame refers to a short, steep-sided, irregular ridge, hill or mound of stratified drift deposited by meltwater in contact with glacier ice.

Kame moraine refers to a group of interconnecting kames, kettles and eskers.

Karst is a type of topography formed within limestone, dolomite or gypsum by dissolving or solution, and that is characterized by sinkholes, caves and underground drainage.

Kettle is a depression in glacial deposits formed by the melting out of ice blocks which were partially or completely buried in the glacial deposits.

Lacustrine pertains to materials deposited at the bottom of a lake.

Levee is a natural bank which confines a stream to its channel.

Loess is a soft, homogeneous, nonstratified deposit consisting predominantly of silt particles deposited by wind.

Longitudinal dune refers to linear-shaped sand dunes aligned parallel to the prevailing winds.

Lowland is a relative term used to indicate lands at lower elevations or more poorly drained.

Luvisol is a moderately-leached soil developed under forest vegetation.

Glossary

Marl are deposits of clay and calcium or magnesium carbonate.

Marsh refers to a wetland with little peat accumulation, periodically inundated with standing or slow-moving water, and often with pronounced seasonal fluctuating water levels exposing mudflats and matted vegetation at water drawdowns. Vegetation consists of non-woody emergent plants such as bulrushes, cattails, sedges, reeds, rushes or grasses interrupted by pools of open water.

Meander scar refers to crescentic cut in the landscape formed by an abandoned stream channel.

Meandering stream is a stream characterized by S-bends and loops, with numerous abandoned channels in the form of oxbow lakes.

Mesotrophic refers to a lake type which is intermediate in character between oligotrophic lakes and eutrophic lakes.

Metasediment is metamorphosed sedimentary rock.

Moraine plateaux are generally subcircular, flat-topped mesa-like mounds composed to till and/or stratified drift.

Morainal veneer is a thin covering of morainal material.

Muskeg is a broad term referring to organic terrain, includes both bogs and fens.

National parks protect representative examples of Canada's natural regions, associated flora, fauna and other natural phenomena for all time. Most of the land in national parks is zoned to protect the environment with relatively small areas devoted to townsites and visitor facilities.

National historic parks are intended to protect historic resources associated with persons, places and events of national historic significance. A **registered** or **provincial historic resource** designation protects an historic area.

National wildlife areas and **migratory bird sanctuaries** are federally legislated and allow some hunting, fishing, trapping and selected agricultural activities, depending upon each site's management.

Natural areas contain natural features representing one or more aspects of the province's biological and physical diversity for non-consumptive nature appreciation.

Nonterrestrial species are organisms not relying on the land for a significant aspect of their life cycle.

Oligotrophic refers to a lake which is usually deep, lacks extensive emergent vegetation and is poor in dissolved nutrients and high in dissolved oxygen.

Order-in-Council refers to decree used as a means of delegated legislation, giving effect in some respect to an Act of Parliament or the Legislative Assembly.

Organic refers to surface deposits composed of partly decomposed peat, also a soil type developed where there is peat accumulation due to poor drainage and saturated conditions.

Oxbow Lake is a term used to describe a crescentic water body formed from a meander of a stream which has been cut off.

Outwash refers to drift deposited by meltwater streams issuing from glacier ice.

Paleodune refers to a now stabilized but once formerly extensive and active sand dune.

Pattered ground is a group term for circles, polygons, nets, steps and stripes that are characteristic of areas which have been subject to intensive frost action.

Parabolic dune refers to a sand dune with a crescentic shape and the points facing into the direction of the prevailing wind.

Pediment is a gently inclined erosion surface, for example the gentle slopes at the base of steeper slopes in badlands.

Periglacial refers to features adjacent to the margin of a glacier.

Peripheral is a term applied to species which barely extend their ranges into Alberta. Areas of peripherality have numerous peripheral species.

Piping feature refers to tubular vertically-oriented features formed by water erosion within bedrock in badland areas.

Plateau is a relatively elevated area of comparatively flat land which is commonly limited on at least one side by an abrupt descent to lower land.

Podzol is a soil with highly-leached upper horizons generally developed under coniferous forest.

Proglacial is applied to features of glacial origin beyond the limits of the glacier itself.

Protected area refers to a geographically defined area which is designated, or regulated, and managed to achieve specific conservation objectives.

Provincial parks protect outstanding recreational resources and provincially significant natural landscapes and features while providing quality recreational and education experiences.

Provincial recreation areas support extensive outdoor recreation opportunities in natural, modified or man-made settings. Traditionally they have met local and regional outdoor recreation needs, been relatively small and largely dominated by recreation facility developments. The trend is now towards larger areas with more emphasis on protecting biophysical resources.

Pseudokarst refers to a large piping feature.

Ramsar Convention acknowledges international concerns about the significant value of a wetlands for its high biological productivity. Alberta's Beaverhill Lake and Hay-Zama Lakes are designated under the Ramsar Convention. The convention is formally referred to as the **Convention on the Conservation of Wetlands of International Importance**.

Raptors refers to birds of prey such as hawks and eagles.

Rational use of biological diversity means the use of components of biological diversity in a way and at a rate that does not lead to their long-term decline.

Regosol is a soil with weakly developed surface horizons usually because of recent deposition or erosion of the surface.

Rill refers to a small channel in a badland slope.

Riverine refers to bands of trees, shrubs and lush vegetation that grow adjacent to rivers, especially in dryer climates.

Sinkhole refers to a funnel-shaped depression in the land surface, characteristic of karst topography.

Sinking creek is an example of karst topography where a stream disappears underground.

Solifluction is the process of slow movement from higher to lower ground of masses of surface material saturated with water.

Solonetz is a grassland soil type with a salinized sub-surface horizon or hard pan layer.

Swamp refers to a wooded wetland with standing to gently flowing water occurring seasonally and often with an abundance of pools and channels. Vegetation cover is coniferous or deciduous trees or tall shrubs, as well as herbs and mosses.

Talus is coarse debris that has collected at the base of a steep slope.

Tarn refers to a small mountain lake or pool, especially one that occupies an ice-gouged basin on the floor of a cirque.

Terrace refers to a former floodplain of a stream, also used occasionally as including an active floodplain.

Terrestrial species are organisms relying on the land for a significant aspect of their life cycle.

Glossary

Thermokarst is topography with a pock-marked appearance in northern landscapes, created by collapse of permafrost features.

Thrust fault is a reverse fault in bedrock, characterized by a low angle of uplift.

Till refers to non-sorted, non-stratified sediment carried by a glacier.

Transverse dune refers to linear-shaped sand dunes aligned at right angles to the prevailing wind.

Tufa is a chemical sedimentary rock composed of calcium carbonate or of silica, deposited from solution in the water of a spring or lake, or from percolating ground water.

Upland is a relative term, used to indicate lands that are at higher elevation or better drained.

U-shaped valley refers to a valley carved by glacial erosion, having steep sides and a characteristic rounded profile.

Vegetation refers to plant communities of an area.

Woodland is any area wooded with trees, interchangeable with forest.

Wild species is a species which has not been deliberately modified by humans.

Wildlife corridors are routes or avenues to ensure completion of life cycles and unimpeded migrations and gene flows.

Wildlife sanctuaries, game bird sanctuaries and wildlife habitat development areas are operated at the provincial level. Hunting and trapping of wildlife is prohibited in Alberta's Sheep River Wildlife Sanctuary and hunting of game birds is prohibited in the seven provincial bird sanctuaries. Habitat development areas are intended to protect and develop key wildlife habitat for waterfowl, upland birds, ungulates and other non-game species and to provide a variety of outdoor education, nature interpretation and recreational used.

World heritage sites are an important international conservation tool aimed at protecting globally significant examples of natural and cultural heritage. Canada signed a 1972 United Nations Educational, Scientific and Cultural Organization (UNESCO) convention that included a commitment to identify, protect and present to both present and future generations the significant heritage resources situated within its territories. Alberta's four world heritage sites are Dinosaur Provincial Park, Head-Smashed-In Buffalo Jump, Wood Buffalo National Park and Canadian Rocky Mountain Parks (Banff and Jasper).

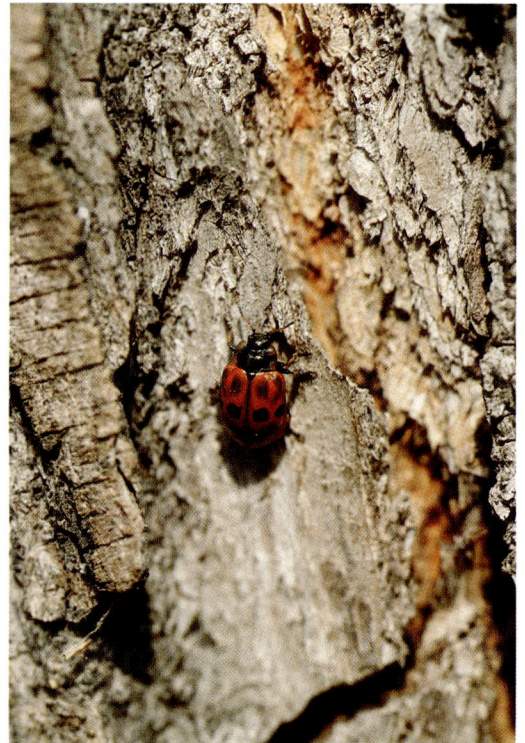

(Wei Yew)

FURTHER READING

Jimmy Simpson — Legend of the Rockies (1991), E.J. Hart, Altitude Publishing, Banff.

Birding: Jasper National Park (1988), Kevin Van Tighem and Andrew A. LeMessurier, Parks and People, Jasper.

A Nature Guide to Alberta (1980), D.A.E. Spalding, Provincial Museum of Alberta, Publication No.5, Hurtig Publishers and Alberta Cultures, Edmonton.

Parks in Alberta (1987), Joy and Cam Finlay, Hurtig Publishers Ltd., Edmonton.

Alberta Wildlife Viewing Guide (1990), Alberta Forestry, Lands and Wildlife, Lone Pine Publishing, Edmonton.

The Lone Pine Picnic Guide to Alberta (1989), Nancy Gibson, John Whittaker, Lone Pine Publishing, Edmonton.

The Discoverer's Guide to Elk Island National Park (1991), Ross Chapman, Lone Pine Publishing, Edmonton.

Handbook of the Canadian Rockies (1986), Ben Gadd, Hignell, Winnipeg.

Nature Alberta: An Illustrated Guide to Common Plants and Animals (1991), James Kavanagh, Lone Pine Publishing, Edmonton.

Trees and Shrubs of Alberta (1990), Kathleen Wilkinson, Lone Pine Publishing, Edmonton.

Mushrooms of Western Canada (1991), Helene M.E. Schalkwijk-Barendsen, Lone Pine Publishing, Edmonton.

Canadian Rockies Super Guide (1991), Graeme Pale, Altitude Publishing, Banff.

Prairie Water: Watchable Wildlife at Beaverhills Lake, Alberta, B.S.T. Publications, Edmonton.

Knee High Nature: Winter in Alberta(1988) Fall In Alberta (1989) Summer In Alberta (1990) Spring in Alberta (1991), Dianne Hayley and Pat Wishart, Knee High Nature, Sherwood Park.

The Kananaskis Valley, Deborah and Robert Enns, Sandra Leckie and John Walper, Wildland Publishing, Duchess.

Dinosaur Provincial Park-World Heritage Site, Deborah and Robert Anns, Sandra Leckie and John Walper, Wildland Publishing, Duchess.

The Tyrrell Museum of Palaeontology and the Drumheller Valley, Deborah and Robert Enns, Sandra Leckie and John Walper, Wildland Publishing, Duchess.

Wildflowers of the Canadian Rockies, George Scotter, Halle Flagar, Hurtig Publishers Ltd., Edmonton.

Birds of the Canadian Rockies, Scotter, Ulrich, Jones, Western Producers Books.

Kananaskis Country Trail Guide, 2nd Edition, Daffern, Rocky Mountain Books.

Guide to the Common Native Trees and Shrubs of Alberta, Alberta Environment Protection Services.

Geology in Peter Lougheed Provincial Park, McMechon, McMechon and Walter, Geological Survey of Canada and Kananaskis Country.

Valley of Rumors ... The Kananaskis, C.Ruth Oltman, Ribbon Creek Publishing.

The Kananaskis Environmental Education Library, Kananaskis Country. Series includes booklets on: Water, Climate, History, Range Management, Mountain-building, Glaciation, Vegetation, Sedimentation, Forests, Resource Management, Non-Renewable Resources. Correlates with school curriculum grades 1 to 12. Available in Calgary schools and Kananaskis Country.

Alberta Bird Atlas, (1992) Recreation, Parks and Wildlife Foundation, Edmonton.

Learning Resource Manuals, Standard Elementary Learning Resources Manual, Standard Junior High Learning Resource Manual. Alberta Provincial Parks Service, Edmonton.

Natural Region Posters, Alberta Provincial Parks Service, Edmonton. Five posters depicting the natural regions.

Further Reading

Information Sources

Alberta Provincial Parks Service, 16th Floor, Standard Life Centre, 10405-Jasper Avenue, Edmonton, AB T5J 3N4

Alberta Provincial Parks Service, West Central Region, Box 920, 2nd Floor, Provincial Building, 5025-55 Street, Rimbey, AB T0C 2J0

Alberta Provincial Parks Service, East Central Region, Box 1019, Provincial Building, 9503 Beaverhill Road, Lac La Biche, AB T0A 2C0

Alberta Provincial Parks Service, Northern Region, Provincial Building, 5102-50 Avenue, Valleyview, AB T0H 3N0

Alberta Provincial Parks Service, Southern Region, P.O. Drawer 930, Pioneer Plaza, Centre Street, Vulcan, AB T0L 2B0

Recreation, Parks and Wildlife Foundation, Park Ventures Fund, 16 Floor, Standard Life Centre, 10405-Jasper Avenue, Edmonton, AB T5J 3N4

Environment Canada - Western and Northern Region, Canada Wildlife Service, 2nd Floor, Twin Atria 2, 4999-98 Avenue, Edmonton, AB T6B 2X3

Canadian Parks Service, Western Regional Office, P.O. Box 2989, Stn. M, 220-4th Avenue SE, Calgary, AB T2P 3H8

Travel Alberta Information: In Alberta 222-6501Outside Alberta 1-800-661-8888

Natural and Protected Areas, Department of Forestry, Lands and Wildlife, 4th Fl. S. Tower, Petroleum Plaza, 9915-108 Street, Edmonton, AB T5K 2C9

Alberta Provincial Museum, 12845-102 Avenue, Edmonton, AB T5N 0M6

Royal Tyrrell Museum of Palaeontology, Box 7500, Midland Provincial Park and Highway 8383, Drumheller, AB T0J 0Y0

Whyte Museum of the Canadian Rockies, 111 Bear Street, Banff, AB T0L 0C0

Organizations Supporting Parks

Canadian Nature Federation, Calgary Branch, 5127 Brisbois Drive, Calgary, AB T2L 2G3. Edmonton Branch, Box 8644, Station L, Edmonton, AB T6C 4J4

Canadian Parks and Wilderness Society (CPAWS) Alberta Chapter, 11759 Groat Road, Groat Building, Edmonton, AB T5M 3K6 Calgary/Banff Chapter, Box 608, Sub P.O. 91, University of Calgary, AB T2N 1N4

Alberta Wilderness Association, Box 6398, Station D, Calgary, AB T2P 2E1

Federation of Alberta Naturalists, Box 1472, Edmonton, AB T5J 2N5

Natural Areas Wilderness Stewards Program, Natural and Protected Areas, Department of Forestry, Lands and Wildlife, 4th Floor, S. Tower, Petroleum Plaza, 9915-108 Street, Edmonton, AB T5K 2C9

Protected Areas Management Program, Faculty of Extension, University of Alberta, 112 St. and 83 Ave., Edmonton, AB T6G 2T4

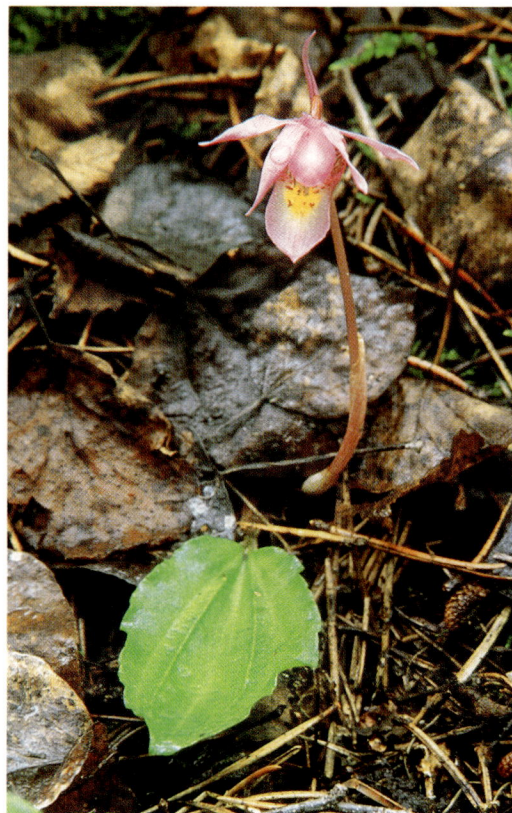

(Rosemary H.L.Calvert, FRPS)

C O N T R I B U T O R S

Acton, Jim
Allen, Sidney
Allers, Wilton
Anderson, Cheryl
Baik, Janice
Bair, A.C.
Bamber, Kevin
Beck, T.
Bennett, G.E.
Bettcher, Ken
Biamonte, Maria
Bird, Wilma
Bocking, Keith
Bosma, Mike
Bovey, Robin
Breier, Heidi
Bruntlet, Chris
Buss, Darryl
Buss, Kathie
Butler, Jim
Cadre, William
Calvert, Rosemary H.L.
Cameron, R.
Cameron, Tom
Campbell, Ian
Campbell, N.
Chabillon, David
Chamney, Ron
Clements, Jack
Clifford, Kyle
Cline, Donn
Cohen, Phil
Cooke, Marilyn
Cooney, Steve
Cooper, Bob
Cornish, Beth
Cox, Carter
Crawford, Glen
Currie, Phillip
Cyncar, Orest
Davison, Howard
Dekker, D.
Deukcher, Linnea
Dodge, David
Drinkwater, Tom
Duffin, Bruce

Durant, Paul
Edmonds, Jan
Eijgel, Heidi
Exell, Harry
Fawcett, Russell
Feick, J.
Findlay, Cam
Findlay, Joy
Finzel, Roy
Foley, Jim
Fraser, Frank
Fryberger, Angela
Gasser, Ellen
Gerding, Hiske
Gerding, Reineke
Gibson, Ray
Glenbow Museum
Gorko, Morris
Grey, Jack
Haggerty, Gordon
Halmrast, Lawrence
Hamill, Mark
Hammer, Fred
Hammond, Ed
Hart, Ted
Harvie, Charlie
Harvey, Glenn
Hass, Frieda
Hass, Wayne
Henderson, Ron
Heschl, Al
Hellum, A.Kåre
Hendry, Alice
Hogan, Daniel
Hommy, Milton
Hope, Kerry
Hoybak, Dennis
Hugill, Rob
Hutchison, Bob
Huseby, Rick
Jappsen, Werner
Jenkinson, Margaret
Johnson, R.
Keith, Nancy
Kennick, Barrie
Klassen, Mike

Kozan, Mel
Kunelius, R.
La Freniere, D.
Landals, Archie
Landals, Blaine
Landals, Maureen
Landry, Marc
Lanz, Carrie
Lavoie, Raymond
Lawson, Wes
Leighton, Doug
Logan, Dianne
Loomis, Stuart
Lyall, Lena
Lychuck, Charles
MacDonald, Chel
MacEwan, Grant
Manchak, Barry
Mannes, D.
Markwart, June
Martin, Glenn
Martin, James
Mason, Allan
McDowall, Maxine
Meynberg, Kelly
Mickleson, Ray
Mills, Bob
Moffatt, Grant
Morberg, Don
Morrison, Gail
Morrison, Maureen
Muir, John
Myers, S.
Nadasde, Wanda
Nesbitt, John
Nordstrom, Wayne
Nowicki, Julian
Ogston, Brian
Olson, Kay
Ost, Donna-Lee
Otto, Kelty
Paetz, Martin
Pare, Joyce
Parenteau, Susan
Peers, Margie
Petruk, Thelma

Contributors

Pike, Rodney
Poirier, Val
Porter, Bill
Pringle, Leslie
Raffael, Norbert
Rasmussen, Ray
Reed-Caron, Shannon
Reilander, Roger
Rennick, Barrie
Robertson, Jim
Robinson, Lorraine
Romanyshyn, Bob
Ross, Chip
Rowed, Scott
Saley, Henry
Schalkwijk-Barendsen, Helene
Schinkel, Dale
Semenchuk, Glen
Senger, Mitch
Shennan, Wes
Shiu, Irene
Skirrow, Stan
Spackman, Dennis
Sparrow-Clarke, Paul
Spelliscy, Rob
Steele, Lynne
Stevenson, Bob
Stewart, Karen
Stroebel, Karen
Sullivan, Leslie
Sullivan, Shirley
Swinnerton, Guy
Swinnerton, Noni
Tarnasky, O'Brien
Telfer, Kathy
Thormin, Terr
Tranter, Gerry
Trompetter, Cora
van Hienen, Theresa
Varty, Jeannine
Vassel, Mike
Verheire, Brenda
Vermeulen, Fred
Vetra, David
von Hauff, Donna
von Hauff, Peter

Wallis, Cliff
Walper, Jon
Walsh, Gary
Want, Rhona
Wark, Kathleen
Wark, Robert R.
Weins, Trevor
Weiss, Larry
Werschler, Cleve
Whitelock, Ed
Wong, Helen
Wood, Vi
Yang, David
Yew, Wei
Yeow, Mary
Zhou, Eric

(Wei Yew)

210

INDEX

Index

Index

(Wei Yew)

215

(Rosemary H. L.Calvert, FRPS)

Alberta Parks — Our Legacy celebrates the 60th anniversary of Alberta's provincial parks. DW Friesen is honored to be a participant in the production of this book. Parks represent one of the great Canadian opportunities for everyone. The publisher, the Recreation, Parks and Wildlife Foundation, wants to make certain that all of us will be able to enjoy Alberta's parklands.

Parks and wilderness areas require proper care so that they will retain their pristine character for our children . . . and our children's children. It is encumbent upon all Canadians to ensure that we leave these unspoiled landscapes in their natural state.

DW Friesen produces quality books of all kinds — coffee table books, educational text books, local history books, school yearbooks, cookbooks and children's books, and corporate communication materials. In 1992 we are also celebrating an important milestone — 85 years of proud service in Western Canada.

Our involvement in this anniversary is our way of saying thank you to our valued customers in Alberta. Let's all work together to preserve and protect Alberta's parks.

DWFriesen